1985

ETHNOGRAPHY IN EDUCATIONAL EVALUATION

SOME PAST VOLUMES IN THE
SAGE FOCUS EDITIONS

ETHNOGRAPHY IN EDUCATIONAL EVALUATION

Edited by
DAVID M. FETTERMAN

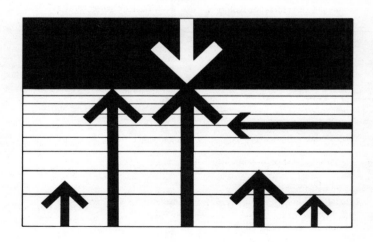

SAGE PUBLICATIONS
Beverly Hills   London   New Delhi

For information address:

SAGE Publications, Inc.
275 South Beverly Drive
Beverly Hills, California 90212

SAGE Publications India Pvt. Ltd.
C-236 Defence Colony
New Delhi 110 024, India

SAGE Publications Ltd
28 Banner Street
London EC1Y 8QE, England

Printed in the United States of America

Library of Congress Cataloging in Publication Data

Main entry under title:

Ethnography in educational evaluation.

(Sage focus editions ; 68)
1. Educational anthropology—Addresses, essays, lectures. 2. Ethnology—Methodology—Evaluation—Addresses, essays, lectures. 3. Education—Research—Evaluation—Addresses, essays, lectures. I. Fetterman, David M.
LB45.E84   1984   370'.7'8   83-24613
ISBN 0-8039-2252-3
ISBN 0-8039-2253-1 (pbk.)

FIRST PRINTING

In Memory of My Father

Irving Fetterman

March 26, 1923–July 11, 1983

Contents

Acknowledgments

This book represents the "state of the art" and, as such, draws from both recently published and unpublished works. In this regard, the editor gratefully acknowledges permission to reprint the following material in part or whole:

Fetterman, D.M. "Ethnography in Educational Research: The Dynamics of Diffusion." *Educational Researcher*, March 1982, pp. 17–29. Copyright 1982, American Educational Research Association, Washington, D.C.

Fetterman, D.M. "Guilty Knowledge, Dirty Hands, and Other Ethical Dilemmas: The Hazards of Contract Research." *Human Organization*, Fall 1983. Copyright 1983, Society for Applied Anthropology, 1983.

Herriott, R.E. and W.A. Firestone. "Multisite Qualitative Policy Research: Optimizing Description and Generalizability." *Educational Researcher*, February 1983, pp. 14–19. Copyright 1983, American Educational Research Association, Washington, D.C.

LeCompte, M.D. and J.P. Goetz. "Ethnographic Data Collection in Evaluation Research." *Educational Evaluation and Policy Analysis*, Fall 1982, pp. 387–400. Copyright 1982, American Educational Research Association, Washington, D.C.

Smith, A.G. and A.E. Robbins. "Structured Ethnography: The Study of Parental Involvement." *American Behavioral Scientist*, September/October 1982, pp. 45–61. Copyright 1982, Sage Publications, Inc.

I would also like to extend my appreciation to Deborah S. Waxman, Stanford University, for her generous assistance in the preparation of this manuscript.

PART I

Overview

1

Doing Ethnographic Educational Evaluation

DAVID M. FETTERMAN

Qualitative data collection techniques have become extremely popular in the field of educational evaluation. In addition, ethnographic techniques in particular have been used successfully to provide useful insights into numerous educational and social problems. Ethnographic educational evaluation projects can be represented along a continuum—some more closely approximate conventional ethnography while others resemble traditional fieldwork-oriented evaluations. Although ethnographic evaluations range from long five-year studies to short projects requiring only a few hundred hours, they share various traditional ethnographic fieldwork techniques and a cultural interpretation of events. Ethnographic educational evaluations, however, are distinguished from conventional ethnography by a number of characteristics.

First, ethnographic evaluations are ultimately evaluations, not ethnographies. These studies begin with the aim of ethnography—to understand. However, they make the next logical step—to assess what is understood. In addition, most ethnographic educational evaluations involve less time on site than traditional ethnographic approaches. Typical ethnographic educational evaluations have been successful without spending an extended or continuous period of time in the field. This may be because, as Wolcott has observed, "We know the school setting so well that, unknowingly, we become our own best informants."

Ethnographic educational evaluation, like ethnography, is both an art and a science. The ethnographer is a human instrument, testing and shaping ideas and insights based on rigorous data collection techniques. The shape of an ethnographic evaluation is based as much on the research design as on the training and personality of the ethnographer. In fact, the role of the ethnographer, as artist and scientist, is the key to understanding ethnographic evaluation's unique contribution both to education and to anthropology. In his classic treatise, *The Interpretation of Cultures*, Clifford Geertz explained it as follows:

> In anthropology, or anyway social anthropology, what the practitioners do is ethnography. And it is in understanding what ethnography is, or more exactly what doing ethnography is, that a start can be made toward grasping what anthropological analysis amounts to as a form of knowledge [1973: 5–6].

Similarly, ethnographic educational evaluation's contribution is best understood by focusing on what ethnographers are doing in educational evaluation. This collection of ethnographic educational evaluation studies has been organized to illustrate what ethnographers have been doing in educational evaluation.

This book is composed exclusively of ethnographic educational evaluation studies as compared with other ethnographic evaluation studies in the areas of drug abuse, housing, and agriculture. At the same time a diverse selection of case studies have been presented to illustrate the intricacies of the issues and concerns that are involved in this process of adaptation. Case studies that addressed theoretical issues and more closely resembled the ethnographic end of the ethnographic-evaluation continuum were selected to demonstrate what can be done without complete assimilation. This structure has been designed to allow a model of ethnographic educational evaluation to emerge from this collection.

Structurally the book is divided into three sections: an overview; a body of illustrative case studies; and a discussion of theoretical and ethical dilemmas. The first section of the book presents an overview of the state of the art and a discussion of ethnographic techniques in evaluation research. Chapter 2, "Ethnography in Educational Research: The Dynamics of Diffusion," examines the transmission of ethnographic elements from anthropology to the field of education. The uses and abuses of ethnography that currently characterize this process of diffusion are discussed in detail, emphasizing the roles of ethnographic methods and a cultural interpretation. This chapter focuses on a national ethnographic evaluation of an alternative high school program for dropouts that offers a multilevel and multidimensional model for ethnographic evaluations. This study applied traditional ethnographic techniques to educational evaluation within the constraints imposed by contract research. The chapter discusses as well the role of federal involvement, evaluation design, and the role of reinforcing world views. The programmatic and policy recommendations generated from this study have broad implications for the conduct of national policy research. By calling for work that deals with issues that transcend academic distinctions and contradistinctions this chapter sets the tone for the collection. Questions of concern to academics and practitioners alike are posed regarding the manner in which qualitative and quantitative techniques are currently being used in evaluation. The following works in this collection respond to these dynamic issues in a step toward the future.

Chapter 3, "Ethnographic Data Collection in Evaluation Research," is designed as a "critical guide to doing ethnographic evaluation for those who now are convinced of its usefulness, rather than as a position paper defending its utility." LeCompte and Goetz demonstrate how ethnographers have collected baseline, process, values, and product data that apply to evaluation research. This chapter briefly discusses methods for recording ethnographic data and criteria for selecting specific recording devices or approaches. The focus of the discussion is on interactive methods for collecting ethnographic data, such as participant observation, key-informant interviewing, career histories, and surveys. Noninteractive methods are also discussed, such as nonparticipant observation, stream-of-behavior chronicles, proxemics and kinesics, interaction analysis protocols, archival and demographic data collection, and physical trace data collection. These methods are discussed within the analytical framework of reliability and validity. This chapter concludes with a discussion of the strengths and weaknesses of conducting a comprehensive ethnography as compared with the selection of a few ethnographic data collection techniques. As such, it serves as a lens through which to view the work of each individual in this collection.

The second section of the book represents the heart of the collection. A series of illustrative case studies of ethnographic evaluations are explored and examined. The case studies include national (multisite) studies, as well as local- and international-level studies. The lead chapter of this section is entitled "Multisite Qualitative Policy Research: Some Design and Implementation Issues." Firestone and Herriott in this chapter discuss "the emergence of a new form of qualitative research, one intended to strengthen its ability to generalize while preserving in-depth description." They report the findings of a National Institute of Education sponsored survey of 25 multisite ethnographic and qualitative evaluation studies. The discussion is divided into two sections. The first presents the formal results of this survey, highlighting institutional and methodological features of the studies. This part is guided by a variety of design issues. The most significant involves structuring data collection efforts to maximize both description and generalizability. This portion of the discussion establishes the foundation for a more comprehensive discussion of this topic in a later chapter. The second half of the discussion focuses on five of these 25 multisite studies. These studies include the Rural Experimental Schools Study, the Experienced-Based Career Education Study, the Career Intern Program Study, the Parental Involvement Study, and the Dissemination Efforts Supporting School Improvement Study. These studies represent a continuum of greater to lesser degrees of formalization in qualitative research. Formalization, the "prespecification of the problem and method" and the "standardization of data reduction and analysis techniques," is the focus of this portion of the discussion. This chapter concludes with a discussion of the future of multisite qualitative research focusing on the opportunities available for more detailed examinations of administrative, methodological, and theoretical features of multisite qualitative research.

Chapter 5, "Federal Bucks for Local Change: On the Ethnography of Experimental Schools," is a review of the voluminous literature generated from one of the longest ethnographic evaluations conducted to date. Messerschmidt's review synthesizes what has been learned in the Experimental Schools Study, based on two project ethnographies, numerous case studies, and over 50 articles in professional journals, among other related publications. This review demonstrates the value of examining a program that failed. The literature examined in this chapter documented what was learned about this innovative educational project: "What it was," "how it operated," and "why it failed." This review also examined what was learned in the process of adapting anthropology to educational evaluation. The key themes that emerge from a review of the literature to guide the discussion are: ethics, power, and time. Ethical obligations and conflicts that characterized the relationship between informant, fieldworker, research corporation, and funding agency are illustrated in this discussion. Similarly, the role of local and federal bureaucratic power is examined in relation to the researcher and the research. In addition, the implications of long-term fieldwork designs in ethnographic evaluation are considered. The chapter concludes with a call for new research and secondary analyses, building on the existing literature reviewed in this chapter.

Chapter 6, "Multimethod Policy Research: A Case Study of Structure and Flexibility," is based on a study of parental involvement in education. This chapter is a pragmatic methodological self-critique of an ethnographic evaluation that combined qualitative and survey studies. Smith and Robbins's discussion is guided by issues of reliability and validity in multisite qualitative research. The first half of the discussion addresses such topics as the local field researcher, selection and training, the analysis packets, the site coordinator, and data reduction and analysis. The second half of the discussion examines the implications of various methodological decisions. These brief excursions into methodological self-examination lead into larger issues. For example, an examination of the decision to employ local field researchers to collect the data raises the question of what makes a good field researcher. Other topics of methodological reflection include the dilemma between structure and flexibility, data quality control, analyzing qualitative data, sequencing and integration of qualitative and survey data, and reporting the results from qualitative research. This chapter is an example of methodological innovation and improvisation, as are most of the case studies presented in this collection. This forthright self-examination, however, reveals the type of methodological concern that represents the undercurrent of every conscientious ethnographic evaluation.

Chapter 7, "Ethnography as Evaluation: Hearing-Impaired Students in the Mainstream," is a sensitive and balanced portrayal of a local-level mainstreaming program for hearing-impaired children. Using traditional anthropological tools, Hemwall provides an understanding and an evaluation of "the everyday experiences facing those involved in mainstreaming." She describes a program in turmoil, where teachers are reluctant to discipline the hearing-impaired, sign interpreters are ineffective communicators, and parents are unsupportive. These maladaptive patterns of behavior reinforced passivity and dependency relationships that erected barriers to the meaningful integration of the hearing-impaired. Her ethnographic insights into the dynamics of this program enabled her to make recommendations that encouraged the development of independence and self-confidence to break through these social barriers. She concludes with a brief review of the problematic nature of applying ethnography to evaluation.

Chapter 8, "Evaluation, Ethnography, and the Concept of Culture: Disadvantaged Youth in an Israeli Town," highlights the theoretical implications of the use of the culture concept in ethnographic evaluation. Goldberg uses three definitions of culture in this chapter to illustrate the dynamics of a government program developed in response to the emerging Israeli Black Panther movement. Culture defined as a way of life is used to evaluate the conflicting relationship between the planners' world view and the social context of the project. A definition of culture as emerging within the project enables the ethnographer to focus on "the specific dynamics of meaning that emerge with the implementation and operation of a program." Culture as "self-reflection" is a third approach to the use of culture in ethnographic evaluation. The self-reflection approach takes into consideration the evaluation design and the program's political context or setting when interpreting what is going on in a project. The culture concept in its varied forms also provides an insight into the often illusory goal of identifying causes and effects in evaluation research. A more appropriate evaluative goal is recommended—viewing evaluation as a "kind of social history" in which "cultural assumptions guiding that history" are identified, traced, and recorded. This chapter concludes the main body of the collection with an international case study that resembles our own domestic programs and research approaches. Moreover, it crystalizes and combines the various implicit definitions of culture individually displayed in the preceding works.

The third section of this book is reflective in nature. This portion of the book addresses theoretical and ethical dilemmas in ethnographic evaluation. Chapter 9, "Ethnographers sans Ethnography: The Evaluation Compromise," underscores the difference between ethnography and evaluation. Basically Wolcott defines ethnography as a tool used to understand, while evaluation is designed to judge a social situation. This chapter suggests that although ethnography could potentially make a more significant contribution to education as an "alternative to, rather than an alternative form of, evaluation," this proposition may be unrealistic at this time. As an ethnographer hired to assist with an evaluation study he, like most other ethnographic evaluators, was asked to follow his customary research style—short of producing a "full-blown" ethnographic study. This is the "evaluation compromise." After exploring a number of theoretical concerns in this regard, the chapter concludes that a university-based academician is able to conduct an ethnographic evaluation using an approach "not inconsistent with the ethnographic tradition."

The last chapter in this collection, "Guilty Knowledge, Dirty Hands, and Other Ethical Dilemmas: The Hazards of Contract Research," examines the social, political, and paradigmatic context of ethnographic evaluation. In addition, this chapter reflects on the ethical hazards faced by fieldworkers in contract research. A few potentially hazardous situations discussed in this chapter include entrance into the field, role conflicts, fieldwork in the inner city, ethnographic reports, and dissemination of findings. In addition, job stress and burnout are discussed. This chapter focuses on how urban fieldwork forces an ethnographer to confront the realities of guilty knowledge, or confidential knowledge of illegal activities; and dirty hands, a situation from which one cannot emerge innocent of wrongdoing. The significance of developing moral decision-making guidelines to deal with these problems and to improve fieldwork is emphasized. The risk-benefit approach, the respect-for-persons ethic, and basic pragmatism are all recommended as guidelines in the field. Other hazards discussed in this chapter range from fieldwork conducted at an accelerated pace, to the reporting of findings in a highly political atmosphere. A review of these issues is presented to guide researchers in this growing field. Moreover, it is hoped that this discussion (like each preceding chapter) will be reflexive, encouraging fieldworkers in various fields to reevaluate their own roles and strategies in their pursuit of knowledge.

REFERENCE

Geertz, C. *The interpretation of cultures.* New York: Basic Books, 1973.

2

Ethnography in Educational Research
The Dynamics of Diffusion

DAVID M. FETTERMAN

Anthropologists have a long tradition of studying the diffusion of cultural innovations (Boaz, 1896/1940; Driver, 1961; Hallowell, 1948; Kroeber, 1931, 1952; Morgan, 1877; Sapir, 1916/1949; Spindler, 1955; Spindler & Goldschmidt, 1952; L. Spindler, 1962; Tylor, 1879). Diffusion occurs during the interaction of two sociocultural systems as in times of war or during trade.

Similarly, the recent interaction of ethnographic and quantitative research methodologies results in an inevitable diffusion of techniques, methods, and values. By viewing these two disciplines as "sociocultural systems" we gain an excellent opportunity to study the dynamics of diffusion between the two fields. Of particular interest is the diffusion of ethnographic techniques, which are among the most visible traits currently being transmitted.

ETHNOGRAPHY AND EDUCATIONAL EVALUATION

Ethnography has become a popular buzz word in education. A number of scholars have observed that researchers with little or no background in anthropology claim to be doing ethnography. In one study, labeled "An ethnographic study of . . . ," observers were on site at only one point in time for five days. In a national study purporting to be ethnographic, once-a-week, on-site observations were made for four months. The methods employed, the researchers' backgrounds, and the data collected and reported in the study were sociological rather than anthropological.

The problem stems largely from the pursuit of scholastic fads. Denenberg (1969) refers to scholastic faddists as Zeitgeister-Shysters.

AUTHOR'S NOTE: I am indebted to Lee J. Cronbach, G. D. Spindler, G. K. Tallmadge, and D. S. Waxman for their assistance in the preparation of this chapter.

They do their research on topics that are scientifically hot and in. They are in the Zeitgeist. What happens when the Zeitgeist changes? These people change their research to conform. As a chameleon changes colors with a shift in the environment so do these researchers change their goals. They lust after research fame and fortune.

Since Zeitgeists often do not last for more than a few years, the work these people publish is exceedingly superficial. They touch the surface of an important problem but rarely study it in depth. They leave in their wake large numbers of papers that add confusion and little else to the field. The signal-to-noise-ratio of their publications ranges from 0.0 to 0.2. Because of the obvious spuriousness of their approach to science, I call these individuals Zeitgeister-Shysters [p. 50].

The result is a proliferation of poorly conducted research or nonscience. This type of activity contributes little to the reputation and credibility of ethnography in particular and less to educational research in general.

Abuses accompany any flurry of interest in novel approaches to research. These abuses, however, have raised the ire of many educational anthropologists. One of the leading figures in this debate (Wolcott, 1980a) charges that

much of what goes on today as educational ethnography is either out and out program evaluation, or, at best, lopsided (and undisciplined) documentation [p. 39].

In response, many researchers have complained of unjust or harsh criticism. They have received much of the "spillover" of the vituperative criticism initially directed at the Zeitgeisters. Moreover, they suggest that many anthropologists have become self-righteous purists. Few educational researchers are aware that they are standing in the middle of a battleground, caught in the crossfire between educational policy decisionmakers on the one hand, and university-based anthropologists of education on the other. They are chastised for using novel techniques inappropriately and are labeled statistical relics or outmoded number crunchers if they do not use the new techniques. These researchers are trying to improve their capabilities by augmenting their research arsenal. Their only transgression is that they have mislabeled their efforts. Rather than conducting ethnographies, they are simply using ethnographic techniques. Moreover, the entire argument over terminology is seen by many individuals as a purely academic affair that gets in the way of getting the job done. Although poorly conducted research requires an honest critique, this process of scholarly criticism has alienated many conscientious individuals rather than serving its intended purpose: sensitizing educators to methodological issues of concern to anthropologists.

A STEP TOWARD THE FUTURE

Constructive criticism is needed. Educational researchers will continue to use ethnographic and other qualitative techniques in the future. Guidance and close individual critiques are required rather than rhetoric and posturing. Anthropologists who criticize are obligated to specify their objections and offer constructive suggestions rather than omnibus condemnations.

Similarly, educational researchers must respect the anthropologist's obligations to see that his or her field is not misrepresented. The use of the term ethnography for any form of qualitative research is a misnomer. Ethnography is a methodological approach with specific procedures, techniques, and methods of analysis. The adoption of random elements of this method without attention to the whole results in the loss of many built-in safeguards of reliability and validity in data collection and analysis.

These difficulties can be considered a result of a faulty or partial transmission of traits from one sociocultural system to another. This is not a new phenomenon. In general, traits rather than entire complexes of sociocultural systems are diffused at a given time. In this instance, only the ethnographic techniques have been transmitted. The values, the most important elements of the anthropological culture system, have been left behind: phenomenology, holism, nonjudgmental orientation, and contextualization. Phenomenology requires that investigators be guided by the insider's viewpoint, the emic perspective. The concept of holism commands our attention to the larger picture and to the interrelated nature of the minute to the whole cultural system. A nonjudgmental orientation prevents the social scientist from making some of the more obvious value judgments in research. Biases are made explicit to mitigate their unintended effects on research. Contextualization demands that we place the data in its own environment so as to provide a more accurate representation.

In addition, anthropology's scientifically substantive concerns with patterns of culture and social organization have been neglected. Ethnographers are guided by these concerns, which in turn lead to the use of such appropriate techniques as participant observation, key informant interviewing, and so on.

Educators are using anthropological tools without understanding anthropology's cosmology. (See McCutcheon, 1981, regarding the role of interpretation in qualitative inquiry.) Much of the current debate will subside when the values and cosmology underlying ethnographic techniques are understood, accepted, and used to guide ethnographic research.

To turn to more substantive issues or at least more substantive arguments about existing issues, one might, for example, ask whether it is the techniques or the cultural interpretation that makes a study ethnographic. Geertz (1973) contends that doing ethnography "is not a matter of methods":

> What defines it [doing ethnography] is the kind of intellectual effort it is: an elaborate venture in, to borrow a notion from Gilbert Ryle, "thick description" . . . consider, he says, two boys rapidly contracting the eyelids of their right eyes. In one, this is an involuntary twitch; in the other, a conspiratorial signal to a friend. The two movements are, as movements, identical; from an I-am-a-camera, "phenomenalistic" observation of them alone, one could not tell which was twitch and which was wink, or indeed whether both or either was twitch or wink. Yet the difference, however unphotographable, between a twitch and a wink is vast; as anyone unfortunate enough to have had the first taken for the second knows. The winker is communicating, and indeed communicating in a quite precise and special way: (1) deliberately, (2) to someone in particular, (3) to impart a particular message, (4) according to a socially established code, and (5) without cognizance of the rest of the company [p. 6].

For Geertz, doing ethnography is a matter of cultural interpretation. Many ethnographic classics have been produced by individuals with little formal training in ethnography. Their work was ethnographic because they were able to make sense out of the data from a cultural perspective (Geertz, 1973). Wolcott (1980b) also emphasizes the role of cultural interpretation as compared with methodology when describing ethnography:

> One could do a participant-observer study from now till doomsday and never come up with a sliver of ethnography . . . . We are fast losing sight of the fact that the essential ethnographic contribution is interpretative rather than methodological [pp. 57, 59].

I argue, however, that both ethnographic techniques and a cultural perspective are needed. A cultural perspective is substantially weakened if the data are collected haphazardly. Similarly, the data, however carefully collected, are unlikely to be ethnographic if analyzed from a purely nomothetic perspective.

Moreover, there are more productive issues that transcend these academic distinctions and contradistinctions. Ethnography is in the process of being diffused into education. The questions of how qualitative and quantitative techniques are currently being used in evaluation and how they can be used more effectively together are of pressing concern to academics and practitioners alike. In addition, the question arises of how the new merger of ethnographic and psychometric orientations can be made relevant to policy concerns. It is time to turn to dynamic rather than static issues regarding these methodological orientations.

DIFFUSION OF TRAITS
AND WHOLE TRAIT COMPLEXES

Single traits or sets of traits are often diffused rather than the whole trait complex in the process of acculturation or diffusion, as discussed earlier. Whole trait complexes like "real" ethnography—using ethnographic methods and a cultural interpretation—can be diffused in a manner that meets the concerns of applied educational research. A brief review of how traits like ethnographic techniques, and whole trait complexes such as ethnography have been diffused in educational research provides an insight into this process of adaptation.

The earliest examples of qualitative methods in evaluation research appeared in the late 1960s (cf. Glaser, 1969; Mech, 1969). The "contract ethnographer" literature has grown since that time. Presently the literature includes discussions of conceptual frameworks, techniques, the role of the ethnographer in evaluation, and procedural suggestions (Brenner, Marsh, & Brenner, 1978; Britan, 1977, 1978; Burns, 1975, 1978; Campbell, 1974; Clinton, 1975, 1976; Colfer, 1976; Coward, 1976; Everhart, 1975; Fetterman, 1980, 1981a, 1981b, 1981c, 1982; Firestone, 1975; Fitzsimmons, 1975; Hall, 1978; Hamilton et al., 1977; Hord, 1978; Mulhauser, 1975; Patton, 1980; Sobel, 1976; Tikunoff & Ward, 1977). This surge of interest in qualitative methodology has been the result of a significant disillusionment with quantitative methods. This disillusionment also has extended to the use of the experimental design, the cornerstone of quantitative methodology in educational evaluation (Cronbach et al., 1980; Scriven, 1978; C. Weiss, 1974; R. Weiss & Rein, 1972, among others). In fact, governmental agencies, most notably the National Institute of Education (NIE), have funded several qualitative evaluation studies over the past five years in response to the problems from the application of experimental design to natural social settings. These studies have generally included ethnographic fieldwork as one component of the evaluation. The ethnographic component has ranged from comprehensive studies of large-scale, federal demonstration projects to more limited ministudies.

One of the more comprehensive studies conducted was the Experimental Schools Program Evaluation (Burns, 1976; Clinton, 1975; Colfer, 1976; Everhart, 1976; Fitzsimmons, 1975; Herriott, 1979a, 1979b). The Experimental Schools Program was a federally funded effort to introduce innovation and change in several school districts throughout the country. The interdisciplinary evaluation used descriptive case studies and traditional survey and psychometric instruments to understand the process of educational change. Abt Associates conducted a portion of the evaluation (Project Rural). In one of their studies they selected an ethnographer to reside in the school district for 3 to 5 years, while the remainder of the team stayed at the firm. In another study, the fieldworker combined efforts with others on the research team at the school site. The study represents the best approximation of a conventional ethnographic approach to research in evaluation. The study was primarily summative in value and the studies produced sizeable ethnographic case studies of the program. One of the drawbacks with this kind of approach, however, is that it is more time consuming than the traditional evaluation procedures and rarely produces reports for policy or administrative decisionmaking in a timely fashion.

The Field Studies in Urban Desegregated Schools Program is another large-scale federal study (see Cassell, 1978; Riffel et al., 1976). However, this study more closely resembled basic research rather than evaluation research and as such is less relevant to the process of ethnographic adaptation to evaluation. There also have been other large-scale evaluation projects outside the field of education that have employed an ethnographic approach such as a recent study of a HUD housing allowance program (Chambers, 1977).

NIE also funded the Far West Laboratory's study of teacher effectiveness, Beginning Teacher Evaluation Study (BTES). The aim of the research was to identify effective teacher behavior and classroom qualities that contributed to achievement in mathematics and reading. The qualitative product of the study was entitled: *An Ethnographic Study of the Forty Classrooms of the Beginning Teacher Evaluation Study Known Sample* (1975). The study provided useful data that was used "to better ensure that beginning teachers receive training in areas that have been empirically demonstrated to affect student learning." The greatest single drawback to the credibility of the findings in this study was that observers were on site for only 1 week. This example represents a partial transmission of anthropological traits.

The Department of Labor funded the Youthwork National Policy Study of Exemplary In-School Demonstration Projects. This large-scale study used the case study approach to address various prespecified policy questions regarding the transition of youth from school to work. The study produced a series of interim reports and professional papers. The results of interviews conducted and questions administered in 40 sites were reported in *Education and Employment Training: The Views of Youth* (Rist et al., 1979). Interviews conducted and questions administered in 36 projects were reported in *Targeting on In-School Youth: Four Strategies for Coordinating Education and Employment Training* (Rist et al., 1980a). Both of these reports were based on an average of once-a-week, on-site observations. In the latter report site visits were made over a period of four months. The final report of this study provided a useful analysis of interinstitutional linkages between education and employment training organizations (Rist et al., 1980b).

Smaller scale evaluations such as the study of an urban alternative school used ethnographers to conduct the research (Wilson, 1977). These studies have been primarily formative in nature. Their most significant contribution has been their ability to provide feedback to those in the programs.

NIE's Experience-Based Career Exploration Program provided an opportunity to explore the utility of ethnographic ministudies. Part-time fieldworkers were selected to conduct short-term fieldwork (approximately 100 hours). A brief report of 20–25 pages was produced by the fieldworkers. The report identified subtle features of program operations, for example, informal education in the learning center (Alvarez & Hishiki, 1974). This approach represents the small-scale or mini application of ethnographic techniques to educational evaluation.

The Career Intern Program (CIP) study represents one of the earliest substantive attempts to apply ethnographic techniques and anthropological insights to a large-scale project within a time frame established to accommodate a more traditional educational evaluation. Ideally, more time and additional ethnographers would have been available for a study of this type. While it must be acknowledged that there are many drawbacks in reducing time normally required to conduct extensive fieldwork, the study suggests what can be done ethnographically within an extremely limited time frame.

THE CAREER INTERN PROGRAM:
A WHOLE TRAIT COMPLEX

The CIP study, similar to the studies discussed above, demonstrates how ethnography can be diffused into applied educational research, in this case as a whole trait complex. The CIP study focused on an alternative high school program for dropouts and potential dropouts. It was selected for study because it represents one of the few exemplary programs for disenfranchised and economically disadvantaged minority youth.

The CIP study consists of four sites, three located in major urban centers—(pseudonyms) New Borough, Plymouth, Oceanside—and a fourth in a small city, Farmington (32,000 population). These sites were organized according to a model developed in Philadelphia by Opportunities Industrialization Centers of America, Inc. (OIC/A), founders of an international skills development organization. OIC/A contracted Gibboney Associates, a social science research organization, to evaluate the prototype. Gibboney's (1977) positive results were corroborated by the Joint Dissemination Review Panel (JDRP), and the program was declared eligible for funding and dissemination. CIP was funded by the Department of Labor; its dissemination was carried out by OIC/A and monitored by NIE. NIE in turn selected RMC Research Corporation, an educational research organization, to evaluate the four CIP sites. The following discussion is based on information derived from the ethnographic component of the RMC evaluation.

As an important social and educational experiment, the CIP is salient to many kinds of audiences. Policymakers have been interested in the program as a viable response to serious labor market problems: high school dropout rates and youth unemployment. Social reformers, however, have viewed the program as a vehicle to redress historically based social inequities and promote upward social mobility for minority groups. The program is also of interest to academicians and researchers because it provides an opportunity to explore the processes of socialization, cultural transmission, and equal educational opportunity in the United States.

The study was subdivided into four tasks: (a) implementation, (b) outcomes, (c) interrelationships, and (d) comparison with similar programs. The ethnographic component of the study task focused on the interrelationships and causal linkages between implementation and outcomes. Ethnographic data collection instruments, methods, procedures and perspectives were employed. The task also relied heavily on information gathered through nomothetic methods and perspectives. Traditional techniques such as participant observation, nonparticipant observation, use of key informants, triangulation, structured and semistructured, and informal interviews, were used to elicit data from the emic or "insider's" perspective. Two-week site visits were made to each site every three months for a period of three years. In addition, regular contact was maintained by telephone, correspondence, and special visits. The study attempted to be nonjudgmental, holistic, and contextual in perspective. A tape recorder and camera were invaluable in collecting and documenting the data. (See Fetterman, 1980 for details regarding the methodology of the study.) In practice, data collection and reporting activities overlapped for each segment of the study.

The study offered a model for ethnographic evaluations, attempting to apply traditional ethnographic techniques to educational evaluation within the constraints imposed by contract research. The most significant contributions the ethnographic component of the study made to educational evaluation included providing a context to interpret meaningfully the data, demythologizing the qualitative-quantitative dichotomy, and producing programmatic and policy recommendations (Fetterman, 1981d).

The study provided a description of the program's neighborhoods to illuminate the program's physical context. A description of the inner city where pimping, prostitution, murder, and theft are common occurrences provides an insight into the influences shaping many urban youth and challenging any educational program. In addition, program attendance statistics were provided with reference to an attendance baseline. For example, a 70 percent attendance figure gains significance when compared with that former dropout's zero attendance baseline figure.

The investigation also attempted to break down the quantitative-qualitative dichotomy by reporting both types of program outcomes. The outcomes included descriptions of attitudinal change and improved self-presentation skills as well as formal quantifiable measures of program success and stability, for example, attendance, turnover, graduation, and placement statistics.

Finally, the study provided programmatic and policy recommendations. For example, the study recommended that the use of the experimental design be abandoned in evaluations of social welfare programs when the no-cause baseline required cannot be established and when empty slots exist in the program. One of the most important problems in the quantitative component of the evaluation was the application of the treatment-control experimental design to a population of dropouts and potential dropouts. The use of this design was methodologically unsound. Assigning students to the control group created a negative treatment, and high attrition rates invalidated the assumption of random equivalence between groups (Fetterman, 1982).

Ethnographic fieldwork helped identify systematic differences between the treatment and control groups—differences traced to differential treatment (knowledge of inclusion or exclusion from the program). Basically, the "nontreatment" condition produced a social organization and a cultural meaning that negatively affected the participants. The rejection from the program was not "the absence of x but a phenomenon in its own right—a y or z." According to a colleague, "Here anthropology's concern with social arrangements and cultural meanings informs our understanding of these real-life settings, and shows the control group condition to be ecologically invalid." On-site observations also documented recruitment difficulties linked to the use of this design. For example, recruitment efforts were dampened when the candidates were informed that their chances of entering the program depended on five hours of testing and a lottery. Ethnographic research also provided the reasons for the continued use of this design, despite site and evaluator protests throughout the study.

The impetus to employ randomized experimental designs and to apply pressures to meet numerical goals, preestablished schedules, and inflexible deadlines stems from the federal bureaucratic climate. Governmental agencies feel they must make the strongest case possible before Congress, on whom they depend for future funds. Since controlled randomized experiments are generally accepted as providing the most credible evidence, it follows naturally that they will be selected regardless of their suitability for the task at hand.

This approach is highly visible in governmental circles today as evidenced by a major document produced by Boruch and Cordray (1980): *An Appraisal of Educational Program Evaluations: Federal, State, and Local Agencies.* Boruch and Cordray, in their executive summary for Congress, recommend that

> the higher quality evaluation designs, especially randomized experiments,
> be authorized explicitly in law for testing new programs, new variations
> on existing programs, and new program components.

Once again this approach is recommended regardless of the study problem (see Cronbach et al., 1980; Fetterman, 1982; Tallmadge, 1979).

Fieldwork, with its close attention to the details of program implementation, can identify causal features and causal linkages that may be overlooked or misattributed on the basis of correlational analysis of survey data or predetermined observational category systems. This study, following those discussed earlier, demonstrates why researchers need not always employ a randomized experimental design to plausibly demonstrate the probability of causation.

The CIP study represents an important shift in emphasis from the urban educational anthropology research of the previous decade because it focuses on school success for minority youth rather than school failure. It differs from the traditional ethnography of schooling in incorporating findings from a multidisciplinary evaluation effort. The research concerns not a single school, but an entire demonstration project in several sites. The analyses examine: classrooms, program components, community environments, local and national affiliates, governmental agencies, and evaluators. The study differs also in its multidimensional emphasis, discussing federal involvement, evaluation design, and the role of reinforcing world views. It represents both an opportunity for and a test of ethnography in its emerging role in educational evaluation.

The study develops an analytical model to explain the programmatic model developed by the CIP. The analytical model holds that educators can treat students particularistically while teaching them skills required to succeed when evaluated by universal criteria of achievement. In analyzing the way educational differences are related to social stratification, the study challenges the traditional assumption of horizontal social mobility by demonstrating how an alternative school can socialize economically disadvantaged youth for vertical (upward) mobility.

The application of ethnographic techniques to educational evaluation remains a new endeavor. The attempt to adapt traditional anthropological techniques to intensive, short-term studies poses many challenges. Thus, each successful application constitutes a significant contribution to the development and refinement of this new methodological approach.

CONCLUSION

Good data is required to "play the causation-identification game." The most appropriate use of ethnography is to borrow the whole trait complex, not a few traits. Securing good data, however, requires the whole trait complex of ethnography and the whole trait complex of traditional evaluation research: "to show broad patterns across a set of sites across time."

Ethnography has been misunderstood and misused in educational research. The misuse of ethnographic techniques, however, is due as much to overzealousness and faddishness as it is to the anthropological tradition of ritualizing methodology. Ethnography is not a panacea. It is one useful methodological tool, among others, used in addressing educational problems. The exploration and development of new frontiers requires adaptations, alterations, and innovations. This does not imply that significant compromises be made in the rigor required to conduct truly ethnographic research. A strict constructionist perspective may strangle a young enterprising new venture, and too liberal a stance is certain to transform a novel tool into another fad in educational research. The traditional anthropological techniques, concepts, and values that have guided the anthropological endeavor thus far still represent the most useful guide to approaching the future. The artful shaping of this adaptation process will contribute to the enrichment and refinement of the fields of anthropology and education.

REFERENCES

Alvarez, R., & Hishiki, P. *Anthropological perspectives of Far West School and students.* San Francisco: Far West Laboratory, 1974.
Boaz, F. *Race, language, and culture.* New York: The Free Press, 1940. (Originally published 1896.)
Boruch, R. F., & Cordray, D. S. *An appraisal of educational program evaluations: Federal, state, and local agencies.* Evanston, Ill.: Northwestern University, 1980.
Brenner, M., Marsh, P., & Brenner, M. (Eds.) *The social context of method.* London: Crown Helm, 1978.
Britan, G. M. *Public school and innovation: An ethnographic evaluation of the experimental technology incentives program.* Washington, D.C.: National Academy of Sciences, 1977.
Britan, G. M. The place of anthropology in program evaluation. *Anthropological and Education Quarterly,* 1978, *51*(2), 119–128.
Burns, A. An anthropologist at work. *Anthropology and Education Quarterly,* 1975, *6*(4), 28–34.
Burns, A. On the ethnographic process in anthropology and education. *Anthropology and Education Quarterly,* 1978, *9*(4), 18–34.
Campbell, D. T. *Qualitative knowing in action research.* Occasional paper, Stanford Evaluation Consortium. Stanford University, 1974.
Cassell, J. *A fieldwork manual for studying desegregated schools.* Washington, D.C.: National Institute of Education, 1978.
Chambers E. Working for the man: The anthropologist in policy relevant research. *Human Organization,* 1977, *36*(3), 258–267.
Clinton, C. A. The anthropologist as hired hand. *Human Organization,* 1975, *34,* 197–204.
Clinton, C. A. On bargaining with the devil: Contract ethnography and accountability in fieldwork. *Anthropology and Education Quarterly,* 1976, *8,* 25–29.
Colfer, C. J. Rights, responsibilities and reports: An ethical dilemma in contract research. In M. A. Rynkiewich & J. P. Spradley (Eds.), *Ethics and anthropology.* New York, John Wiley and Sons, 1976.
Coward, R. The involvement of anthropologists in contract evaluations: The federal perspective. *Anthropology and Education Quarterly,* 1976, *7,* 12–16.
Cronbach, L. J., Ambron, S. R., Dornbusch, S. M., Hess, R. D., Hornik, R. C., Phillips, D. C., Walker, D. F., & Weiner, S. S. *Toward reform of program evaluations: Aims, methods, and institutional arrangements.* San Francisco: Jossey-Bass, 1980.
Denenberg, V. Prolixities A. Zeitgeister. *Psychology Today,* 1969, *3*(1), 50.
Driver, H. E. *Indians of North America.* Chicago: University of Chicago Press, 1961.
Everhart, R. B. Problems of doing fieldwork in educational evaluation. *Human Organization,* 1975, *34*(3), 183–196.

Everhart, R. B. Ethnography and educational policy: Love and marriage of strange bedfellows? *Council on Anthropology and Education Newsletter*, 1976, 7, 17–24.

Fetterman, D. M. Ethnographic techniques in educational evaluation: An illustration. In A. Van Fleet (Ed.), *Anthropology of education: Methods and applications. Journal of Thought* (special topic edition), 1980, *15*(3), 31–48.

Fetterman, D. M. *Study of the Career Intern Program. Final report–Task C: Program dynamics: Structure, function, and interrelationships.* Mountain View, Calif.: RMC Research Corporation, 1981. (a)

Fetterman, D. M. Blaming the victim: The problem of evaluation design and federal involvement, and reinforcing world views in education. *Human Organization*, 1981, *40*(1), 67–77. (b)

Fetterman, D. M. New perils for the contract ethnographer. *Anthropology and Education Quarterly*, 1981, *12*(1), 71–80. (c)

Fetterman, D. M. *A shift in allegiance: The use of qualitative data and its relevance for policy.* Unpublished manuscript, 1981. (d)

Fetterman, D. M. Ibsen's baths: Reactivity and insensitivity (a misapplication of the treatment-control design in a national evaluation). *Educational Evaluation and Policy Analysis*, 1982, *4*(3), 261–279.

Firestone, W. A. Educational field research in a "contract shop." *The Generator*, 1975, *5*(3), 3–11.

Fitzsimmons, S. J. The anthropologist in a strange land. *Human Organization*, 1975, *34*(2), 183–196.

Geertz, D. *The interpretation of cultures.* New York: Basic Books, 1973.

Gibboney Associates, Inc. *The Career Intern Program: Final Report* (vol. 1 and 2). Blue Bell, PA: Author, 1977.

Glaser, E. *A qualitative evaluation of the Concentrated Employment Program (CEP) in Birmingham, Detroit, Los Angeles, San Antonio, Seattle, and South Bronx, by means of the participant observation method.* Final report to the Office of Education, Manpower Administration, U.S. Department of Labor. Los Angeles: Human Interaction Research Institute, 1969.

Hall, G. *Ethnographers and ethnographic data, an iceberg of the first order for the research manager.* Austin, Tx.: University of Texas, Research and Development Center for Teacher Education, 1978.

Hallowell, A. I. Acculturation processes and personality changes. In E. Kluckhohn & H. A. Murray (Eds.), *Personality in nature, society, and culture.* New York: Alfred A. Knopf, 1948.

Hamilton, D., McDonald, B., King, C., Jenkins, D., & Parlett, M. *Beyond the numbers game: A reader in educational evaluation.* Berkeley, Calif.: McCutchan, 1977.

Herriott, R. E. The federal context: Planning, funding, and monitoring. In R. E. Herriott & N. Gross (Eds.), *The dynamics of planned educational change.* Berkeley, Calif.: McCutchan, 1979. (a)

Herriott, R. E. *Federal initiative and rural school improvement: Findings from the experimental school program.* Cambridge, Mass.: Abt, 1979. (b)

Hord, S. *Under the eye of the ethnographer: Reactions and perceptions of the observed.* Austin, Tx.: University of Texas, Research and Development Center for Teacher Education, 1978.

Kroeber, A. L. Historical reconstruction of culture growths and organic evolution. *American Anthropologist*, 1931, *33*, 149–156.

Kroeber, A. L. *The nature of culture.* Chicago: University of Chicago Press, 1952.

McCutcheon, G. On the interpretation of classroom observations. *Educational Researcher*, 1981, *10*(5), 5–10.

Mech, E. *Participant observation: Toward an evaluative methodology for Manpower programs*. Final report to the Office of Education, Manpower Administration, U.S. Department of Labor. Tempe, Az.: Arizona State University, 1969.

Morgan, L. H. *Ancient society*. New York: Holt, Rinehart, & Winston, 1877.

Mulhauser, F. Ethnography and policymaking: The case of education. *Human Organization*, 1975, *34*, 311.

Patton, M. *Qualitative evaluation methods*. Beverly Hills, Calif.: Sage, 1980.

Riffel, R., Ianni, F., Orr, M., Reuss-Ianni, E., Savavoir, A., & Sparks, A. Research on desegregation in school and classroom settings. In *The desegregation future: A critical appraisal*. Washington, D.C.: National Institute of Education, 1976.

Rist, R., Hamilton, M., Holloway, W., Johnson, S., & Wiltberger, H. *Education and employment training: The views of youth*. Interim report No. 2, Youthwork National Policy Study. Ithaca, N.Y.: Cornell University, 1979.

Rist, R., Hamilton, M., Holloway, W., Johnson, S., & Wiltberger, H. *Targeting on in-school youth: Four strategies for coordinating education and employment training*. Youthwork National Policy Study. Ithaca, N.Y.: Cornell University, 1980. (a)

Rist, R., Hamilton, M., Holloway, W., Johnson, S., & Wiltberger, H. *Patterns of collaboration: The CETA/school linkage*. Youthwork National Policy Study, Ithaca, N.Y.: Cornell University, 1980. (b)

Sapir, E. Time perspective in aboriginal American culture: A study in method. In D. G. Mandelbaum (Ed.), *Selected writing of Edward Sapir*. Berkeley, Calif.: University of California Press, 1949. (Originally published 1916.)

Scriven, M. Two main approaches to evaluation. In R. M. Bossone (Ed.), *Proceedings, second national conference on testing*. New York: Center for Advanced Study in Education, City University of New York, 1978.

Sobel, L. *An assessment of the use of qualitative social science methods in program evaluation research*. Unpublished manuscript. Seattle: University of Washington, 1976.

Spindler, G. *Sociocultural and psychological processes in Menomini acculturation*. University of California Publications in Culture and Society, No. 5. Berkeley, Calif.: University of California Press, 1955.

Spindler, G., & Goldschmidt, W. R. *Experimental design in the study of culture change*. Southwestern Journal of Anthropology, 1952, *8*, 68–83.

Spindler, L. Menomini women and culture change. *American Anthropological Association Memoir*, 1962, *91*, 1–92.

Tallmadge, G. K. Avoiding problems in evaluation. *Journal of Career Education*, 1979, *5*(4), 300–308.

Tikunoff, W., & Ward, B. (Eds.). Exploring qualitative/quantitative research methodologies in education. *Anthropology and Education Quarterly*, 1977, *8*, 37–163.

Tylor, E. B. On the game of patolli in ancient Mexico, and its probably Asiatic origin. *Journal of the Royal Anthropological Institute of Great Britain and Ireland*, 1879, *8*, 116–131.

Weiss, C. H. (Ed.). Alternative models of program evaluation. *Social Work*, 1974, *19*, 675–681.

Weiss, R. S., & Rein, M. The evaluation of broad-aim programs: Difficulties in experimental design and an alternative. In C. H. Weiss (Ed.), *Evaluation action programs: Readings in social action and education*. Boston: Allyn & Bacon, 1972.

Wilson, S. The use of ethnographic techniques in educational research. *Review of Educational Research*, 1977, *47*(2), 245–265.

Wolcott, H. PA Comments: Ethnography and applied policy research. *Practicing Anthropology*, 1980, *3*(2), 39. (a)

Wolcott, H. How to look like an anthropologist without really being one. *Practicing Anthropology*, 1980, *3*(2), 6–7, 56–59. (b)

3

Ethnographic Data Collection in Evaluation Research

MARGARET D. LeCOMPTE
JUDITH P. GOETZ

During the past decade, interest in the application of ethnographic research strategies has increased among educational policy and evaluation researchers. The growth of educational ethnography as a subfield of anthropology and education (e.g., Comitas & Dolgin, 1978) and dissatisfaction with limitations of traditional quantitative designs (e.g., Eisner, 1979; Filstead, 1979) have contributed to the increasingly common phenomenon of incorporating an ethnographic component into evaluation research. The systems-analysis approach (Rivlin, 1971), commonly used in economics and industry and which has dominated federally funded educational evaluation, emphasizes measurement of variables that are scaled or quantified easily and that generate highly reliable data. In many cases, this approach has been inappropriate to the phenomena under investigation and has produced data of uneven and questionable validity (Guttentag, 1977; Helfgot, 1974; House, 1979; LeCompte, 1970). The results have failed to satisfy those involved in programs and their evaluations, to explain success or failure of innovations, or even to define success adequately. Constructs and models lacking meaning for participants have been used in evaluation designs; goals assessed often have been insignificant to program planners; and final reports have addressed few questions important to participants. Process data on problems and successes of program implementation rarely have been reported. Because of their higher internal validity (Crain, 1977; Denzin, 1978; Erickson, 1977; Reichardt

AUTHORS' NOTE: This chapter is based on a paper presented at the annual meeting of the American Educational Research Association, Boston, April 1980. Its revision has benefited from the comments of our colleagues: C. R. Berryman, M.J.M. Brown, L. Galda, M. Ginsburg, C. D. Glickman, A. D. Pellegrini, D. O. Schneider, J. Taxel, and two anonymous EEPA reviewers.

& Cook, 1979), ethnographic research strategies recently have been advocated to correct these deficiencies. Literature encouraging the use of ethnography in educational evaluation has become abundant (e.g., Koppelman, 1979; Patton, 1980). This article is designed as a critical guide to doing ethnographic evaluation for those who now are convinced of its usefulness, rather than as a position paper defending its utility.

Ethnographies are analytic descriptions or reconstructions of intact cultural scenes and groups (Spradley & McCurdy, 1972) which delineate the shared beliefs, practices, artifacts, folk knowledge, and behaviors of some group of people. The design of ethnographic studies mandates investigatory strategies conducive to cultural reconstruction. First, these strategies elicit data that are phenomenological. They represent the world view of the participants being investigated. Second, ethnographic research strategies are empirical and naturalistic. They involve acquisition of firsthand, sensory accounts of phenomena as they occur in real world settings. Third, ethnographic research is holistic. Ethnographers seek to construct descriptions of total phenomena within their various contexts and to generate from these descriptions major variables affecting human behavior and belief toward the phenomena. Finally, ethnography is multimodal; ethnographic researchers use a variety of research technologies (Wilson, 1977).

Three kinds of data provided by ethnographic research strategies are useful in assessing the impact of an intervention program or curricular innovation (for alternative schemes for classifying evaluation research according to overall evaluative purposes, highlighting case study or ethnographic methods, see Patton, 1980; Stufflebeam & Webster, 1980):

(1) Baseline data: information about the human and technological context of the research population and program setting. Social, psychological, cultural, demographic, and physical features of the context should be identified, both for assessing intervention impact and for establishing parameters that could affect generalizability to other settings and populations. The institutional framework and its relationships with other institutions should be examined for the variety of countervailing influences impinging upon change and stability (cf., e.g., Apple & King, 1977; Sharp & Green, 1975).

(2) Process data: information determining what happened in the course of a curricular program or innovation. The way the program or intervention and the evaluation was approached and handled by participants provides data for assessing the impact and success of an intervention (Suchman, 1967).

(3) Values data: information about the values of the participants, the program administrators, and the policymakers who financed the program. The values implications of an innovation, whose values the intervention supports and whose are neglected, may affect decisions about further dissemination (Krathwohl, 1980; Suchman, 1967).

The characteristics of ethnographic research outlined above contribute to providing more integrated baseline and process data and generating more comprehensive parameters for values data than do conventional evaluation designs (Guba, 1980). Because ethnography uses multiple data collection strategies, it provides the flexibility needed for the variety of situations that evaluators are requested to assess. Research designs based on combinations of data collection strategies also provide more complete and complex data on phenomena than do unimodal research designs. They possess more credibility because they enhance reliability and validity of the research results (Denzin, 1978). They may assess processes as well as provide specific information on effects of programs.

To the extent that an evaluator wishes to collect baseline, process, values, and even product evaluation data that are phenomenological, naturalistic, and holistic—generated through multimodal research designs—ethnographic research strategies may be useful. This discussion delineates ways ethnographers traditionally collect data of this nature and indicates how these data collection methods may be applied to curriculum and program evaluation.

METHODS FOR RECORDING ETHNOGRAPHIC DATA

To the traditional evaluator, accustomed to a wide variety of instruments, rating scales, and tests, the data collection techniques most commonly used by ethnographers may seem absurdly simple. The primary tools of the ethnographer are eyes and ears and other sensory abilities, augmented by a collection of mechanical aids such as video- and audiotape recorders and still and motion-picture cameras (e.g., Collier, 1973).

The material recorded includes what investigators observe themselves, what they can induce participants to record, and what they and participants photograph, tape record, film, or videotape. These create a data bank of field notes, formal and informal reviews, questionnaires, written records, newspapers, memos, diaries, letters, recollections and reminiscences, myths, and folktales, as well as more standardized instruments for recording values and perceptions such as projective devices.

Recording methods must be chosen according to a number of criteria. Some, like videotapes, are more obtrusive than others and may be obviated in sensitive settings. Others may be complicated to use or may record data not readily usable. Whichever means of recording data are chosen, researchers should select only what they can use well. Complex, sensitive cameras and comparable equipment may interfere with the data collection procedure unless they are used by skilled practitioners. Novices are served better by simpler devices which provide the data required, albeit less artistically. Second, although use of cameras and recorders may increase the reliability of a study by registering data that the researcher might forget or overlook, such equipment records only uncodified and unclassified data. Huge amounts of data are generated that require organization(Goetz & LeCompte, 1981). Third, they induce strong reactions from subjects; they can affect seriously the degree to which the recorded behavior is natural (LeCompte & Goetz, 1982) and thus may reduce the validity of a study. A final problem is that cameras and recorders are as selective in what they register as are the researchers who use them; they present only abstractions from an entire social context.

Field notes and other handwritten records are less complete than mechanically produced records. Because they may be idiosyncratic, reflecting the interests of a particular researcher, and because they represent data preselected to some degree, they are less amenable to accurate enumerative coding than are films, tapes, and photographs. Such data may obstruct efforts to establish quantitative measures for intercoder reliability. Properly conducted, however, recording observations in field notes may be less reactive than mechanical strategies, eliciting less contrived behavior from participants. Field notes also may generate data that are more flexible than are records produced by mechanical means: Field notes may be coded informally during the process of data collection and used to generate categories and constructs about phenomena at the moment they are observed.

METHODS FOR COLLECTING
ETHNOGRAPHIC DATA

In their seminal work on ethnographic research techniques, Pelto and Pelto (1978) distinguish two categories of research tools. One group consists of methods for collecting data that involve interaction between researcher and participant and that produce, as a result, reactions from participants that may affect the data collected. Unobtrusive and other less reactive techniques (Webb, et al., 1966), necessitating little or no interaction between investigator and participant, comprise the second category.

INTERACTIVE METHODS

All four strategies discussed below—participant observation, key informant interviewing, career histories, and surveys—depend in some degree on the investigator questioning participants and eliciting data from them. They share an advantage over most unobtrusive measures in that procurement of information is controllable: through elicitation, the investigator is better able to obtain appropriate data. However, they are more reactive or obtrusive. The so-called observer effect may lead participants, deliberately or unconsciously, to supply false or misleading data.

Participant Observation. Participant observation is the primary technique used by ethnographers to gain access to data. In this mode the investigator lives as much as possible with and in the same manner as the subjects being investigated. Researchers take part in the daily activities of people, reconstructing their interactions and activities in field notes taken as soon as possible after their occurrence (for detailed presentations of participant observation, see McCall & Simmons, 1969; Spradley, 1980). Included in the field notes are interpretive comments based on researcher perceptions; these are affected by the social role taken by the researcher within the group and by the way people react as a consequence of that social role. Many of these interpretive notes are based on the empathy which investigators develop with subjects in the process of taking a variety of roles in the course of the investigation. Janes (1961) discusses the differential data to which he had access as his role underwent progressive redefinition during eight months of field-work in a small midwestern town. Everhart (1977), whose field residence extended over a two-year period in a junior high school, documents changes in his sensitivity to data as a function of participants' redefinition of his role.

Participant observation serves to elicit from subjects their definitions of reality and the organizing constructs of their world. Because these are expressed in particular linguistic patterns, it is crucial that the ethnographer be familiar with the language variations or argot used by subjects. Evaluators studying children and teenagers in schools should be familiar with and imperturbable toward current juvenile word usage; they should recognize the tendency for teacher talk to center around descriptions of what is socially acceptable, rather than of what teachers actually do (Keddie, 1971).

One problem researchers may encounter is that subject or participant reports of their activities and beliefs often are widely discrepant from their observed behavior. As a means of determining how subjects view and behave within their world, participant observation enables the researcher to verify that the subjects are doing what they or the researcher thinks they are doing. In curriculum evaluation, participant observation enables the researcher to determine whether subjects are processing information or reacting to a curricular innovation in the manner intended. The more probable discovery is that participants respond to innovations in a variety of unintended ways. In their ethnography of the development of an innovative elementary school, Smith and Keith (1971) document the myriad ways implementations of innovations differ from intended designs of innovations. Their study stands as a classic exemplar of discontinuities between the goals and objectives of educational reform and the means available to achieve these ends (cf., e.g., Smith & Carpenter, 1972; Smith & Schumacher, 1972).

The contribution of participant observation to gathering process data in evaluation studies has been demonstrated by a number of educational ethnographies. The Center for New Schools (1972) used participant observation and interviewing to evaluate faculty-developed goals during the initial two years of a public alternative high school. The school's failure to achieve one such goal, student participation in institutional decisionmaking, was documented from the perspective of the students and was explained by the researchers as caused by historical and maturational factors beyond the control of the school's teachers. Combining participant observation and interviewing with questionnaires and other standardized instruments, Deal (1975) reported a comparative evaluation of two alternative high schools in which organizational success and failure depended on the resolution of authority problems. Richberg's evaluation (1976) of a Follow Through Program in a Choctaw Indian community identified comparable obstructions to effective program implementation, deriving from conflicting authority jurisdictions. Trend (1979) demonstrated how resolving discrepancies between participant observation data and conventionally quantified outcome measures in an evaluation of a federal housing program for a low-income families contributed to a more comprehensive explanation for problems arising in such programs. La Belle, Moll, and Weisner (1979) have proposed a research strategy that allows participant observers to refine the collection of process data so as to produce valid and reliable data on program effects. Other investigators (e.g., Burns, 1975; Center for New Schools, 1976; Everhart, 1976;

Herriott, 1977), in examining problems of implementing participant-observation components of evaluation designs, have identified areas of discrepant value orientations, patterns of social interaction, and methods for conflict resolution among program participants, program developers and evaluators, and policymakers that obstruct achievement of program objectives.

Less obvious is the role of participant observation in collecting baseline data. The ethnographer's entry to the field, both in evaluation studies and in traditional fieldwork, is accompanied by an informal process of "shagging around" (LeCompte, 1969), sometimes designated "mapping" (Schatzman & Strauss, 1973). Shagging around involves "casing the joint": getting acquainted with the participants, learning where they congregate, recording demographic characteristics of the population, mapping the physical layout, and creating a description of the context of the phenomenon or the particular innovation under consideration.

More formally, shagging around consists of taking a census of the people involved in a group or program—determining such factors as their number, ages, training, socioeconomic status, sex, racial and ethnic identity, and organizational status position, both formal and informal. It involves an informal process of eliciting participant constructs by means of careful listening and subsequent recording of what has been heard. In this way, the investigator examines how people categorize each other, the central issues of importance to participants, and any potential areas of conflict and accord.

In the process of shagging around, key informants can be identified, and a map of time use and episodes or daily events can be developed so that parameters are established for later, more detailed mapping strategies. Most important is the collection of stories, anecdotes, and myths, such as are found in the daily round of gossip in the teachers' lounge or among student groups, with which a sense of the dominant themes of concern to teachers, parents, and children can be developed. These data indicate what is important and unimportant, how people view each other, and how they evaluate their participation in groups and programs. They provide the basis for determining the extent to which a particular innovation is being implemented, or not implemented, according to plan. Nelson (1979), for example, in her analysis of special education directors in a Midwestern state, analyzed goal statements exchanged between the directors and their hierarchical superiors in accounting for the directors' success in promoting their programs and agendas.

Another task accomplished during the early stages of a study is parallel to recording components of the external environment. Ethnographers customarily note their initial subjective reactions to the group under investigation. These reactions and evaluations often form the basis for preliminary analytic categories and constructs; they provide a means by which other scholars may assess possible sources of bias arising from the individuality of the researcher. Geer's account (1964) of the entry period in a study of midwestern undergraduates (Becker et al., 1968) documents both her developing relationship with the study participants and the early evolution of constructs and hypotheses which became central to the study's conclusions.

Shagging around facilitates the development of more formal means of data collection such as structured and unstructured interviewing. Denzin (1978) differentiates three forms of interview: the scheduled standardized interview, the nonscheduled standardized interview, and the nonstandardized interview (cf., Patton, 1980 for an alternative approach to classifying interviews and for an extensive discussion of ethnographic interviewing in evaluation research). Some researchers refer to the latter two instruments as interview guides in which general questions to be addressed and specific information desired by the researcher are anticipated, but may be addressed during the interview informally in whatever order or context they happen to arise. Whether interviews are structured or unstructured, standardized or nonstandardized, they include the following specialized forms: key informant interviewing, career or life histories, and surveys.

Key Informant Interviewing. Key informants are individuals who possess special knowledge, status, or communicative skills and who are willing to share that knowledge and skill with the researcher (Zelditch, 1962). They frequently are chosen because they have access—in time, space, or perspective—to observations denied the ethnographer (for detailed presentations of key informant interviewing, see Freilich, 1979; Spradley, 1979). They may be atypical individuals and should be chosen with care so as to ensure that representativeness among a group of key informants is achieved (see Dean et al., 1967, for a discussion of common types of informants).

Key informants have been used in a variety of ways in educational ethnography. Carroll (1977) developed his discussion of participant constructs in the domains of work and play by interviewing children as he and they observed ongoing classroom activities. Jackson (1968) used interviews with the students he studied as a means to corroborate his own observations of classroom exchanges. Smith and Geoffrey (1968) provided a model for investigator-participant teamwork in their analysis of the behavior of a classroom teacher and his rationale for his actions; this research partnership has a lengthy history in ethnography (e.g., Malinowski, 1935; Whyte, 1955). Data collected from key informants may add material to baseline data otherwise inaccessible to the ethnographer because of time constraints in a study. Because key informants are often reflective individuals, they may contribute insights to process variables not evident to the investigator. Finally, key informants may sensitize the researcher to value dilemmas and implications.

Career Histories. Anthropologists use the term life history interviewing to refer to the elicitation of the life narratives of participants, which then are used to formulate questions or inferences about the culture of a people (for detailed discussions of life history interviewing, see Denzin, 1978; Langness, 1965). In educational research, life histories may be unnecessary for most purposes, but career histories may be useful devices for determining how participants respond to settings, events, or particular innovations. Career histories consist of narrative accounts of individuals' professional lives.

One element of Wolcotts's study (1973) of an elementary school principal is the participant's account of his or her career to the time when the researcher entered the field. A variation on this method was developed by Fuchs (1969) who followed the emerging career histories of novice teachers in inner city school settings through intermittant interviewing. Career histories may be used to assess differences in life and training experiences (e.g., Newman, 1979, 1980) or as evidence for predicting which teachers might be most amenable to participating in a given innovative program. They can supply significant baseline data to an evaluation study and provide a source for inferences about value contrasts in school settings.

Surveys. Survey instruments and procedures are among the most common research strategies. In ethnographic studies, they are based on information first gathered through the less formal and more unstructured methods described above. They generally take one of three forms: confirmation instruments, participant-construct instruments, and projective devices.

Confirmation Surveys. Structured interviews or questionnaires verifying the applicability of key informant and other data to the general population are used frequently by ethnographers. In that surveys are based on formal instrumentation, they facilitate replication of studies and comparison of results with other, larger groups (for detailed discussions of confirmation surveys, see Colson, 1954; Gordon, 1975). Confirmation surveys are mandated in curriculum evaluation where an innovative program involves large numbers of participants, whether teachers or students. They are based on a variety of sampling procedures to ensure representativeness. Their purpose is to assess the extent to which participants hold similar beliefs, share specific constructs, or execute comparable behaviors. They may provide material for baseline, process, and values data or for production of a final report on program effects. One caveat needs to be mentioned: Self-reports of behavior should be corroborated by observational data because they are sometimes inaccurate indicators of actual behavior (see Dean & Whyte, 1958, for sources of interviewee bias and distortion). Self-reports are useful for assessing how individuals make judgments about people and events, and they do register what people think or do or what they think is socially acceptable to do.

In her analysis of differential teaching patterns among urban schools serving different racial and socioeconomic groups, Leacock (1969) used confirmation surveys to establish concurrent validity of her observations in classrooms. Ogbu (1974) sampled more widely than Leacock in his interviews with teachers, parents, students, and other community participants in order to demonstrate common attitudes toward and beliefs about education in a lower-class, ethnically mixed, urban neighborhood.

Participant-Construct Instruments. A second category of survey commonly used by ethnographers consists of instruments designed to elicit participant constructs. Measuring value judgments, or the strength of feeling people have about phenomena, or eliciting the categories into which people classify items in their physical world involves the determination of the set of "agreed upons" which inform the world of each participant. These consist of categories of knowledge deemed important by the group, the canons of discrimination used to sort items into categories, and processes that are a function of the way variables are seen to relate to one another (Kimball, 1965). Participant-construct surveys thus provide material for both process and values data (for a more detailed discussion of participant construct surveys, see Spradley, 1972).

Researchers can request participants to sort and classify any number of items. Teachers may sort children according to their popularity, to their desirability as students (Feshbach, 1969; Silberman, 1971), or to their ascribed intelligence (Rist, 1970). Teachers may group children into whatever categories they feel exist in a class and explain what those groups are and how they are defined. Goetz (1976b) used this procedure with third graders, identifying child-designated and defined categories of good and bad students. This is a particularly efficient way to elicit participant constructs. It resembles the technique of linguistic elicitation in which lexical and other items of vocabulary are obtained from informants and sorted into like, unlike, and related categories. Such requests for participant sorting and classification should be preceded by preliminary fieldwork so that the investigator can structure the task initially for the informant. Pelto and Pelto (1978) restrict the use of participant-construct surveys to situations where fieldwork and accompanying strategies for reliability and validity support the credibility of the data gathered.

A variation of the participant-construct survey is participant enumeration and listing. In this method, participants are asked to tell the investigator what all members are of a particular category of things. In classic community studies, the analogy is a request to enumerate all the types of birds found in the area, all the kinds of food eaten by community people, or all the gift-exchanging occasions throughout the calendar year.

In order to develop a typology of kindergarten children's perceptions of student and teacher roles, LeCompte (1980) asked them to tell her all the things they thought they and their teachers could do in kindergarten. Fetterman (1979) used photographs of familiar neighborhood sites and settings to elicit the ways in which adolescent informants categorized their own community. Such techniques can be developed further by asking participants to sort and arrange given sets of items to see which belong together and which do not, eliciting through conversation the parameters of categories and the canons of discrimination used to determine them. Sorting and arranging techniques customarily are reserved for physical items, but they can form the basis for sociograms, where participants sort and arrange names of their fellows along any number of dimensions.

Projective Devices. Often, placing individuals into the context to be assessed is impossible. In this case, indirect or projective techniques may be substituted (for detailed discussions of projective strategies, see Anastasi, 1976; Lindzey, 1961). Photographs, drawings, or games often can elicit people's opinions or reactions or enable the researcher to determine patterns of social interaction nonobservable in the natural setting. LeCompte (1980) was faced with the difficulty of asking four- and five-year-old children to imagine what kindergarten would be like before they had attended school. She used photographs of typical classroom situations as stimuli for what otherwise would have been a task too abstract for children of that age to perform. Pelto and Pelto (1978) discuss the use of games, naturally occurring and contrived, as projective techniques designed to elicit interaction styles among groups of people. Spindler (1973, 1974) used abstract drawings of familiar rural and urban scenes and activities to assess the school's role in a German village's transition from rural context to urban community (see Collier, 1973, for an extended discussion of using concrete visual stimuli for responses).

More familiar to many researchers is the use of vague or indirect stimuli to elicit statements about people's values or images of themselves. Spindler and Spindler (1958) used the Rorschach technique to develop hypotheses about the relationship between personality types and acculturation to white society among the Wisconsin Menominee. Educational ethnographers more often use participant-constructed abstractions such as the Draw-a-Man test. Hostetler and Huntington (1971) used this technique to examine subcultural differences in the effectiveness of curricula in Amish and mainstream schools. It also was used by Minuchin, Biber, Shapiro, and Zimiles (1969) to assess differences in the effect of classroom environment and authority structure on the self-concept and level of social and emotional maturity of elementary school children in New York City.

SUMMARY

One advantage of the strategies discussed in the preceding section of this chapter is that, properly conducted, they yield data with high validity. They customarily are used in natural, noncontrived settings. Their formats are concrete and elicit empirical, participant categories. Because they often are used over a long period of time, most provide a continual opportunity to match and refine scientific categories with participant reality.

Conversely, they can yield data that are less replicable or reliable than that produced by noninteractive strategies. For example, inferences drawn from projective devices are less amenable to interobserver agreement than are inferences drawn from more concrete data. Participant constructs, which are grounded in particular times, settings, and populations, may fail to replicate precisely. Confirmation surveys, based on questionnaires or scheduled standardized protocols, can be controlled more stringently for reliability than most other interactive methods. Reliability for career histories, key informant interviewing, and participant observation depends on (1) clear exposition of the role taken by the ethnographer in the field and the precise techniques used for data collection and analysis and (2) the clarity with which constructs developed in a study are presented (see LeCompte & Goetz, 1982, for a more detailed discussion of reliability and validity in ethnographic research).

NONINTERACTIVE METHODS

Noninteractive strategies for collecting ethnographic data allow the researcher to gather material with little or no exchange with the participants or subjects of a study. The three methods discussed below—nonparticipant observation, archival and demographic collection, and physical trace collection—are less reactive or obtrusive than interactive strategies (Webb et al., 1966). The researcher is less likely to influence participant responses. On the other hand, noninteractive methods are more fortuitous. Investigators may or may not locate sufficient data to address initial themes and questions.

Nonparticipant Observation. Treated by Pelto and Pelto (1978) and others (e.g., Gold, 1958) as a category separate from participant observation, nonparticipant observation involves merely watching what is going on and recording events on the spot. As a completely distinct category, nonparticipant observation exists only where interaction is viewed from hidden cameras and recorders or through one-way mirrors. Interaction is impossible to avoid in social situations. Whenever researchers are observing on the scene, they acquire some role and status. In school settings where curriculum evaluation is conducted, investigators necessarily will interact with the teachers and pupils under consideration, even if only nonverbally, and will become, to some extent, participants. This need not be a liability: It simply means that estimated consequences of being a participant should be noted in the research report. Three forms of nonparticipant observation commonly are used by educational ethnographers: stream-of-behavior chronicles, analysis of proxemics and kinesics, and interaction analysis.

Stream-of-Behavior Chronicles. The recording and analysis of streams of behavior in narrative chronicles, delineated by Barker (1963), requires accurate, minute-by-minute accounts of what a participant does and says. These may be filmed, taped, or recorded by hand on the spot. Barker and Wright's account (1951) of a day in the life of a seven-year-old boy may be the most extreme exemplar of this strategy. More commonly, ethnographers sample across participants, events, and settings, collecting chronicles pertinent to major study themes and questions. Peshkin (1972) sampled for stream-of-behavior narratives in his study of the effects of schooling on children in a traditional African culture. Patterns of behavior among children were compared with six cultures by Whiting and Whiting (1975) who analyzed behavior streams sampled from children in these cultures. Goetz (1976a, 1976b) developed a taxonomy of classroom behavior among third graders, based on stream-of-behavior narratives intermittently sampled from her study participants. LeCompte (1978), on the other hand, took continual stream-of-behavior records in her comparative analysis of the normative behaviors of four elementary schoolteachers. Studies such as these facilitate the delineation of categories of activities, the study of time and motion use, and the mapping of movement and physical environment. Stream-of-behavior chronicles can generate invaluable process data for curriculum evaluation where researchers are concerned with factors such as actual manipulation of materials and applications of particular teaching strategies. Pelto and Pelto (1978) qualify the use of data collected through stream-of-behavior strategies, noting that the interpretation of such material should be validated through participant observation, key informant interviewing, or surveys. Similarly, Smith and Brock (1970) note the philosophical biases inherent in choices of observational and recording strategies and in the use of units of analysis, which may be neither meaningful to nor shared by the research subjects.

Proxemics and Kinesics. These approaches are concerned, respectively, with social uses of space and with bodily movement (for detailed discussions of proxemics and kinesics, see Birdwhistell, 1970; Hall, 1974). Educational ethnographers tend to incorporate observational records of movement and space use informally with other narratives (e.g., Goetz, 1976b; Larkins & Oldham, 1976; Rist, 1970). Shultz and Florio (1979), however, focused primarily on an analysis of classroom space use in their investigation of the development of social competence among primary-level students. Guilmet (1978, 1979) drew from kinesic analysis in his comparison of the differing behavior styles of Native American and white children and of differential teacher reactions to such styles. Incorporating observational records that focus on proxemics and kinesics may be particularly useful where a curriculum evaluation entails a new use of classroom space or new patterns of teacher-student interaction.

Interaction Analysis Protocols. Finally, nonparticipant observation may include any of a variety of interaction analysis protocols (for detailed discussions of interaction analysis protocols, see Medley & Mitzel, 1963; Rosenshine & Furst, 1973). These range in structure from informal sociograms devised on the spot by the observer to standardized behavioral rating systems such as that developed by Flanders (1970). The focus here is on collecting records of ways participants interact with one another. Educational ethnographers tend to reject Flanders-like systems, despite their reliability and generalizability, because such systems record only a few, narrowly defined categories of behavior and because they rarely match emerging patterns of concern. More frequently, investigators devise their own protocols, based on early observations in the field. Borman (1978) coded group participation according to numbers of individuals involved, in examining patterns of social control across differentially structured classroom environments. Although most such analyses have focused on student-student or teacher-student interaction patterns, comparable examinations of inter-action styles among and between groups of teachers, administrators, curriculum developers, and policymakers may contribute both process data and values data to studies in curriculum evaluation (cf., e.g., Hymes, 1967; Sinclair & Coulthard, 1975).

Archival and Demographic Collection. Based on the preliminary mapping described above, ethnographers discover the range of written and symbolic records kept by or on participants in a social group (for detailed discussions of archival and demographic collection, see Pitt, 1972; Webb et al., 1966). Official demographic material may reveal characteristics of the population under investigation that provide a framework for baseline data. The collection and analysis of textbooks, curriculum guides, memos, enrollment records, student and teacher handbooks, student classroom products, lesson plans, correspondence, government documents, and such researcher-stimulated archives as teacher diaries, logs, and recollections can provide invaluable resources for baseline, process, and values data.

In assessing community participation in educational decision mak-ing, specified as an objective by one of the projects in the Experimental Schools Program, Mercurio (1979) analyzed attendance records and minutes of a citizen advisory board for data that substantiated information from surveys, interviews, and participant observation. He concluded that community involvement, in this instance, was nonrepre-sentative and generally ineffective, but useful in providing an outlet for the concerns of influential community members. Lee's analysis (1955) of teachers' manuals and guides used in high school home economics programs is a provocative statement about the discrepancies between program objectives and the means advocated to implement such programs. Similarly, content analysis of textbooks can delineate social and philosophical biases in curricular goals (Fitzgerald, 1979; Zeigler &

Peak, 1970). The application of data drawn from school enrollment records, community-action group documents, student personnel files, school board meeting minutes, and school annual reports strengthened many of the conclusions reported by Ogbu (1974) in the study cited above.

Physical Trace Collection. Among the least obtrusive of the noninteractive data collection methods is the collection of physical traces, the erosion and accretion of artifacts and natural objects used by people in groups (for a detailed discussion of physical trace collection, see Webb et al., 1966). This also may be the method most neglected by educational ethnographers, despite its potential for generating valuable process and baseline data.

Curriculum evaluators may examine such factors as what equipment is used the most—and thus requires the most repair, according to school records—and what equipment is ignored. What materials remain in teachers' closets, covered with dust months after they were to be used? Who has access to equipment and supplies? Problems of access may explain why planned innovations fail to materialize. Evaluators also can examine what is discarded and what is retained. Occasionally, this garbage-dump strategy adapted from archeologists can result in educational gains. The 1967 Woodlawn Experimental School Project (LeCompte, 1969) discovered that low attendance patterns were related both to glass debris, which littered the school grounds and which children and parents regarded as unsafe, and to the existence of street gangs whose members harrassed children on their way to school. Attendance figures rose when increased police surveillance curtailed gang activity and local merchants were persuaded to sell soft drinks in cans, rather than in breakable bottles.

SUMMARY

Noninteractive strategies for data collection possess several advantages for ethnographic researchers. In most cases, many types of data are collected or generated in raw form and consequently are relatively amenable to reanalysis by either the collector or by other researchers. Such reprocessing may be used to establish reliability coefficients or to generate new constructs and hypotheses. Noninteractive strategies also tend to be more easily replicated than interactive strategies, partially because observer effects are controlled more easily. On the other hand, access to the records and written materials comprising much of this type of data may be contingent on the development of rapport between researcher and subjects. In those cases, the type, amount, and quality of data collected may be as dependent on the special characteristics of the researcher as are data derived from more interactive and obtrusive strategies. In these situations, the special role occupied by the researcher should be delineated clearly.

Unfortunately, the very richness of data drawn from archives or from stream-of-behavior chronicles can be a disadvantage. At issue are decisions regarding the appropriateness of given data to the research question and the suitability of the analytic strategies proposed for their reduction. Such decisions determine which data are relevant and facilitate production of the final report (Goetz & LeCompte, 1981). The Whiting and Whiting data (1975) were collected in such an unselected manner that the final analysis was published over 20 years after the data had been gathered. Overcollection of unselected data is a serious problem in the use of both noninteractive and interactive methods of data collection.

CONCLUSION

Ethnographic data collection strategies can be used in curriculum and program evaluation in two ways: comprehensive adoption of the entire ethnographic process or strategic selection of a few data collection techniques (for a statement of problems and issues in ethnographic evaluation, see Knapp, 1979). Choice between these alternatives is informed by the objectives of the research. If the goal is a descriptive product intended to document shared beliefs, practices, artifacts, environments, folk knowledge, behaviors, subtle patterns of interaction, and a comprehensive inventory of program effects, then the appropriate choice is the development of an ethnography of the entire intervention program. Smith and Keith's analysis (1971) of the establishment of an innovative elementary school and Wax's documentation (1982) of the process of desegregation in five public schools are ethnographies comparable to traditional investigations conducted by anthropologists and sociologists. They offer implicit or explicit explanations to account for the patterns observed. Such ethnographies of organizational or curricular innovations differ from community and tribal studies only in their focus. They are costly, requiring liberal financing and highly trained personnel. Results may be inaccessible until several years after the innovation has been either disseminated or rejected.

A second objective is the selective use of one or a few ethnographic techniques of data collection in what is otherwise a traditional quasi-experimental or survey design. Such limited applications may provide some baseline, process, and values data or may strengthen the validity of standardized instrumentation. For example, Hall and Loucks (1977) used limited nonparticipant observation to assess the validity of a teacher questionnaire, designed to determine the extent to which instructors actually use educational innovations in their classrooms. Limited use of ethnographic techniques also may be used to highlight specific program effects of interest to developers or program participants. Applications such as these have the advantage of reducing required time and resources while producing useful results soon available to policymakers.

The significance of the distinction between overall versus limited ethnographic design lies principally in interpretation of their results. Conclusions based on 9 to 18 months of fieldwork, grounded in a variety of collection and analytic techniques, must be assessed differently than one-time, nonparticipant observations of a variety of classrooms or social scenes. The more limited the design, the less credible and valid are the results. Decisions by evaluators as to which design to choose must be based on all factors identified: the research problem; goals of participants; credibility of the investigator, methods, and design; and the time and resources available.

REFERENCES

Anastasi, A. *Psychological testing* (4th ed.). New York: Macmillan, 1976, chap. 19.

Apple, M. W., & King, N. K. What do schools teach? *Curriculum Inquiry.* 1977, *6,* 341–369.

Barker, R. G. *The stream of behavior: Explorations of its structure and content.* New York: Appleton-Century-Crofts. 1963.

Barker, R. G. & Wright, H. F. *One boy's day: A specimen record of behavior.* New York: Harper, 1951.

Becker, H., Geer, B., & Hughes, F. *Making the grade: The academic side of college life.* New York: John Wiley, 1968.

Birdwhistell, R. *Kinesics and context.* Philadelphia: University of Pennsylvania Press, 1970.

Borman, K. Social control and schooling: Power and process in two kindergarten settings. *Anthropology and Education Quarterly,* 1978, *9,* 38–53.

Burns, A. An anthropologist at work: Field perspectives on applied ethnography and an independent research firm. *Anthropology and Education Quarterly,* 1975 (4), 28–33.

Carroll, T. C. Work and play: A probe of the formation, use and interaction of adult and child activity domains (Doctoral dissertation. State University of New York at Buffalo, 1976). *Dissertation Abstracts International,* 1977, *38,* 5211A–5212A. (University Microfilms No. 77–3520)

Center for New Schools. Strengthening alternative high schools. *Harvard Educational Review,* 1972, *42,* 313–350.

Center for New Schools. Ethnographic evaluation in education. *Journal of Research and Development in Education,* 1976, *9*(4), 3–11.

Collier, J., Jr. *Alaskan Eskimo education: A film analysis of cultural confrontation in the schools.* New York: Holt, Rinehart & Winston, 1973.

Colson, E. The intensive study of small sample communities. In R. F. Spencer (Ed.). *Method and perspective in anthropology.* Minneapolis: University of Minnesota Press, 1954.

Comitas, L. & Dolgin, J. On anthropology and education: Retrospect and prospect. *Anthropology and Education Quarterly,* 1978, *9,* 165–180.

Crain, R. L. Racial tensions in high schools: Pushing the survey method closer to reality. *Anthropology and Education Quarterly,* 1977, *8,* 142–151.

Deal, T. E. An organizational explanation of the failure of alternative secondary schools. *Educational Researcher,* 1975, *4*(4), 10–16.

Dean, J. P., Eichhorn, R. L. & Dean, L. R. Fruitful informants for intensive interviewing. In I. T. Doby (Ed.). *An introduction to social research* (2nd ed.). New York: Meredith, 1967.

Dean, J. P. & Whyte, W. F. How do you know if the informant is telling the truth? *Human Organization,* 1958, *17*(2), 34–38.

Denzin, N. K. *The research act: A theoretical introduction to sociological methods* (2nd ed.). New York: McGraw-Hill, 1978.

Eisner, E. W. The use of qualitative forms of evaluation for improving educational practice. *Educational Evaluation and Policy Analysis,* 1979, *1*(6), 11–19.

Erickson, F. Some approaches to inquiry in school-community ethnography. *Anthropology and Education Quarterly,* 1977, *8,* 58–69.

Everhart, R. B. Ethnography and educational policy: Love and marriage or strange bedfellows? *Anthropology and Education Quarterly,* 1976, *7*(3). 17–25.

Everhart, R. B. Between stranger and friend: some consequences of "long term" fieldwork in schools. *American Educational Research Journal,* 1977, *14,* 1–15.

Feshbach, N. D. Student teacher preferences for elementary school pupils varying in personality characteristics. *Journal of Educational Psychology,* 1969, *60,* 126–132.

Fetterman, D. M. *Ethnographic techniques and concepts in educational evaluation.* Paper presented at American Anthropological Association, Cincinnati, December 1979.

Filstead, W. J. Qualitative methods: A needed perspective in evaluation research. In T. D. Cook & C. S. Reichardt (Eds.), *Qualitative and quantitative methods in evaluation research* . Beverly Hills, Calif: Sage, 1979.

Fitzgerald, F. *America revised: History schoolbooks in the twentieth century.* Boston: Little, Brown, 1979.

Flanders, N. A. *Analyzing teacher behavior.* Reading, Mass.: Addison-Wesley, 1970.

Freilich, M. (Ed.) *Marginal natives: Anthropologists at work.* New York: Harper & Row, 1970.

Fuchs, E. *Teachers talk: Views from inside city schools.* New York: Anchor Books, 1969.

Geer, B. First days in the field: A chronicle of research in progress. In P. E. Hammond (Ed.) *Sociologists at work.* New York: Basic Books, 1964.

Goetz, J. P. Behavioral configurations in the classroom: A case study. *Journal of Research and Development in Education,* 1976, *9*(4). 36-49. (a)

Goetz, J. P. Configuration in control and autonomy: A microethnography of a rural third-grade classroom (Doctoral dissertation, Indiana University, 1975). *Dissertation Abstracts International,* 1976. *36,* 6175A. (University Microfilms No. 76–6, 275) (b)

Goetz, J. P. & LeCompte, M. D. Ethnographic research and the problem of data reduction. *Anthropology and Education Quarterly,* 1981, *12,* 51–70.

Gold, R. L. Roles in sociological field observations. *Social Forces,* 1958, *36,* 217–223.

Gordon, R. L. *Interviewing: Strategy, techniques, and tactics* (Rev. ed.). Homewood, Ill.: Dorsey Press, 1975.

Guba, E. G. *Naturalistic and conventional inquiry.* Paper presented at the annual meeting of the American Educational Research Association, Boston, April 1980.

Guilmet, G. M. Navajo and Caucasian children's verbal and nonverbal-visual behavior in the urban classroom. *Anthropology and Education Quarterly,* 1978, 9, 196-215.

Guilmet, G. M. Instructor reaction to verbal and nonverbal-visual styles: An example of Navajo and Caucasian children. *Anthropology and Education Quarterly,* 1979, *10,* 254–266.

Guttentag, M. Evaluation and society. *Personality and Social Psychology Bulletin,* 1977, *3,* 31–40.

Hall, E. *Handbook for proxemic research.* Washington D.C.: Society for the Anthropology of Visual Communication, 1974.

Hall, G. E. & Loucks, S. F. A developmental model for determining whether the treatment is actually implemented. *American Educational Research Journal,* 1977, *14,* 263–276.

Helfgot, J. Professional reform organizations and the symbolic representation of the poor. *American Sociological Review,* 1974, *39,* 475–492.

Herriott, R. F. Ethnographic case studies in federally funded multidisciplinary policy research: Some design and implementation issues. *Anthropology and Education Quarterly,* 1977, *8,* 106–115.

Hostetler, J. A. & Huntington, G. E. *Children in Amish society: Socialization and community education.* New York: Holt, Rinehart & Winston, 1971.

House, E. R. The objectivity, fairness, and justice of federal evaluation policy as reflected in the Follow Through evaluation. *Educational Evaluation and Policy Analysis,* 1979, *1,* 28–42.

Hymes, D. Modes of interaction of language in social settings. *Journal of Social Issues,* 1967, *23,* 8–28.

Jackson, P. W. *Life in classrooms,* New York: Holt, Rinehart & Winston, 1968.

Janes, R. W. A note on phases of the community role of the participant observer. *American Sociological Review,* 1961, *26,* 446–450.

Keddie, N. Classroom knowledge: In M. F. D. Young (Ed). *Knowledge and control: New directions for the sociology of education.* London: Collier Macmillan, 1971.

Kimball, S. T. The transmission of culture. *Educational Horizons,* 1965, *43,* 161-186.

Knapp, M. S. Ethnographic contributions to evaluation research: The Experimental Schools Program evaluation and some alternatives. In T. C. Cook & C. S. Reichardt (Eds.), *Qualitative and quantitative methods in evaluation research.* Beverly Hills, Calif.: Sage, 1979.

Koppelman, K. L. The explication model: An anthropological approach to program evaluation. *Educational Evaluation and Policy Analysis,* 1979, 1(4), 59–64.

Krathwohl, D. R. The myth of value-free evaluation. *Educational Evaluation and Policy Analysis,* 1980, *2*(1), 37–45.

La Belle, T. J. , Moll, L. C. & Weisner, T. S. Context-based educational evaluation: A participant research strategy. *Educational Evaluation and Policy Analysis,* 1979, *1*(3), 85–94.

Langness, L. L. *The life history in anthropological science.* New York, Holt, Rinehart & Winston, 1965.

Larkins, A. G. , & Oldham, S. E. Patterns of racial separation in a desegregated high school. *Theory and Research in Social Education,* 1976, *4*(2), 23–38.

Leacock, E. B. *Teaching and learning in city schools: A comparative study.* New York: Basic Books,1969.

LeCompte, M. D. *The dilemmas of inner city school reform: The Woodlawn Experimental School Project.* Unpublished master's thesis, University of Chicago, 1969.

LeCompte, M. D. The uneasy alliance of community action and research. *School Review,* 1970, *79,* 125–132.

LeCompte, M. D. Learning to work: The hidden curriculum of the classroom. *Anthropology and Education Quarterly,* 1978, *9,* 22–27.

LeCompte, M. D. The civilizing of children: How young children learn to become students. *The Journal of Thought,* 1980, *15*(3), 105–127.

LeCompte, M. D. & Goetz J. P. Problems of reliability and validity in ethnographic research. *Review of Educational Research,* 1982, *52,* 31–60.

Lee, D. Discrepancies in the teaching of American culture. In G. D. Spindler (Ed.), *Education and anthropology.* Stanford, Calif.: Stanford University Press, 1955.

Lindzey, G. *Projective techniques and cross-cultural research.* New York: Appleton-Century-Crofts, 1961.

Malinowski, B. *Coral gardens and their magic.* London: George Allen Unwin, 1935.

McCall, G. J. & Simmons, J. L. (Eds.), *Issues in participant observation: A text and reader.* Reading, Mass.: Addison-Wesley, 1969.

Medley, D. M. & Mitzel, H. E. Measuring classroom behavior by systematic observation. In N. L. Gage (Ed.), *Handbook of research on teaching.* Chicago: Rand McNally, 1963.

Mercurio, J. A. Community involvement in cooperative decision making: Some lessons learned. *Educational Evaluation and Policy Analysis,* 1979, *1*(6), 37–46.

Minuchin, P., Biber, B., Shapiro, E. & Zimiles, H. *The psychological impact of school experience.* New York: Basic Books, 1969.

Nelson, A. G. Information makes might: The relationship between information and power explored. *Anthropology and Education Quarterly,* 1979, *10,* 96–108.

Newman, K. K. Middle-aged experienced teachers' perceptions of their career development (Doctoral dissertation, Ohio State University, 1978). *Dissertation Abstracts International,* 1979, *39,* 4885A–4886A. (University Microfilms No. 7902196)

Newman, K. K. Stages in an unstaged occupation. *Educational Leadership,* 1980, *37,* 514–516.

Ogbu, J. U. *The next generation: An ethnography of education in an urban neighborhood.* New York: Academic Press, 1974.

Patton, M. Q. *Qualitive evaluation methods.* Beverly Hills, Calif.:Sage, 1980, chaps. 1-5, 7.

Pelto, P. J. & Pelto, G. H. *Anthropological research: The structure of inquiry* (2nd ed.), Cambridge, England: Cambridge University Press, 1978.

Peshkin, A. *Kanuri schoolchildren: Education and social-mobilization in Nigeria.* New York: Holt, Rinehart & Winston, 1972.

Pitt, D. C. *Using historical sources in anthropology and sociology.* New York: Holt, Rinehart & Winston, 1972.

Reichardt, C. S. & Cook, T. D. Beyond qualitative *versus* quantitative methods, In T. D. Cook & C. S Reichardt (Eds.), *Qualitative and quantitative methods in evaluation research.* Beverly Hills, Calif.: Sage, 1979.

Richberg, J. A. Dual jurisdiction and political conflict: A case of the Choctaw Follow Through Program. *Journal of Research and Development in Education,* 1976, *9*(4), 91–101.

Rist, R. C. Student social class and teacher expectations: The self-fulfilling prophecy in ghetto education. *Harvard Educational Review,* 1970, *40,* 411–451.

Rivlin, A. *Systematic thinking for social action.* Washington, D.C.: The Brookings Institution, 1971.

Rosenshine, B. & Furst, N. The use of observation to study teaching. In R. M. W. Travers (Ed.), *Second handbook of research on teaching.* Chicago: Rand McNally, 1973.

Schatzman, I. & Strauss, A. I. *Field research: Strategies for a natural sociology.* Englewood Cliffs, N.J.: Prentice-Hall, 1973.

Sharp, R. & Green, A. *Education and social control.* London: Routledge & Kegan Paul, 1975.

Shultz, J. & Florio, S. Stop and freeze: The negotiation of social and physical space in a kindergarten/first grade classroom. *Anthropology and Education Quarterly,* 1979, *10,* 166–181.

Silberman, M. L. Teachers' attitudes and actions toward their students. In M. L. Silberman (Ed.), *The experience of schooling.* New York: Holt, Rinehart & Winston, 1971.

Sinclair, J. & Coulthard, R. *Towards an analysis of discourse.* London: Oxford University Press, 1975.

Smith, L. M. & Brock, J.A.M. *"Go, bug, Go": Methodological issues in classroom observational research.* St. Louis: Central Midwestern Regional Educational Laboratory, 1970.

Smith, L. M. & Carpenter, P. C. *General Reinforcement Package Project: Qualitative observation and interpretation.* St. Louis: Central Midwestern Regional Educational Laboratory, 1972.

Smith, L. M. & Geoffrey, W. *The complexities of an urban classroom: An analysis toward a general theory of teaching.* New York: Holt, Rinehart & Winston, 1968.

Smith, L. M. & Keith, P. M. *Anatomy of educational innovation: An organizational analysis of an elementary school.* New York: John Wiley, 1971.

Smith, L. M. & Schumacher, S. *Extended pilot trails of the Aesthetic Education program: A qualitative description, analysis, and evaluation.* St. Louis: Central Midwestern Regional Educational Laboratory, 1972.

Spindler, G. D. *Burgbach: Urbanization and identity in a German village.* New York: Holt, Rinehart & Winston, 1973.

Spindler, G. D. Schooling in Schönhausen: A study of cultural transmission and instrumental adaptation in an urbanizing German village. In G. D. Spindler (Ed.) *Education and cultural process: Toward an anthropology of education.* New York: Holt, Rinehart & Winston, 1974.

Spindler, G. D. & Spindler L. Male and female adaptations in culture change. *American Anthropologist,* 1958, *60,* 217–213.

Spradley, J. P. (Ed.). *Culture and cognition: Rules, maps, and plans.* New York: Chandler, 1972.

Spradley, J. P. *The ethnographic interview.* New York: Holt, Rinehart & Winston, 1979.

Spradley, J. P. *Participant observation.* New York: Holt, Rinehart & Winston, 1980.

Spradley, J. P. & McCurdy, D. W. (Eds.), *The cultural experience: Ethnography in complex society.* Chicago: Science Research Associates, 1972.

Stufflebeam, D. L. & Webster, W. J. An analysis of alternative approaches to evaluation. *Educational Evaluation and Policy Analysis,* 1980, *2*(3). 5–20.

Suchman, F. A. *Evaluation research.* New York: Russell Sage, 1967.

Trend, M. G. On the reconciliation of qualitative and quantitative analyses: A case study. In T. C. Cook & C. S. Reichardt, (Eds.), *Qualitative and quantitative: methods in evaluation research.* Beverly Hills, Calif.: Sage, 1979.

Wax, M. L. (Ed.). *When schools are desegregated: Problems and possibilities for students, educators, and the community.* New Brunswick, N.J.: Transaction Books, 1982.

Webb, E. J. , Campbell, D. T., Schwartz, R. D. & Sechrest, L. *Unobtrusive measures: Nonreactive research in the social sciences.* Chicago: Rand McNally, 1966, chaps. 3, 4.

Whiting B. B., & Whiting J.W.M. *Children of six cultures: A psycho-cultural analysis.* Cambridge, Mass.: Harvard University Press, 1975.

Whyte, W. F. *Street corner society: The social structure of an Italian slum* (2nd ed.). Chicago: University of Chicago Press, 1955.

Wilson, S. The use of ethnographic techniques in educational research. *Review of Educational Research,* 1977, *47,* 245–265.

Wolcott, H. F. *The man in the principal's office: An ethnography.* New York: Holt, Rinehart & Winston, 1973.

Zelditch, M. Some methodological problems of field studies. *American Journal of Sociology,* 1962, *67,* 566–576.

Zeigler, H. & Peak, W. The political functions of the educational system. *Sociology of Education,* 1970, *43,* 129–142.

PART II

Case Studies

4

Multisite Qualitative Policy Research
Some Design and Implementation Issues

WILLIAM A. FIRESTONE
ROBERT E. HERRIOTT

The classical qualitative educational research design is the case study. Studies of school life (Cusick, 1973; Wolcott, 1973), of the larger social forces affecting schooling (Ogbu, 1974), and of efforts to promote planned educational change (Smith & Keith, 1971) have used qualitative data in describing a single social setting. Typically, such studies emphasize in-depth description but provide a weak basis for generalization to other settings.

The last decade, however, has seen the emergence of a new form of qualitative research, one intended to strengthen its ability to generalize while preserving in-depth description. These *multisite* qualitative studies address the same research question in a number of settings using similar data collection and analysis procedures in each setting. They consciously seek to permit cross-site comparison without necessarily sacrificing within-site understanding. Although having some roots in academic social sciences (e.g., see Clark, 1970; Whiting, 1963; Whiting & Whiting, 1975), multisite qualitative research arose primarily in response to pressures from the federal government in the 1970s for studies that could overcome some of the weaknesses of large quantitative evaluations without being limited by the particularism of the single-site case study. Like many hybrids, it is today quite robust. However, these multisite qualitative studies were typically expensive endeavors and were done for specific policy purposes which the current federal administration seems neither to value nor to feel it can afford.

AUTHORS' NOTE: This chapter is based on work done for the National Institute of Education under contract 400-80-0019. It does not, however, necessarily reflect the view of that agency. We are particularly indebted to Fritz Mulhauser, formerly of the NIE's staff, for his unfailing facilitation of our research.

There are two important reasons for reflecting on the historical development and potential utility of multisite qualitative policy research at this time. Although it is unwelcomed by most social scientists, the current hiatus in commissioning policy research at the federal level provides researchers and policymakers with an opportunity to consider these issues in some detail. Further, the field of policy research has matured to the point where such considerations can be very fruitful. In recent years qualitative researchers have moved beyond the need to defend the legitimacy of their craft in the policy arena (Rist, 1977; Smith, 1978; Stake, 1978). Moreover, quantitative researchers are beginning to acknowledge a role for qualitative research in policy and evaluation studies (Cronbach, 1982; Hoaglin et al., 1982) and to consider the proper balance of qualitative and quantitative techniques (Cook & Reichardt, 1979; Smith & Louis, 1982). In addition, practitioners of multisite qualitative policy research now exhibit sufficient confidence in their craftsmanship to begin a process of public self-criticism with an eye to improving their methods (Firestone & Herriott, 1983; Miles, 1979; Smith & Louis, 1982; Yin, 1981).

Efforts to examine multisite qualitative policy research suffer, however, from the absence of descriptive data about the field's status and growth. While there are useful first-person accounts of individual projects (e.g., see Fetterman, 1982; Herriott, 1982) the field lacks systematic knowledge about a range of studies. The sections that follow offer a start in that direction. First we review the historical context associated with the use of this innovative design in the 1970s and present the results of a formal survey of 25 studies to highlight some of its institutional and methodological features. We then examine in detail the degree of "formalization" within five of these studies. Finally we consider ways in which current understandings of the strengths and weaknesses of multisite qualitative methods might be extended by academically oriented social scientists.

HISTORICAL CONTEXT

The tremendous growth of social programs in the 1960s led to even greater growth in the sponsorship of research about them in the 1970s. Initially, federally funded policy research concentrated on program outcomes, but gradually an expansion occurred to include an interest in program processes and implementation. Associated with this broadening of interest was a shift from the use of research designs that were exclusively quantitative to those that mixed quantitative and qualitative techniques and even to ones that were exclusively qualitative. In the sections that follow we describe factors that contributed to this expanded interest in qualitative policy research and consider concerns about its validity and utility.

THE INTEREST IN QUALITATIVE RESEARCH

Increased interest in qualitative research within the policy arena seems to have stemmed largely from a reaction against exclusively quantitative approaches. The reasons for this reaction have not been well documented, but they involve a mixture of considerations focused on issues of political utility, scientific validity, and forms clearance. One federal official notes a concern that early evaluation designs in the field of education were "findings poor" because they could not help policymakers understand why programs like Head Start and Follow Through had null effects or how to improve the programs (Datta, 1982). Another argues that the discontent was also with the content of the findings, "few of which were liked by program advocates" (Smith, personal communication, 1982).

The validity concerns with quantitative studies related to both outcomes and "treatments." In education, for example, the outcome problem focused on the potential cultural bias in existing measures of pupil performance which, it was argued, mitigated against showing positive effects (with even the strongest quantitative designs) for the minority group members who were the object of the most ambitious federally funded efforts (Cohen, 1975). In a variety of fields, there was also a question as to whether the treatments (i.e., the federal programs) were sufficiently faithful to the intentions of their designers or enacted in a sufficiently uniform manner across sites to permit a meaningful test of their effects (Weiss & Rein, 1970). This latter concern in particular contributed to a growing interest in the study of program implementation (Pressman & Wildavsky, 1973).

A further contributor to the interest in qualitative studies was the growth of a cumbersome forms-clearance process for instruments used in federal evaluation contracts. Introduced originally to protect private industry from redundant federal data collection for regulatory purposes, forms clearance by the Office of Management and Budget in the 1970s was embroiled in issues of federal-state relations and of individual privacy. The review process became a major obstacle to standardized data collection efforts—often requiring delays of six months or more between initial study design efforts and the initiation of data collection (Carter, 1977; Datta, 1982).

Over the course of the decade, qualitative studies increasingly came to be seen as a way to overcome the apparent limitations of quantitative studies. A former official of the National Institute of Education reports that qualitative studies were attractive to policymakers and program advocates because "case study approaches . . . tend to yield less controversial findings, ones with conclusions on both sides of a political decision" (Smith, personal communication, 1982). Qualitative studies also assisted in efforts to reconceptualize the issue of program implementation (Greenwood et al., 1975). One official responsible for the Follow Through planned variation experiments reports an increasing reliance on qualitative studies to understand why Follow Through "models" were implemented so differently in different schools (McDaniels, personal communication, 1982). Finally, by the end of the decade, many federally funded projects—particularly in the field of education—relied at least in part on unstandardized data collections to minimize or eliminate the "forms clearance hassle."

CONCERNS ABOUT QUALITATIVE RESEARCH

Inspite of such pressures favoring the increased use of qualitative studies in federally funded policy research, qualitative approaches in their most highly developed academic form—that of anthropological ethnography—were often seen as having limited applicability to the policy context. A congressional aide who later became an official at the National Institute of Education (NIE) reflected on the early experiences of that agency with the sponsorship of multisite ethnographic studies and openly questioned their relevance to the immediate needs of policymakers (see Mulhauser, 1975). However, an experienced ethnographer who was serving as an advisor to one of NIE's contractors argued that ethnography would lose its credibility as a form of scholarship if it attempted to be evaluative (see Wolcott, 1975).

Concurrently, *quantitative* researchers questioned the ways that qualitative methods dealt with the problems of generalizability and reliability (e.g., see Campbell, 1974). Their concern was with the larger domain, if any, to which the findings from qualitative policy research could be applied. Often the question focused on the relationship of the sample under study to a larger population of policy interest (generalization from sample to population), but it also focused on the relationship of what was being learned in individual sites to that at the "typical" location (generalization from case to sample). Moreover, some researchers and policymakers were quick to note that such a concern about "statistical generalizability" failed to consider the fact that policymakers seldom were concerned solely about the effects of a specific treatment on a specific population at a specific point in time. Rather they were continually attempting to extrapolate from current experience to future aspirations. Cronbach (1982, p. 76), for example, argues that "the evaluation of a program [should lead] to a statement about what to expect if a certain plan of action is adopted (or continued) in a certain site or class of sites." Such *forecasting* requires inferences that go well beyond statistical generalization and is problematic for all forms of research.

Traditional ethnography ignores issues of generalization and forecasting; it is radically particularistic. Spradley and McCurdy (1972, p. 3) define ethnography as " the task of describing a particular culture" and differentiate it from ethnology which compares and explains. To Wolcott (1975, p. 112) "an ethnography is, literally, an anthropologist's 'picture' of the way of life of some interacting group." Such a research tradition avoids efforts to explain, generalize, or draw lessons for application in other settings.

Sociologists doing qualitative research tend to be more willing to go beyond description. They have written a great deal about how qualitative research can be used to build theory, including concepts and explanations. Glaser and Strauss (1967), for example, do not limit themselves to the study of a single "case." They and other qualitatively oriented sociologists proceed by generating explanations about a single social system intuitively and then disaggregating that case to individuals or events in order to seek confirmation or disconfirmation (Campbell, 1975).

One problem with this approach is that it throws very little light on generalizability beyond the particular case or on the conditions under which explanations derived from that case are likely to hold. All generalizations are, of course, tentative. However, one federal official suggested that the strength of generalizations from case studies can be increased when many cases are included and when the sample meets criteria such as substantial variety among cases, many similarities to the larger population of interest, and few unique characteristics (Kennedy, 1979). This line of reasoning was a major force behind the increasing federal interest in *multicase* qualitative studies.

The reliability issues for qualitative research has to do with the accuracy and stability of measurement. Quantitative researchers typically give great attention to these by carefully designing and documenting procedures and instruments (Selltiz et al., 1976). In traditional *qualitative* studies, there is less prespecification of data collection procedures in order to permit the researcher to interact with the setting and gain insights in the process. This is one reason for the observation that qualitative research often increases construct validity at the expense of reliability (McGrath, 1982). Such a view does not imply that qualitative researchers are not concerned with accuracy. Rather they seek to improve it through nonquantitative means. These include extensive immersion in a setting, triangulation to check insights and hypotheses via multiple sources, socialization to a relativistic viewpoint, and especially the habit of introspection to check against personal bias (Wolcott, 1975).

While the ethnographer's approach to accuracy is well accepted within the community of qualitative researchers, it was not viewed positively by most quantitative researchers—at least not initially (see Campbell & Stanley, 1966). Moreover, it encountered two problems in the policy world not faced in the academic world. The first stemmed from the adversarial nature of some policy research. Findings that are unpopular or disadvantageous to an interest group are often attacked on methodological grounds. The researcher must be able to describe and defend data collection and analysis procedures. Further the data may have to withstand extensive methodological critique and secondary analysis as has happened with two of the Coleman studies (see Mosteller & Moynihan, 1972; Hallinan & Olneck, 1982). Historically, qualitative researchers have had great difficulty disseminating their procedures and data in sufficient detail to make their studies amenable to either replication or secondary analysis.

The second problem associated with the reliability issue was specific to multisite research. Given the many sites needed to increase generalizability, the researchers seemed to lack the flexibility of single-site designs. With more than one site, comparability of data collection, reduction, and analysis procedures across all sites tended to be given priority over in-depth description at individual sites. In general this was done to ensure that whatever similarities and differences were noted among sites stem from intersetting rather than interresearcher variation (Pelto & Pelto, 1978).

Such questions about the validity and utility of qualitative research created new demands on qualitative policy researchers in the 1970s. They led to the introduction of the multisite design as a way to cope with the problems of generalizability and to the "formalization" of those designs as a way to cope with that of reliability.

A SURVEY OF MULTISITE
QUALITATIVE STUDIES

To learn more about the expansion of multisite qualitative methods in the 1970s we undertook a formal telephone survey of federal officials and qualitatively oriented researchers. Through a snowball sampling process we identified 25 projects that (1) were federally funded via a competitive "request for proposals" (RFP) process, (2) involved the application of qualitative methods of data collection within at least a major part of the overall design, and (3) intended to compare two or more research sites.[1] Although the sampling process was clearly nonrandom it led to the selection of 25 projects of considerable diversity.

One of the most noticeable features of these projects is that whereas single-site case studies arise almost exclusively within academia all but four of these multisite projects were located within the type of private research firm that was specializing at that time in *quantitative* policy research (Table 4.1). With only five exceptions each of these projects contained two or more distinct substudies with varing degrees of qualitative or quantitative emphasis. Overwhelmingly their qualitative substudies were imbedded within multimethod endeavors having quantitative components as well, thus providing opportunities not only for cross-site qualitative synthesis but for the integration of qualitative and quantitative data (see Louis, 1982a). The funding for these projects was rather extensive (typically over $1 million) and their duration lengthy (typically at least three years).[2]

While the intent of *multisite qualitative* policy research is to optimize description and generalizability, there is a persistent tension between these two objectives that permeates all research (Cook & Campbell, 1979; McGrath, 1982). In multisite qualitative research this tension seems to revolve around four design issues. The most prominent of these issues is the degree to which the data collection effort should be "structured." Cross-site comparison and generalization require researchers at all sites to use shared definitions of concepts and common data collection procedures to ensure that cross-site similarities and differences are characteristics of the sites and not the result of measurement procedures or researcher bias (Pelto & Pelto, 1978). Yet such standardization encourages researchers to ignore the unique aspects of each site and to overlook processes and contexts that may make special contributions to the phenomena of interest. They also encourage the researchers to impose their definitions of the situation through premature conceptualization (Blumer, 1969).

A high degree of structuring of data collection is obtained through the use of closed-end, precoded questionnaires and interview schedules. Unstructured modes of data collection include unobtrusive observation and schedule-free interviewing. These are the primary forms of data collection for most traditional case studies. Our snowball sampling

TABLE 4.1 Distribution of 25 Federally Funded Policy Research Projects on Five Context Variables

Context Variable	Number of Projects
A. The contractor organization:	
Diversified private firm	12
Specialized private firm	9
University	4
B. The number of distinct substudies:	
None (i.e., a single unified project)	5
Two	5
Three	9
Four or more	6
C. The methodological emphasis:	
Exclusively qualitative	8
Primarily qualitative	12
Equal qualitative and quantitative emphasis	3
Primarily quantitative	2
D. The project's total budget:	
Less than $500,000	6
$500,000 to $1 million	6
$1 to 2 million	5
More than $2 million	8
E. The project's duration:	
Less than 2 years	7
2 to 3 years	5
3 to 4 years	6
More than 4 years	7

process excluded projects that relied primarily on highly structured data collection. Nevertheless, when we examined the data collection procedures employed by a major qualitative study within each of these 25 projects, we were surprised to find that only 5 relied primarily on unstructured data collection techniques. The other 20 employed primarily a variety of semistructured procedures, including site-visit guides which specify the questions that must be answered but not the specific data sources to be used, open-end interview guides, and instructions for focused observation (Table 4.2).

A second design issue concerns the number of sites to be studied. To a point, generalizability is enhanced by the inclusion of many sites (Kennedy, 1979). However, for any given budget level, increasing the number of sites limits the resources that are available for describing and analyzing events at any one site or for cross-site comparison. Within this sample, the fewest sites studied was 3 and the most was 60 with a

TABLE 4.2 Distribution of 25 Qualitative Policy Research Studies on Four
Design Variables

Design Variable	Number of Studies
A. The predominant data collection approach:	
Primarily semistructured	14
Semistructured with some unstructured	6
Primarily unstructured	5
B. The number of sites being studied:	
3 to 6	7
8 to 22	13
30 to 60	5
C. The degree of on-site presence:	
One or two short visits	10
Several intermittent visits	7
Many repeated visits or continuous presence	8
D. Analytic emphasis of report narrative:	
Primarily site-specific	12
Primarily cross-site with some site-specific	3
Exclusively cross-site	10

median of 11. The 25 studies seem to cluster into three distinct groups: those with 3 to 6 sites (7 instances), those with 8 to 22 sites (13 instances), and those with 30 to 60 sites (5 instances). The 5 studies with over 30 sites raise an interesting question: How does one synthesize the mass of qualitative data from so many locations when attempting to draw generalizations? One risk in attempting such a cross-site analysis is that the analyst will draw on the sites selectively, thus reducing data complexity but at the expense of representativeness. One alternative to such selectivity is to quantify the qualitative data through the use of rigorous coding schemes so that formal statistical models can be used in carrying out the cross-site analysis. Yet such quantification can undermine the descriptive value of qualitative research that the multisite design is intended to exploit.

A third issue is the length of time to be spent at each site for purposes of data collection. Long-term immersion (generally of over one year) is the hallmark of classical ethnography (Wolcott, 1975) and is an important means of ensuring valid description (Dawson, 1982). However, increasing the amount of time at any one site limits the resources available for studying other sites and for cross-site comparison and generalization. On-site presence in this sample of 25 studies fell into three broad categories: one or two short visits to each site (10 instances), several intermittent visits (7 instances), and more continuous fieldwork (8 instances).

Finally, the research team can emphasize site-specific reporting or cross-site, issue-specific reporting. Site-specific reporting is a literary device that enhances description but tends to mask similarities and differences across sites, thereby inhibiting generalization. Cross-site, issue-specific reporting facilitates generalization, but often at the expense of site-specific context. Although most of the 25 studies we surveyed used both site-specific and cross-site qualitative reporting formats, 12 emphasized the former and 13 the latter.[3]

FORMALIZATION IN QUALITATIVE RESEARCH

While our survey provided a rough outline of these features of multisite qualitative studies, it raised a number of questions about how those features were combined and the extent to which they were complementary. To learn more, we conducted our own multisite qualitative study of five of these projects. This more intensive examination suggested one pervasive dimension underlying the methodological arrangements used in all of the projects: formalization. Formalization affects three aspects of the research process:

- Whereas traditional qualitative research tends to emphasize the discovery of relevant questions and variables while in the field, these multisite studies tended to emphasize the *codification* of questions and variables before beginning fieldwork.

- Whereas traditional qualitative research tends to emphasize unstructured questioning and observation, these multisite studies tended to emphasize the *standardization* of data collection procedures through the use of semistructured interview and observation protocols.

- Whereas traditional qualitative research tends to emphasize extended presentation of verbal narrative, these multisite studies tended to emphasize the *systematic reduction* of verbal narrative to codes and categories.

While any one of these shifts alone would constitute simply a minor adaptation to the policy arena, the simultaneous occurrence of all three produced a radical transformation in the way qualitative research is conducted. This transformation has been driven in part by the need to coordinate data collection in many sites and to ensure responsiveness to a client's need for cross-site conclusions. In addition, some advocates of such coordination argue that problem-driven research using standardized techniques for data collection and analysis increases the truth or accuracy of qualitative research by responding to standards of validity and reliability traditionally associated only with *quantitative* research

TABLE 4.3 Distribution of 25 Qualitative Studies by Length of Time on Site and the Number of Sites

Length of Time on Site	Number of Sites		
	2–5	6–15	16+
One or two short visits	2	3	5(EBCE)
Several intermittent visits	1	5(DESSI)	0
Many repeated visits or continuous presence	3(CIP)	3(RES)	3(PI)

NOTE: The five studies selected for intensive study are identified parenthetically. For the identity of all 25 studies, see Herriott & Firestone (1982: Appendix A).

(Huberman & Miles, 1983). To them, what we have characterized as "formalization" represents a major improvement in the way that qualitative research is conducted and appraised.

The advantages and disadvantages of this dramatic shift in the conduct of qualitative research are currently being debated by many of the principals (e.g., see Louis, 1982a; Miles, 1979; Rist, 1980; Wolcott, 1980; Yin, 1981). Our research does not enter that debate directly. Rather it seeks to inform it by describing the degree to which the five policy research projects we examined formalized their research approaches. In the following sections we present the organizational context and structure of each project, describe variation in the degree of formalization across them, and consider the utility of highly formalized designs.

FIVE MULTISITE PROJECTS

We began the intensive phase of our research by arraying all 25 projects in terms of two variables obtained via the telephone survey: the number of sites, and the length of time spent in collecting data at each site (see Table 4.3). We then selected for detailed study one project from each of the five cells where either variable was relatively high.[4] Each of the five projects used research teams to carry out qualitative fieldwork at multiple sites with the intent of making cross-site generalizations. They differed substantially, however, in their methodological approach. The five projects are as follows:

- *The Rural Experimental Schools (RES) Study.* Initiated in 1972, this complex multimethod project at Abt Associates Inc. explored the utility of *comprehensive* change efforts for reforming schools. In one of its five major substudies, ethnographic field work was conducted in 10 rural school districts over a three-year period by full-time "on-site researchers" trained in the discipline of anthropology or sociology.

The field work was coordinated by Stephen J. Fitzsimmons, Robert E. Herriott, and Michael B. Kane.[5]

- *The Experienced-Based Career Education (EBCE) Study.* This research by The Huron Institute was inaugurated in 1976 to learn if EBCE "models" developed by four regional educational laboratories would be effective when exported to a wide variety of public school settings. Attention was also given to learning about program implementation as a social process. Over a three-year period three social scientists made several short visits to 45 schools. The amount of time spent at each school site varied from 1 to 12 person-days. Fieldwork was conducted by Peter Cowden, John DeSanctis, and Eleanor Farrar with David Cohen serving as senior advisor.

- *The Career Intern Program (CIP) Study.* The CIP program originated at one site as a promising way to train minority youth to be employable workers or enter higher education. In 1978 it expanded to four geographically scattered site. Through a multimethod study the RMC Corporation investigated what happens when an attempt is made to replicate the prototype in new settings, what produces "successful" program outcomes, and what those outcomes were. For purposes of an ethnographic substudy, approximately seven rounds of two-week visits were made to each site by a trained anthropologist. Key senior staff members included David Fetterman, Kasten Tallmadge, and Peter Treadway.

- *The Parental Involvement (PI) Study.* Begun in 1978, this large-scale project conducted by System Development Corporation described the form and extent of parental involvement within four federal educational programs. Data were collected at 57 sites over a four-month period by half-time, on-site field researchers. The formal academic training of these fieldworkers varied from the prebachelor to the postdoctoral level. All fieldwork was coordinated by a staff of social scientists which included Ward Keesling, Ralph Melarango, Al Robbins, and Allen Smith, each of whom played an active role in cross-site data analysis.

- *The Dissemination Efforts Supporting School Improvement (DESSI) Study.* This complex multimethod study was commissioned in 1978 to reconsider assumptions underlying federal dissemination strategies, to learn how school districts undertake planned change, and to examine whether the federal government should promote fidelity to externally developed program models or local adaptations. Under the direction of David P. Crandall, The Network Inc. coordinated the work of a series of subcontractors, one of whom undertook case studies of 12 schools. Fieldwork of approximately eight days per site was carried out over a three-month period by Jo Ann Goldberg, A. Michael Huberman, Matthew B. Miles, and Beverly Taylor, with Huberman and Miles subsequently conducting the cross-site analyses.

Three of these five projects (RES, EBCE, and CIP) were supported by the National Institute of Education, and two (PI and DESSI) by the Office of Planning, Budget and Evaluation in the Office (later Department) of Education. All five were carried out by private corporations and were multimethod endeavors that included quantitative surveys in addition to the "case studies" we focused on. The projects ranged in duration from 33 months (PI) to eight years (RES) and in total budget level from $1 million (CIP) to $5 million (RES).

VARIATION IN FORMALIZATION

As noted above, what we are referring to as "formalized" qualitative research projects tend to have more codified research questions at the beginning, more standardized data collection procedures, and more systematic means to reduce verbal data to categories for analysis. Table 4.4 summarizes variation among the five projects we studied in terms of each of these definitional elements.[6]

Classical qualitative research begins with only the most tentative research problem, and the first days in the field become an important time for fleshing out an understanding of the phenomena of interest (Geer, 1969). Formalized qualitative research begins with well-specified conceptual models and uses early fieldwork to refine the conceptualization, to check the feasibility of questions, or simply to collect the necessary data. Within the five projects we studied, RES embraced the traditional ethnographic fieldwork model most fully, delegating the task of designing case studies to the individual on-site researchers, each of whom was an experienced fieldworker. Thus, there was never a central guiding conceptualization for its qualitative research. The EBCE team reported to us that in retrospect they could see the seeds of their major findings in their earliest proposal—perhaps reflecting ideas they had developed in doing other studies of implementation—but neither they nor the CIP team developed any formal a priori conceptualization to guide the research. PI and DESSI operated very differently. One staff member from the PI team devoted the first few months of the project to generating a model that elaborated five dimensions of parental involvement; he devoted less attention to specifying its causes and consequences. The DESSI team developed a comprehensive model of the major variables thought to affect educational change efforts and explicated 34 research questions. The RES, EBCE, and CIP teams each used early fieldwork to become grounded conceptually. Each made explicit reference to using the first year to develop their theory along the lines suggested by Glaser and Strauss (1967). The PI and DESSI teams moved more quickly to collecting the data called for by their

TABLE 4.4 Descriptive Characterization of Five Projects on Eight Indicators of Formalization

Indicator of Formalization	Project				
	RES	EBCE	CIP	DESSI	PI
Codification					
(1) Formal a priori conceptualization	None	Implicit based on thinking on implementation	Minimal, mostly from proposal	Detailed explication of the major variables thought to affect educational change efforts	Detailed explication of five dimensions of parental involvement
(2) Purpose of earliest fieldwork	To become grounded in the site and its larger sociocultural context	To explore the phenomenon of experience based career education at each site	To become acquainted with the key personnel of each site	To collect initial data on the various a priori variables and refine the conceptualization	To collect initial data on each of the five dimensions
Standardization					
(3) Dominant early data collection format	Unstructured observation and interviewing	Unstructured observation and interviewing	Mostly unstructured interviewing and observation loosely guided by proposal	Informal interviewing and observation, some semistructured	Highly structured extensive "analysis packets" based on conceptualization
(4) Dominant later data collection	Unstructured observation and interviewing	Semistructured observation and interviewing	Mostly unstructured interviewing and observation guided by emerging conceptualization	Semistructured interview guide based on conceptualization	Semistructured extensive "analysis packets" based on conceptualization

(5) Site-specific data reduction approach	Left to discretion of each fieldworker at each site	Transfer of field notes into a notebook for each site and rating of each site on a series of emergent variables.	Summaries by site on programmatic topics	Systematic coding of field notes and preparation of a standardized site summary for each site	Site summaries by fieldworkers and synthesis by central staff
(6) Site-specific data presentation approach	Extended narrative case studies for eight sites. Brief semistructured case studies for five sites	Frequent use of illustrative quotes and vignettes for unidentified sites	Chapter-length case studies in topical report	Standardized charts for each site: Semistructured case studies for each site	Standardized verbal tables comparing sites on variables; Frequent use of illustrative quotes and vignettes
(7) Cross-site data analysis procedures	Traditional literature reviews by various non-fieldworkers of draft case studies	Intuitive analysis by the three field workers as a team	Intuitive analysis by the single fieldworker responsible for cross-site analysis	Display and systematic analysis of data using pictorial techniques by two of the four fieldworkers	Formation of analysis committees of non-fieldworkers to systematically sort sites and variables
(8) Intersubjective checks on data reduction and analysis	Multiple independent synthesizers	Informal discussion by the two fieldworkers when on site trips. Collaborative review of field notes and draft analyses by the three fieldworkers	Informal discussion of facts of each case by research team	Collaborative review of field notes and draft analyses	Periodic discussion between fieldworkers and their supervisors. Creation of "analysis committees" of supervisors
Overall Index of Formalization	Low	Moderate	Moderate	High	High

conceptual models, although those models were modified somewhat over time (see Table 4.4, indicators 1 and 2).

As noted in the previous section, data collection techniques can vary on a continuum from unstructured (where researchers simply observe and ask questions), to highly structured (where closed-ended precoded instruments are used). The RES study never had a centrally imposed structure for its qualitative data collection. However, over time some of the on-site researchers became progressively more structured in their approach, but only one developed formal interview guides (see Firestone, 1980). In contrast, such progressive focusing was the rule on EBCE and CIP. At the end of the first round of site visits the EBCE team took time to reassess its research objectives and to write position papers. They used the insights gained from that collective process to guide later fieldwork. Fieldwork for CIP was done in seven rounds of site visits. What was learned in the first was checked later. PI and DESSI relied primarily on semistructured guides. PI developed theirs before the fieldwork from the a priori conceptualizations. DESSI finalized forms after the first, brief round of site visits. In both cases fieldwork was geared to completing those guides, and there was frequent monitoring by senior researchers on both teams to assure that adequate data were collected to answer each question at each site (Table 4.4, indicators 3 and 4).

Data reduction is the task of condensing information about each site to manageable proportions, and it too can vary in its prespecification, with more standardized modes generally thought to facilitate cross-site analysis. RES essentially left this task to the discretion of the individual on-site researchers, and no formalized procedures were used in CIP as a single fieldworker covered all four sites. EBCE experimented with a number of techniques, including creating a three-ring binder for each site in which field notes were cut up and organized by standard topics, and the use of wall charts to portray sites and topics in matrix form. In PI each fieldworker prepared a narrative summary of data and observations for his or her site. These were followed by site-specific syntheses done by the central staff following a standard outline and using the summaries and various interview forms as data. Before completing its fieldwork, the DESSI team generated "interim" summaries of some sites and a case-study outline with detailed data displays including dummy tables and tentative causal flow charts. These were subsequently completed for each case (Table 4.4, indicator 5).

Generally, traditional qualitative approaches show their rigor through extensive presentation of data close to its raw form, while formalized qualitative approaches emphasize presenting primarily higher order data—one or more steps removed from the original field notes. RES reported its qualitative site data through book-length case studies (e.g., see Clinton, 1979; Firestone, 1980). EBCE presented illustrative quotes and vignettes in the cross-site analysis, but the reader cannot form an understanding of any specific site (see Farrar, DeSanctis, & Cowden, 1980). CIP used a similar approach but also presented chapter-length case studies of each site (see Fetterman, 1981). PI presented some site-specific vignettes, but displayed most of its data in extensive narrative tables with variables as rows and sites as columns (e.g., see Smith & Nernberg, 1981). DESSI prepared case studies which are available to interested reviewers, but its public document features summary graphic displays for specific sites that were distilled from field notes during case-study development (see Huberman & Miles, 1984; see also Table 4.4, indicator 6).

The credibility of cross-site qualitative analysis can often be increased by the use of explicit preplanned procedures, including rules and displays for coded data, and by intersubjective checks requiring that there be consensus within the research team on the accuracy of coding and analysis (Firestone & Dawson, 1982). RES did not use standardized procedures for cross-site analysis, but its use of multiple independent synthesizers of the case-study narratives (and in one instance the simultaneous presentation of five syntheses in a single report—see Herriott & Gross, 1979) enhanced the credibility of its approach. EBCE and CIP relied on a similar form of intuitive cross-site analysis, although only one synthesis was done within each project. The use of a team of three researchers on the EBCE study provided some checks and created the opportunity for each researcher to have to defend his or her conclusions. Teamwork was less evident in the CIP case, but the overall project director aggressively reviewed and challenged all reports. PI required that all conclusions be apparent in cross-site analysis tables and that both table entries and the verbal patterns be defended in formal analysis committee meetings organized by conceptual element and by program studied (Smith & Robbins, 1982). Within PI both attacks and defenses of conclusions were extremely spirited. The DESSI senior researchers developed complex and thorough procedures for sorting sites and variables and for displaying the results (Huberman & Miles, 1983). They checked each other's work but not with the same degree of open review required by the group context of PI (Table 4.4, indicators 7 and 8).

In order to summarize the narrative picture of these five projects we read across the eight rows of Table 4.4 several times to get a sense of the range of variation on each indicator. We then read down each of the five columns to discover the modal tendency within each project. Although our original intent was simply to divide the five projects into two ordered categories (low formalization and high formalization) the data reflected three (low, moderate, and high). The RES study stayed close to the traditional ethnographic approach by delegating the data collection and case study writing to individual on-site researchers and by deemphasizing standardized cross-site analysis. It was at the low extreme. DESSI and PI, with their early conceptualization, extensive instrumentation and standardized data reduction, analysis, and reporting techniques, were at the opposite extreme. CIP and EBCE were intermediate (Table 4.4).[7]

THE UTILITY OF HIGHLY FORMALIZED DESIGNS

What can be said on the basis of our research about the utility of highly formalized multisite qualitative studies? In some ways such an assessment is premature because this approach is still so new. We have seen useful research conducted at all three levels of formalization that we observed. Nevertheless, formalization (at least to a point) seems to have distinct advantages for both those who commission and those who conduct policy research. However, it is not a panacea for either.

The strengths of formalization are most apparent for researchers doing etic research. In anthropology, etic research relies on concepts generated from outside the phenomena of interest; the strength of formalization is in clarifying the relationships among such predetermined concepts, although generating new ones is not precluded. This is not surprising as those who developed formalized approaches are well versed in quantitative—usually survey—approaches to research. They want to show, sometimes even test, relationships among concepts. However, formalized research techniques are not particularly useful for emic research where the objective is to identify and clarify the concepts or meanings of the people being studied. If the researcher is intent on constructing "thick descriptions" and interpreting cultures (Geertz, 1973), less formalized approaches are likely to be more appropriate.[8] Thus, there are limits to the utility of formalized approaches to qualitative research. Such a limitation is not serious; something designed to serve one purpose well will probably not serve others as well. Still, it is important to know of such limits; when one starts a task that needs a hammer, one does not want to depend on a screwdriver.

Formalization does have distinct advantages when doing etic research. The development of an initial conceptual framework and its operationalization through a series of open-ended instruments is an extremely useful way to ensure comparability in data collection across sites. More formal data reduction and analysis techniques also facilitate drawing conclusions. They provide a much more precise language through which members of a research team and reviewers from the sites studied can describe and debate conclusions about specific settings and then about cross-site patterns. This language forces the team to confront differences of perception so that conclusions can be "audited" (Lincoln & Guba, 1982), and the agreement of a group of well-informed experts becomes a major claim for the credibility of findings.

Whether these techniques constitute a major advance in the reliability and validity of qualitative research is more open to question. By themselves, they cannot constitute stronger "proof" for the uninformed reader. A great deal of judgment goes into the development of the type of ratings utilized by both the PI and DESSI teams—much more than goes into the numbers analyzed in survey or experimental studies. The reader must take it on faith that these judgments are correct. Typically, such judgments are less well justified in the final report of a highly formalized study than in that of research using a more traditional ethnographic approach where substantial excerpts from original field notes are shared with the reader. The authors of some formalized studies point out that case study materials are available for external audit (e.g. see Huberman & Miles, 1982), but these are generally difficult to use by individuals who did not do the original field work.

For those who commission research, formalization provides assurance early in the study that the research will be "on target." Early papers detailing the conceptual framework and the semistructured instruments give a research monitor some basis for anticipating what data will be collected and what policy questions will be answered. With less formalized techniques (where the problem is refined in the field) the monitor has fewer intermediate products from which to judge the direction the study is taking. To obtain a concrete sense of the contents and quality of the research effort he or she must wait for draft final reports (Herriott, 1977). The intermediate products from formalized research do not necessarily give a project monitor more control over the study (Firestone & Herriott, 1983), but they do provide a sense of initial comfort. This comfort may have contributed to the lower researcher-sponsor tension in the two more formalized projects we examined.

One might expect formalization to increase the timeliness and economy of a policy study; the heavier emphasis on early planning, it might be argued, should give greater control over the research schedule. This is not the case. The reduction of qualitative data can be an exhausting and time consuming process, and the reduced data provide more options for analysis rather then fewer. Moreover, by providing a common language for discussion within the research team, they permit analysis to become a more collective process and force analysts to justify conclusions to colleagues on the team. We could see no noticeable improvement in the timeliness of formalized research. In fact, the final report of one of the formalized studies was not completed until well after the contractual deadline. Moreover, the extended time period made the costs of formalized analysis substantial, although we lacked data precise enough to compare the more and less formalized approaches in this regard.

In sum, techniques of formalization in multisite qualitative studies have advantages and disadvantages as means to bolster the credibility and utility of a research report. Their wider use will depend in part on time and cost implications. Because they are fairly expensive to employ, we venture the prediction that they will become an important part of the "tool kit" of multisite qualitative researchers without becoming the sine qua non of good practice. The issue for those who commission and conduct qualitative policy research seems to be one of deciding how much formalization is appropriate under what combination of various scientific and political conditions (Cronbach, 1982; Firestone & Herriott, 1983).

DISCUSSION

The introduction of multisite qualitative research to the policy world was part of the methodological eclecticism that characterized that field as it expanded rapidly in the 1970s. Although this design had its precursors in academic social science, it was largely an invention of federally funded contract research. By the end of the 1970s, multisite qualitative studies were a fragile part of the policy scene. There was clearly "something in the air" that made this type of study useful to federal research sponsors, but there was great ambiguity on the part of both sponsors and researchers on matters of study design and implementation (Firestone & Herriott, 1983). From a historical perspective, the formalization that took place in the 1970s was an adaptation to the demands of the policy context. Just as quantitative researchers were seeking to enrich their understanding by incorporating qualitative elements into their work (e.g., see Cook & Reichardt, 1979) so qualitative researchers borrowed some techniques and invented others in order to address canons of good work widely accepted in the quantitative world (Smith & Louis, 1982).

Now that the federal government is commissioning fewer large-scale policy research studies, academically oriented social scientists have an opportunity to reexamine the strengths and weaknesses of this approach. In the process multisite qualitative research may have to be adapted back to the academic setting which, unlike the federal policy context, generally requires that research be done at more modest cost but with longer time lines.

Academic researchers can facilitate the development of multisite qualitative research by examining a broad range of methodological issues in greater detail than was possible in this study. For example, one current need is to understand better the consequences of different procedures for standardizing data collection across sites. This is an especially important issue in qualitative research where the investigator is often the crucial "instrument" (Sanday, 1979). The dilemma is to find ways to increase simultaneously two contradictory qualities: reliability and depth of understanding. At the extreme we see two basic ways to increase reliability. One is to use a single investigator to carry out all fieldwork in all sites (see Metz, 1978). Such an approach standardizes the data collection "instrument" across sites without sacrificing the potential for in-depth understanding, but it seems limited to situations involving no more than three or four sites. The opposite way is to provide greater standardization of data collection across multiple field workers through the use of detailed, extensive field manuals (Campbell & LeVine, 1973). There are also a number of intermediate solutions that need exploration. For instance, one can have different fieldworkers prepare case study narratives for their sites using a common format agreed to after conducting some fieldwork (see Herriott & Gross, 1979). We need systematic efforts to generate the full range of possibilities and to identify the advantages and disadvantages of each. Although there has been some effort to compare various approaches, it has not been as systematic or as extensive as it could be (Perlman, 1973).

Another crucial task is to map different approaches to the standardized reduction of unstandardized data. Such reduction is a necessary first step to any analysis within or across sites (Goetz & LaCompte, 1981). The potential of any study for useful, valid description and generalization depends on the analysts' ability to reduce data to a manageable form without distortion or loss of meaningful detail. Studies with a large number of sites, or where the principal investigator is not intimately familiar with all locations are especially dependent on their approaches to data reduction. While we currently have some craft discussion of how data reduction was done in specific projects, we need to know more about the advantages and disadvantages of the quantification of qualitative data (see Louis, 1982b; Talmage & Rasher, 1981) and of verbal, tabular, and graphic data reduction devices (see

Huberman & Miles, 1983; Smith & Nernberg, 1981). Miles and Huberman (1984) provide the first systematic compilation of the latter techniques, but a great deal more practical research experience and analytic work will be needed to clarify the strengths and weaknesses of various approaches.

A third area for exploration is the "management" of qualitative research. Some of the unanswered questions in this area are, What are the advantages of trained researchers versus local residents as field researchers? Under what conditions is it advantageous to include field researchers in cross-site analysis and when should the task be done by outside "experts" who work only with site-specific narratives? When is it better to maintain a continuous field presence and when can intermittent visits be made? For what purpose it is important to control total elapsed time for fieldwork and under what conditions is the number of days on site most important? Such staffing and organizational issues have cost implications, yet the experience to date suggests they also have profound but poorly understood implications for the quality of data collected and the analyses that result.

Major methodological issues of the type illustrated above are discussed in subsequent chapters of this volume. However, due to the press of time they have seldom been explored systematically in the course of policy studies. Academically oriented methodological studies represent an opportunity to more fully explicate the logic of this developing research form and to examine in detail its utility in both academic and policy contexts.

NOTES

1. The snowball sampling process began with several highly visible qualitative researchers (Karen S. Louis, Matthew B. Miles, Ray C. Rist, Robert Yin) and federal officials (Edward Glassman, Frederick Mulhauser, Marshall Smith, James Vanecko). Through their recommendations—and the recommedations of persons suggested by them—a roster of approximately 100 candidate projects was created. Subsequent telephone calls to a person more knowledgeable about each project led to the elimination of approximately 75 projects, in most cases due to a failure to satisfy all three of the sampling criteria. For those projects meeting all criteria, arrangements were made for a one-hour telephone interview, generally with the project's director. At the time of the interview the informant was queried about his or her project using a highly structured "project profile" sheet as a guide. After the interview was finished a draft copy of the complete profile was sent to the informant and modifications requested if necessary. After the full set of 25 profiles had been created and reviewed, they were used to code each project in terms of a series of summary categories. The key informants then reviewed that coding and suggested whatever further modification of the profile sheets or summary tables seemed warranted.

2. For a detailed description of each of the 25 projects, see Herriott & Firestone (1982, Appendix A).

3. Only in the case of the number of sites and the emphasis on site-specific reporting (a negative relationship) was their a statistically significant association between two or more of these four design variables. For details, see Herriott & Firestone, 1982, Appendix C.

4. No effort was made to achieve a random sample of projects within each of the five relevant cells of Table 4.3. Instead we endeavored to select a sample representative of the field of qualitative policy research in the 1970s by emphasizing variation of the following seven factors: the funding agency, the contractor organization, the date of contract award, the size of the contract, the length of the funding period, the previous experience of key federal monitors, and the disciplinary background of key project staff. We also gave priority to projects that our informants in the snowball sampling process suggested were methodologically sophisticated. For comparable data on all 25 projects, see Herriott & Firestone, 1982, Appendix A.

5. The on-site researchers included Allan F. Burns, Charles A. Clinton, A. Michael Colfer, Carol J. Pierce Colfer, William L. Donnelly, Ronald P. Estes, Jr., William A. Firestone, Lawrence Hennigh, Stephen J. Langdon, Donald A. Messerschmidt, Marilyn C. Richen, Charles I. Stannard, and C. Thompson Wacaster. In addition to their case-study reports these anthropologists and sociologists produced a lively literature on the stresses and strains of qualitative fieldwork in the policy research setting — see Messerschmidt's chapter in this volume for illustrative citations.

6. To learn about each project we reviewed such documents as requests for proposals, the proposals themselves, assorted planning documents, final reports, and published books and articles. In four cases we conducted extensive interviews with key project staff at their offices to learn about things not apparent in the documents. The interviews focused on the natural history of each project, the interests of project staff and relevant outsiders, and a series of methodological and administrative dilemmas that we anticipated would arise frequently in multisite qualitative policy research. We spent from six to twelve hours talking with several members of each project team. (This step was not taken with the RES study because we had been members of its staff, Herriott as the project's director and Firestone as one of the on-site researchers.) For all five projects we later talked to at least one of the federal officials responsible for its monitoring to understand the project's history better and to obtain a client perspective.

7. Elsewhere we have considered three competing explanations for such variation in formalization: the technical requirements of the research, the demands of the research sponsors, and the interests of the research teams and their professional networks (see Firestone & Herriott, 1983).

8. Becker & Geer (1960) describe formalizing techniques that can assist emic analysis.

REFERENCES

Becker, H.S. & Geer, B. Participant observation: The analysis of qualitative field data. In R.N. Adams & J.J. Preiss (Eds.), *Human organization research: Field relations and techniques*. Homewood, Ill.: Dorsey Press, 1960.

Blumer, H. *Symbolic interactionism: Perspective and method*. Englewood Cliffs, N.J.: Prentice-Hall, 1969.

Campbell, D.T. *Qualitative knowing in action research*. Kurt Lewin Award Address, Society for the Psychological Study of Social Issues, 1974.

Campbell, D.T. "Degrees of freedom" and the case study. *Comparative Political Studies*, 1975, *8*, 178–93.

Campbell, D.T. & LeVine, R.A. Field-manual anthropology. In R. Naroll & R. Cohen (Eds.), *A handbook of method in cultural anthropology*. New York: Columbia University Press, 1973.

Campbell, D.T. & Stanley, J.C. *Experimental and quasi-experimental designs for research.* Chicago: Rand McNally, 1966.

Carter, L.F. Federal clearance of educational evaluation instruments: Procedural problems and proposed remedies. *Educational Researcher,* 1977, *6*(5), 7–12.

Clark, B.R. *The distinctive college: Antioch, Reed & Swathmore.* Chicago: Aldine, 1970.

Clinton, C.A. *Local success and federal failure: A Study of community development and educational change in the rural South.* Cambridge, Mass.: Abt Books, 1979.

Cohen, D.K. The value of social experiments. In A.M. Rivlin & P.M. Timpane (Eds.), *Planned variation in education: Should we give up or try harder?* Washington, D.C.: Brookings Institution, 1975.

Cook, T.D. & Campbell, D.T. *Quasi-experimental design: Design and analysis issues for field settings.* Chicago: Rand-McNally, 1979.

Cook, T.D. & Reichardt, C.S. (Eds.). *Qualitative and quantitative methods in evaluation research.* Beverly Hills, Calif.: Sage, 1979.

Cronbach, L.J. *Designing evaluations of educational and social programs.* San Francisco: Jossey-Bass, 1982.

Cusick, P.A. *Inside high school: The student's world.* New York: Holt, Rinehart & Winston, 1973.

Datta, L. Strange bedfellows: The politics of qualitative methods. *American Behavioral Scientist,* 1982, *26*(1), 133–144.

Dawson, J.A. *Qualitative research findings: What do we do to improve and estimate their validity?* Paper presented at the Annual Meeting of the American Educational Research Association, 1982.

Farrar, E., DeSanctis, J.E. & Cowden, P. *The walls within: Work, experience and school reform.* Cambridge, Mass.: The Hurton Institue, 1980 (ERIC Document Reproduction Service No. ED 203 193).

Fetterman, D.M. *Study of the Career Intern Program: Final report task C. Program dynamics: Structure, function and interrelationships.* Mountain View, Calif.: RMC Corp., 1981 (ERIC Document Reproduction Service No. ED 206 843).

Fetterman, D.M. Ethnography in educational research: The dynamics of diffusion. *Educational Researcher,* 1982, *11*(3), 17–22, 29.

Firestone, W.A. *Great expecations for small schools: The limitations of federal projects.* New York: Praeger, 1980.

Firestone, W.A. & Dawson, J.A. *Approaches to qualitative data analysis: Intuitive, procedural and intersubjective.* Paper presented at the annual meeting of the American Educational Research Association, March 1982.

Firestone, W.A. & Herriott, R.E. The formalization of qualitative research: An adaptation of "soft" science to the policy world. *Evaluation Review,* 1983, 7(4), 437–466.

Geer, B. First days in the field. In P.E. Hammond (Ed.), *Sociologists at work.* Garden City, NY: Doubleday, 1967.

Geertz, C. *The interpretation of cultures.* New York: Basic Books, 1973.

Glaser, B.G. & Strauss, A.L. *The discovery of grounded theory: Strategies for qualiative resarch.* Chicago: Aldine, 1967.

Goetz, J.P. & LeCompte, M.D. Ethnographic research and the problem of data reduction. *Anthropology and Education Quarterly,* 1981, *12*(1), 51–70.

Greenwood, P.W., Mann, D. & McLaughlin, M.W. *Federal programs supporting educational change,* vol. III: The process of change. Santa Monica: Rand Corporation, 1975.

Hallinan, M.T. & Olneck, M.B. (Eds.). Special issue on *Public and Private Schools, Sociology of Education*, 1982, *55*, 63–182.

Herriott, R.E. Ethnographic cases studies in federally-funded multi-disciplinary policy research: Some design and implementation issues. *Anthropology and Education Quarterly*, 1977, *9*(2), 106–115.

Herriott, R.E. *Federal initiatives and rural school improvement: Findings from the Experimental Schools Program.* Cambridge, Mass.: Abt Associates Inc., 1980 (ERIC Document Reproduction Service No. ED 192 961).

Herriott, R.E. Tensions in research design and implementation: The Rural Experimental Schools Study. *American Behavioral Scientist,* 1982, *26*(1), 23–44.

Herriott, R.E. & Firestone, W.A. (Eds.) *Multisite qualitative policy research in education: A study of recent federal experience.* Concord, Mass.: Authors, 1982 (Final Report No. NIE-400-80-0019).

Herriott, R.E. & Firestone, W.A. Multisite qualitative policy research: Optimizing description and generalizability. *Educational Researcher*, 1983, *12*(2), 14–19.

Herriott, R.E. & Gross, N. (Eds.). *The dynamics of planned educational change: Case studies and analyses.* Berkeley, Calif.: McCutchan, 1979.

Hoaglin, D.C., Light, R.J., McPeek, B., Mosteller, F. & Stoto, M.A. *Data for decisions: Information strategies for policymakers.* Cambridge, Mass.: Abt Books, 1982.

Huberman, A.M. & Miles, M.B. *Innovation up close: How school improvement works.* New York: Plenum, 1984.

Huberman, A.M. & Miles, M.B. Drawing valid meaning from qualitative data: Some techniques of data reduction and display. *Quality and Quantity*, 1983, *17*(4), 281–340.

Kennedy, M.M. Generalizing from single case studies. *Evaluation Quarterly*, 1979, *3*, 661–678.

Lincoln, Y.S. & Guba, E.G. *Establishing dependability and confirmability in naturalistic inquiry through an audit.* Paper presented at the American Educational Research Association Annual Meeting, New York, March 1982.

Louis, K.S. Multi-site/multi-method studies: An introduction. *American Behavioral Scientist*, 1982, *26*(1), 6–22. (a)

Louis, K.S. Sociologist as sleuth: Integrating methods in the RDU Study. *American Behavioral Scientist*, 1982, *26*(1), 101–120. (b)

McDaniels, Garry L. Telephone interview with Robert E. Herriott, July 27, 1982.

McGrath, J.E. Dilematics: The study of research choices and dilemmas. In J.E. McGrath, J. Martin, & R. Kulka (Eds.), *Judgment calls in research.* Beverly Hills, Calif.: Sage, 1982.

Metz, M.H. *Classrooms and corridors: The crisis of authority in desegregated secondary schools.* Berkeley: University of California Press, 1978.

Miles, M.B. Qualitative data as an attractive nuisance: The problem of analysis. *Administrative Science Quarterly*, 1979, *24*, 590–601.

Miles, M.B. & Huberman, A.M. *Qualitative data analysis: A sourcebook of new methods.* Beverly Hills, Calif.: Sage, 1984.

Mosteller, F. & Moynihan, D.P. (Eds.) *On equality of educational opportunity.* New York: Random House, 1972.

Mulhauser, F. Ethnography and policy-making: The case of education. *Human Organization*, 1975, *34*, 311–15.

Ogbu, J.U. *The next generation: An ethnography of education in an urban neighborhood.* New York: Academic Press, 1974.

Pelto, P.J. & Pelto, G.H. *Anthropological research: The structure of inquiry* (2nd ed.). Cambridge: Cambridge University Press, 1978.

Perlman, M.L. The comparative method: The single investigator and the team approach. In R. Naroll & R. Cohen (Eds.), *A handbook of method in cultural anthropology.* New York: Columbia University Press, 1973.

Pressman, J.L. & Wildavsky, A. *Implementation.* Berkeley: University of California Press, 1973.

Rist, R. On the relations among educational research paradigms: From disdain to detente. *Anthropology and Education Quarterly,* 1977, *8*(2), 42–49.

Rist, R. Blitzkrieg ethnography: On the transformation of a method into a movement. *Educational Researcher,* 1980, *9*(2), 8–10.

Sanday, P.P. The ethnographic paradigm(s). *Administrative Science Quarterly,* 1979, *24,* 527–539.

Selltiz, C., Wrightsman, L.S. & Cook, S.W. *Research methods in social relations (3rd ed.).* New York: Holt, Rinehart & Winston, 1976.

Smith, A.G. & Louis, K.S. (Eds.). Multimethod policy research: Issues and applications. *American Behavioral Scientist,* 1982, *26*(1), 1–144.

Smith, A.G. & Nerenberg, S. *Parents and federal educational programs, Vol. 5: Follow Through.* Santa Monica, Calif.: System Development Corporation, 1981 (ERIC Document Reproduction No. ED 218 787).

Smith, A.G. & Robbins, A.E. Structured ethnography: The study of parental involvement. *American Behavioral Scientist,* 1982, *26*(1), 45–61.

Smith, L.M. An evolving logic of participant observation, educational ethnography and other case studies. In L. Schulman (Ed.). *Review of Research in Education: Vol. 6.* Chicago: Peacock, 1978.

Smith, L.M. & Keith, P.M. *Anatomy of educational innovation: An organizational analysis of an elementary school.* New York: John Wiley, 1971.

Smith, Marshall S. Letter to Robert E. Herriott, June 28, 1982.

Spradley, J.P. & McCurdy, D.W. (Eds.). *The cultural experience: Ethnography in complex society.* Chicago: Science Research Associates, 1972.

Stake, R.E. The case study method in social inquiry. *Educational Researcher,* 1978, *7*(2), 5–8.

Talmage, H. & Rasher, S.P. *Quantifying qualitative data: The best of both worlds.* Paper presented at the Annual Meeting of the American Educational Research Association, 1981.

Weiss, R.S. & Rein, M. The evaluation of broad-aim programs: Experimental design, its difficulties, and an alternative. *Administrative Science Quarterly,* 1970, *15,* 97–109.

Whiting, B.B. (Ed.). *Six cultures: Studies of child rearing.* New York: Wiley, 1963.

Whiting, B.B. & Whiting, J.W.M. *Children of six cultures: A psycho-cultural analysis.* Cambridge, Mass.: Harvard University Press, 1975.

Wolcott, H.F. *The man in the principal's office: An ethnography.* New York: Holt, Rinehart & Winston, 1973.

Wolcott, H.F. Criteria for an ethnographic approach to research in schools. *Human Organization,* 1975, *34,* 111–128.

Wolcott, H.F. How to look like an anthropologist without really being one. *Practicing Anthropology,* 1980, *3*(2), 6–7, 56–59.

Yin, R.K. The case study crisis: Some answers. *Administrative Science Quarterly,* 1981, *26,* 58–65.

5

Federal Bucks for Local Change
On the Ethnography of Experimental Schools

DONALD A. MESSERSCHMIDT

Out of touch, write the critics. Useless. Ineptly designed. Poorly administered. Tragicomedy. Failure.

All of this has been said about the potentially innovative but largely unsuccessful "Experimental Schools" Program (ESP) of the 1970s. The program was a $6.4 million, nine-year (1970–1978), federally funded attempt to improve both urban and rural American education. This chapter concentrates mostly on the rural ESP. The program embodied several agendas and important objectives. Of the major ones, critics like Peter Cowden and David Cohen (in a draft report) have concluded, for example, that

> despite its promising beginnings, ESP did not escape the fate of other federal programs. The central notion of ESP—comprehensive change—failed . . . The policy of local autonomy also failed . . . Similarly, the federal evaluation scheme fell on dark days [1979: 3].

These critics are not alone in concluding lack of success; see also Clinton (1979a), Firestone (1980), Messerschmidt (1981b) and Orlich (1979), among others. Most agree that ESP did not work well, that it failed to bring significant and lasting improvement to education. But those who studied the program in depth—the many anthropologists, sociologists, educational researchers and organizational behaviorists who have attempted to bring an ethnographic perspective to ESP—have gone one important step beyond mere criticism of its failure to document *what* it was, *how* it operated, and *why* it failed.

To all of those social scientists, then, Cowden and Cohen's most damning conclusion is that this venture in educational federalism and ethnographic research "was *unable to provide new social science knowledge* about the program and the local change process" (1979: 3; emphasis added). Their detached perspective and criticism reflect the dirth of substantive social science study available on ESP at that time. (The same criticism holds for the comments of Orlich, 1978, 1979, and Hansen & Orlich, 1980.) In light of more recent publications by the social science researchers of ESP, such conclusive finality about the lack of results is, in a word, premature. Major reports, books, and articles documenting and analyzing the program—especially from the ethnographic perspective—were only available from 1979 onwards. By design, these publications are summative in nature and were available only following closure of the ES program (in 1978). Substantive conclusions about the what, how, and why of ESP as an educational change program were not ready before that although studies of methodology, history, and community life did appear earlier. Hence, recent ethnographic materials that have been generated about its failures and its limited successes—especially those by the rural ES researchers, based on long-term fieldwork and data analysis spanning much of the decade—are not reflected in the earlier conclusions of *total* program failure.

Far from providing no new social science knowledge, the more recent ethnographic studies reflect considerable new insight and appreciation for what happened. Some of them are the product of a rewarding new application of anthropological research methodology and theory to the American scene (see Hennigh, 1981; Messerschmidt, 1981a, 1981b, 1981c, and 1981d). This chapter addresses and reviews several of the major ethnographic efforts to date, and points out the importance of this social research effort to the future of educational and rural development planning in America.

WHAT IS ESP?

The Experimental Schools program was launched in 1971 by the U.S. Office of Education (USOE), under its discretionary funding authority. It was formally initiated at selected urban sites in 1971 and at rural sites in 1972. Rural site selections were based on the competitive response from 319 school districts nationally out of approximately 7000 eligible districts with 2500 students or less. Rural school funding was targeted in the realization that past funding had tended to ignore small schools and in the belief that small districts were more amenable to change (Firestone 1980: 7–8). Initially, 12 rural districts were funded for one year, after which 10 received funds to continue the full five years of the program. During the first planning year each project site was funded by a direct grant, while the five-year implementation period was funded by a more binding contract between each site and NIE. The NIE was the National Institute of Education, the agency in which the

ES program was housed for most of its short life. The NIE/site contract was both innovative and problematic, for the small districts were by and large unfamiliar with the conditions and uncomfortable with the constraints that a contract implies. The states in which ES rural project sites were located are Alaska, Washington, Oregon, Arizona, Wyoming, South Dakota, Michigan, New Hampshire, Kentucky, and Mississippi.

The program embodied two components, one in funding and one in research. The funding component was designed to test the overall hypothesis that comprehensive educational change is more likely to lead to enduring improvement in the quality of schooling than the piece-meal, categorical, and incremental (and primarily curriculum-oriented) change programs of the past. The funding component, in turn, incorporated the objectives of comprehensive change and local autonomy. By comprehensive change, ES planners meant simultaneous changes in school curricula, staffing, use of time, space and facilities, community involvement, evaluation, and administration and organizational structures throughout each school system.

The emphasis on local autonomy grew out of a concern that federal educational programs of the 1960s had been "too directive and too fragmented"; hence, federal planners concluded that "a new change strategy was needed, one that would give greater autonomy to local school officials to plan and implement innovations which they thought would best address local needs" (Herriott, 1979: 50–51). ES program officials in Washington, D.C., instructed rural educators to design projects that not only addressed their local needs but would ensure community involvement in the process of creating comprehensive and systemic changes in the schools. Local planning and autonomy and high levels of funding gave incentive to apply. Local leaders interpreted the ESP design as having a minimum of red tape, and they perceived in it a chance for their rural districts to catch up to their more innovative urban counterparts. They understood ES to be "a new approach for federal change efforts, involving local school districts and the federal government as 'partners' in a cooperative effort of 'field experiments' in *comprehensive* educational change" (Herriott, 1979: 51).

The research component required each local project site to host an on-site researcher (at no local expense) who would document and evaluate local efforts over most of the five-year period. Abt Associates Inc., an applied social research firm located in Cambridge, Massachusetts, conducted the outside evaluation under contract to NIE. The research firm was encouraged by NIE officials to go beyond traditional educational evaluation methods and to employ a wide variety of social research strategies including long-term ethnographic fieldwork. The research was to be holistic and contextual, in the fashion of traditional ethnographic case studies. Altogether 13 sociologists and anthropologists were employed by Abt Associates between 1972 and 1978 to conduct this part of the research design at the rural sites.

THE RESEARCH EFFORT

Ethnographic research on education is not new, but the in-depth ethnographic study of 10 rural American school districts involved in ESP brings a new dimension to the subject. The descriptive and analytic literature generated by the social science researchers out of the nationwide rural ES program now totals eight full-length site case studies, seven cross-site and synthesis studies, two dissertations, several edited collections, more than 50 articles in journals, collections and research monographs, and at least 30 papers presented at professional meetings.[1]

This large collection reached its zenith recently in the formal publication of two of the project ethnographies—one by anthropologist Charles A. Clinton, *Local Success and Federal Failure: A Study of Community Development in the Rural South* (1979a), and one by sociologist William A. Firestone, *Great Expectations for Small Schools: The Limitations of Federal Projects* (1980). These researchers have chronicled and analyzed the often painful and protracted steps taken by educators, bureaucrats, and rural community folk to comply with a federal contract to implement the massive reordering of their small school systems. The Clinton and Firestone ethnographies both cap and augment the work of a multidisciplinary team of 13 ethnographers at the 10 rural ES project sites, backed up by social scientists of several disciplines at Abt Associates' headquarters in Cambridge, within the federal agency itself, and outside of the ES program at major U.S. universities.

In addition to the two ethnographies, the publication of a set of short case studies in a book entitled *The Dynamics of Planned Educational Change: Case Studies and Analyses*, (edited by education sociologists Robert Herriott and Neal Gross, 1979) is also important.[2] Their volume presents descriptive and analytical materials about the ES program experience of five rural sites prepared by on-site researchers Clinton (1979b), Donnelly (1979a), Firestone (1979), Messerschmidt (1979b), and Wacaster (1979). It also accounts for the heretofore unconsidered federal site—the ES program's host agency, the National Institute of Education in Washington. Herriott and Gross have included several analytical essays prepared by various educational administration and social research professionals along with chapters on the program's historical context and on policy recommendations. Michael Knapp, in a recent article entitled "Ethnographic Contributions to Evaluation Research," has taken a critical look at the work represented in the Herriott and Gross volume (Knapp, 1979).

The present chapter reviews and discusses the Clinton and Firestone ethnographies in some detail. It also points out the importance of other social science findings from the ES program experience, particularly those studies employing the ethnographic method.

THREE LINES OF RESEARCH
AND PUBLICATION

The ES program attracted social science researchers along three lines of interest and analytical effect: the research experience, the site experience, and the national experience. Each is discussed in turn.

(1) The Research Experience: On Problems of Rapport and Constraint. Descriptions and analyses of the problems of rapport on site and of the constraints and contingencies of working for a firm like Abt Associates and a government agency like NIE began to appear early in the project—in 1975. By mutual understanding, this was one of the few topics the researchers could write about until project funding and the experiment were over in 1978. Only papers and articles about methodological or substantive issues not specific to the rural ES sites or project were permitted for publication. All other studies that discussed, analyzed, evaluated, or in any other way assessed the projects were to be held until the end to retain the experimental nature of the project and to protect researcher rapport and credibility on-site.

Anthropologists and sociologists are an introspective lot. They tend to examine the turf on which they roam and the context and impacts of their work as much as the substantive issues. ESP was little different in this regard, and the first published comments by the rural researchers presented some critical appraisals of the research experience itself. The implications of large-scale, long-term, applied, contract-directed, ethnographic research were scrutinized from many angles. Many of the resulting publications reflect concern and considerable discomfort with the constraints on fieldwork that often accompany multidisciplinary government research. Some titles in this genre are, themselves, informative and even provocative; for example, "The Anthropologist as Hired Hand" and "On Bargaining with the Devil" (Clinton 1975, 1976), and "The Anthropologist in a Strange Land" (Fitzsimmons, 1975). Others were more neutral in tone, such as "An Anthropologist at Work" (Burns, 1975) and "The Anthropologist as Key Informant" (Hennigh,

1981). (See also Burns, 1976, 1982; Colfer, 1976; Firestone, 1975; Herriott, 1977, 1982; Messerschmidt, 1981b; Wacaster & Firestone, 1978.) All of these were written in an attitude of positive and constructive criticism, and some reflect legitimate compromise in what was a unique experience for each researcher involved. It is important to note that despite an emphasis on *problems* encountered in conducting ESP research—reflecting very real problems in the field—much good and useful social science insight came from these early publications.

Three critical issues emerge from them that deserve further elaboration. They are the issues of ethics, power, and time in the fieldwork enterprise. Each is intertwined with the others.

The ethics issue was a topic of discussion by virtually all of the rural ES researchers at one or another time during their tenure on-site. Carol Colfer (1979b) has published the most detailed analysis of the most serious issue of professional ethics—the question of "secret" reporting.

What was so secret about ES program research? Initially, nothing— and virtually everything! By program design, the contract and research-er understanding, nothing would be reported in secret. The intent of the research was to study the local projects for summative evaluation; substantive findings would be reported only at the end of the program. No formative feedback before 1978, neither secret nor public, would be allowed to influence the quasi-experimental nature of the program. In another way of looking at it, virtually everything of a substantive, evaluative nature that the rural researchers studied would remain secret—unreported, unpublished—until the end. The greatest concern was to keep project and site evaluations away from NIE until that agency's power to influence the projects, or defund them, was nil. This was an essential stance which allowed researchers to establish credibili-ty on their sites; it was critical to the maintenance of their value-free role as neutral observers and recorders. As I have described it elsewhere,

> Above all, no substantive reports about individual projects would go to
> NIE until after June 1978, when the whole ES program would be over.
> By avoiding formative feedback, the researchers at each site assumed that
> concerns about evaluation and the threat of reprisals to local projects (by
> the funding agency) would not arise [1981b: 196].

Researchers had to be able to establish trust on site; otherwise their studies would be suspect, the local projects would be undermined, their sources closed to them, and the data valueless.

Above all, the stricture against secret reporting is a basic tenet of the American Anthropological Association's Code of Ethics:

no reports should be provided to sponsors that are not also available to the general public . . . [the anthropologist] should not communicate his findings secretly to some and withold them from others . . . Specifically, no secret research, no secret reports or debriefings of any kind should be agreed to or given [1971: 1–2].

Despite the code and the initial good intentions, however, the "eternally shifting sands of bureaucracy . . . [and] the overall instability of the system" (Colfer, 1979b: 34) threatened to destroy the basis of researcher viability and to test the researcher's professional morality. In the fall of 1973, Colfer reports, a high official from NIE visited her research site: "He immediately began asking us questions requiring evaluative answers, apparently unaware of the relevant agreements between our company and his Bureau. We were taken completely by surprise" (1979b: 39).

In fact, this officer's request only previewed a much more serious change in NIE's official stance toward the field research activity:

A year into the research, officials at NIE changed the rules and suddenly demanded that on-site researchers report their findings regularly to the funding agency. The reasons and the timing of their demands were clearly related to NIE's own need to account to Congress about its activities [Sproull, Weiner, & Wolff 1978]. When NIE faced a congressional threat to cut funding in 1974, officers within the institute responded by raising questions about the accountability of many of their programs, including experimental schools. Within ES it was thought necessary to require reports from all contracting organizations. That meant, in turn, that each on-site researcher with Abt Associates would have to submit reports for immediate evaluation, well before the end of the research period [Messerschmidt, 1981b: 197].

In light of these changes the researchers found themselves faced with three options. As Colfer tells it, they had several options: They could quit, in defiance of the breach of ethics; they could acquiesce and prepare the requested reports secretly and without the knowledge of the local public; or they could make the "secret" reports public, thereby avoiding the personal and professional discomforts of the first two options (1979b: 41–43). None of these options was ideal; each had its disadvantages. But faced with the fact that the preferred course—the now null option to abstain from all substantive reporting until the end—some choice had to be made. Colfer took the third option, submitting the required reports to the agency and to the local public, simultaneously. As co-researchers, she and her husband wrote on topics that they thought would have little or no negative feedback. Apparently, they encountered no serious repercussions. Other researchers pursued similar strategies, some with quite different results (cf. Messerschmidt, 1981b).

The power issue, like the ethics issue, pervades this genre of critical writings about the research experience. It typically emerges in the complex relationships that develop between researchers, informants, and bureaucrats. One of the best recent statements of the power dilemma and of an innovative and insightful resolution of the issue in similar research is that by Light and Kleiber (1981) about their study of a Canadian health program. Within the ES program research, the power issue is most directly addressed in my own work (Messerschmidt, 1981b).

The applied contract research of rural ESP provides an object lesson in the impact and influence of power on the research and project experience. The rural ES program was riddled with power relationships, any one of which would have made interesting ethnographic study. They included the interface between students, teachers, administrators, the school board, and the public on the one hand, to those between the researcher, research firm, and the funding agency, and between the researcher and local informants (i.e., the host public and school officials) on the other.

The potential power of NIE over ESP school district authorities was awesome, threatening, and disruptive to the smooth running of most local projects. The threat of withdrawing project funds or of not renewing the NIE/site contract after the mid-contract evaluations of 1975, was an especially constant worry at my research site; and local perspectives of my role in affecting the funding condition—positively or negatively—clouded and confounded the maintenance of good rapport that was so essential to the fieldwork.

Most of the rural on-site researchers found themselves involved in one way or another with the issue of their own power as perceived by others. On some sites, like mine, the researchers[3] were considered a potential threat, sometimes as the enemy.[4] On other sites, researchers were sometimes considered as allies and, cautiously, as friends. To my knowledge, no on-site researcher was ever viewed as a mere passive or neutral actor in the ES program drama. Circumstances varied, but all implied a certain access to power and the potential threat or promise of its use.

In an earlier discussion "On Power," I note that power is intimately tied to the issues of ethics and time:

> Applied anthropologists . . . frequently find themselves in situations in
> which the dictates of the powerful and the constraints of the contract

severely limit their ability to function well. Humanistic solutions to social problems get lost in the shuffle to conform to rules (at root, ethical issues) and the typical rush to get a job done (the time issue). Despite the best intentions of the people involved, concerns for maintaining institutional agendas or for defending the host organization or agency against threats—particularly by keeping the processes of power and authority secret and unapproachable to outsiders—tend to undermine individual human integrity and good purpose [1981b: 200–201].

Future research of this nature must more clearly reflect the honest attempt of planners and researchers alike to confront the serious, omnipresent issue of power in the research equation. The lesson of ESP is especially cogent as we apply the ethnographic methods tried and tested in societies not our own—where power relationships between researcher and others are not usually a serious issue in the study—to research relationships in our own society (where they *are*).

The time issue is one that continually confronts anthropologists and other social scientists engaged in applied research. It has two dimensions: Either there is too little time to do the work well, or too much. Constraints due to shortness of time and pressures to produce results quickly are the most frequently encountered; see Feldman (1981) for an especially cogent example. Short-term deadlines only occasionally confounded the rural ES research efforts. The opportunity for very long-term fieldwork in applied social science is less often encountered, but in rural ES research it was the expectation.

ESP was intended as a five-and-one-half-year program. In that span of time the local environment on each site was not expected to change greatly given the generally conservative nature of rural America. But as Herriott has recently pointed out, it was anticipated that some aspects of the nonlocal context *would* surely change:

> [I]f there is any iron law in policy research, it is that a long timeline means numerous changes in the political context of the research, in its most important policy questions, in the audience for whom answers are intended, and in the sponsors' personnel responsible for monitoring the linkage between answers and questions [1982: 38–39].

In order to facilitate so much change, Abt Associates' directors designed six distinct substudies. The case study was designed to produce 10 qualitative ethnographies, 1 from each site. The other 5 were an organization study, a community study, a pupil study, site histories, and a set of special research studies (see Herriott, 1980, 1982, for synopses).

Initially, the rural researchers were expected to stay on site for most of the five years. In fact, however, few stayed on much longer than three years (the longest was closer to four). Fieldwork of that duration constituted "an extreme case" that provided two unique opportunities—first, to assess the effects of time on the fieldwork enterprise itself (i.e., on fieldworkers) and second, to study change over the long run (Wacaster & Firestone, 1978: 270).

Wacaster and Firestone (1978) have analyzed the effects of long-term, continuous fieldwork in the ESP rural case. They describe experiences with which most of their follow researchers could identify. Four issues of promise and problems emerge.

The first is what they call "the conceptual promise." It concerns the impact that "extended immersion" can have on theory—potentially positive and constructive, for the most part (1978: 270–271). The authors discuss a four-stage model of change that guided much of the thinking about ESP in the field (after Hage & Aiken, 1970):

Evaluation ➡ Initiation ➡ Implementation ➡ Routinization

Unlike typical short-term fieldwork which tends to focus on all or parts of only one stage, the length of ES rural research allowed time to observe the social change process over more than one stage, in depth, and to compare the behavioral reality with the formal theory. Hence researchers and by extension policymaker and planners had the opportunity to comprehend better the conceptual discrepancies that tend to emerge between ideal and real processes of change. Research based on formally designed and staged planning, they say, "may run into some severe difficulties," especially when attempts to measure the degree of completeness or success of a particular stage precedes completion of that stage. This sort of short-term perspective, they conclude, "may lead to premature judgements of project failure" (1978: 270–271).

For the rest of their paper, Wacaster and Firestone concentrate on the problems. In a section entitled "The Problem of Role Maintenance" they deal with the relationship between length of stay and rapport on site. Ethnographic field researchers typically give great attention to rapport; few, however, have the opportunity to test the maintenance of roles over the long run. Wacaster and Firestone note that as ESP fieldtime increased, so did their intimacy and closeness with the locals, both to the benefit and the detriment of their work. On the one hand, long-term presence in the community allows some social barriers to fall, resulting in a much freer flow of information (hence, more data). On the other hand, openness creates pressures on researchers to reciprocate, increasing the risk of biasing the data (hence, the objectivity) and of saying too much (betraying confidences).

In their discussion of "Psychological Stress and Physical Fatigue," the authors relate the tensions created by trying to balance expected closeness to informants with the need to maintain distance and objectivity. They tell it best, as follows:

> A sense of being continually on stage; the accompanying paranoia; the felt need always to be attending to impression management even with "friends"; the compulsion not to miss anything significant and thus the tyranny of site events in our life; the consequent ever expanding pile of field notes and documents; the problem of "insight madness" as events refused to leave our minds (even while taking showers) and we mulled those events over, trying to see conceptual patterns, piecing together the conceptual models; the inevitable and expending boredom that eventually comes in so many social situations from "having seen all this before"— all of this was enormously tiring, physically and mentally [1978: 273].

The resulting stress is unavoidable, discomforting, and at times highly personal:

> [W]e were faced with the necessity of maintaining, for research purposes, close, on-going relationships with blackguards, bigots, well-intentioned Baptists, and a variety of other individuals we would otherwise have avoided. What this meant tactically was that we accepted these people no matter what they were; we socially rewarded them . . . In short, we affirmed their beings. At the same time, we suppressed our own values, our own moral voice. Under such conditions for a long period of time, one may develop a devastating sense of losing one's own soul [1978: 272–273].

In discussing their fourth topic, "Problems of Write-Up in the Field," Wacaster and Firestone note several issues. Not the least of these issues is the conflict that often arises between loyalty to project demands, professional responsibility, and personal sensitivity. They describe the common dilemma of what to put into the final report and what to leave out. They also express concern about the "debunking" function of research that "tends to bring an irreverent perspective to things held sacred within the social system studied" (1978: 273).[5] To publish some kinds of information might contribute to local conflict and undermine local beliefs and self-image. Reports are powerful tools with potentially negative consequences.

Finally, Wacaster and Firestone express a particular sensitivity about the impacts of long-term isolation on the overall professional approach of their research. The isolation on rural ESP sites led, as they put it, to a "withering" of ties to the professional community:

> The problem this posed during our second and third years in the field was that we became less and less dependent upon such audiences for psychic support and more so on local people. Since it was during these years that we moved more and more into analysis of data and write-up of findings, we became aware that the setting in which those activities take place could significantly influence the long-term field-worker's decisions in regard to balancing the demands of his diverse audiences. That setting may bias his research findings by making him overly susceptible to the interests of the local audience and, therefore, prone to excessive self-censorship [1978: 274].

For Wacaster, those last words were prophetic. His was one of the two site case studies that were never finished. Herriott (1982: 33) attributes this to ethical and professional reasons associated with federal and local politics. Certainly, personal sensitivities were also part of Wacaster's decision.

Further discussion of research experience issues appear in Burns (1975, 1982), Clinton (1975, 1976), Firestone (1975), Fitzsimmons (1975), Hennigh (1981) and Herriott (1977, 1982). See also the brief methodological postscripts to the ethnographies of Clinton (1979a: 169–77) and Firestone (1980: 189–200).

(2) The Site Experience: On Community Case Studies and Project Ethnographies. Work on substantive evaluation and analysis of sites and projects came to print in two phases. Early on, a number of case studies appeared that provide the detailed contextual (descriptive) data through which subsequent project activities are appreciated and understood. This phase started with the publication of *Rural America*, a bulky two-volume document featuring social and educational histories of the 10 rural ES program communities (edited by Fitzsimmons et al., 1975). Researchers on every site contributed to this effort.

Three years later, a smaller set of short ethnographic case studies written by Burns, Clinton, Colfer, Colfer, and Hennigh appeared in a special issue of the journal *Rural Sociology* on "Aspects on the Rural Community" edited by Wolcott (1978). Other ethnographic case material also appeared in special studies by Colfer (1977, 1979a) and Hennigh (1978).

Meanwhile, from 1972 to 1976 the on-site researchers collected data on local ESP experiences in preparation for the final, summative evaluations of local project activities. The bulk of this work is ethnographic in methodology and style, and appeared in 1979 and 1980.

Site-specific final reports were prepared by Burns (1979), Clinton (1979a), Colfer and Colfer (1979), Donnelly (1979b), Firestone (1980), Hennigh (1979), Messerschmidt (1979a), and Stannard (1979). See also Hennigh (1978, 1981), Herriott (1980), Herriott and Gross et al. (1979), and Messerschmidt (1981b).

Of these reports two were eventually published in book form, one by Clinton (1979a) and one by Firestone (1980). They are both exemplary accounts of the rural ES experience. Each provides ample evidence of the serious problems encountered by local educators, rural townspeople, and government bureaucrats to produce comprehensive educational change. In fact, the case studies produced by Abt Associates' researchers at all of the sites depict elements of confusion, tension, conflict, and outright failure of NIE to fulfill its mandate to help improve rural schooling. The same case studies provide important insights into the program generally, of the specific projects, and of the change process and its barriers.

Charles A. Clinton's ethnography, *Local Success and Federal Failure*, is a richly illustrated and insightful glimpse of the internal workings of a southern county called Shiloh (a pseudonym) engaged in community and educational development. It compliments an already well-established regional literature from the American South (see Hill 1977). This book fulfills four functions. It is, first, a sociocultural change study strongly oriented toward the sociology of small town American politics. Second, it is a community study—distinctly problem-oriented and focused on industrial growth, the remodeling of a local government system, and the ambitious restructuring of the local school system. Third, it presents a challenging and well-documented critique of a federal project gone awry and subverted by local ambitions, an issue important to community developers and educational planners. And fourth, it is a prime example of insider research by an anthropologist at home in his or her own society.

Clinton's thesis is about the nature of politics in developmental change. He postulates that "local political decisions are responsible for developmental change in Shiloh, even when the agent of change is federal policy or a federal agency" (1979a: 37). He pursues this hypothesis through several interesting themes. To begin with, Shiloh (like much of the rural South) is split along traditional lines of community, neighborhood, religion, and familism, and is factionalized politically by differing approaches to development and change. In Shiloh, struggling for change, these various parts are interwoven by a series of what Clinton calls "systemic linkages" among actors and issues, both locally forged and externally imposed, between town, county, school district, and federal agency. It was the skillful adaptation of these linkages by local leaders that set the pace and form of Shiloh's transformation in the early 1970s from a sleepy community to a progressive one. Among several agencies involved in this transformation, the NIE's Experimental Schools program played a critical role. Within the politics of change, Clinton identifies several key individuals who wielded various amounts of social control and political clout, contending for attention and power. Among the principal actors in this political arena was the superintendent of schools, an aggressive individual appropriately named Wheeler (pseudonym). Despite the best efforts of the ES administrators in Washington, D.C., to push program goals and to reorder Shiloh's school system along lines that they had defined from outside, Wheeler managed to dominate local events until his constituency became suspicious of his motives, dropped their support, cut him out of local linkages, and ultimately drove him out of office.

According to Clinton, decision making at all levels—in and out of schools; local, national, and international— proceeds along similar lines. Although the stakes may be relatively higher or lower in particular instances and although the players may command more or less resources, when it comes to explaining development action Clinton's thesis holds true: Political decisions are responsible for developmental change. Furthermore, political decisions are the work of political creatures, individuals who wield power and dictate action with more or less authority. Every political decision that Clinton describes (in a book repleat with examples) is at root the action of one or two key persons. There is no "force" for change, and no "system" save that defined and acted upon by the leaders and would-be leaders of each faction or community group (Clinton 1979a: 37ff.).

The primary focus of the book is the manner in which Shiloh's school system and government leaders made political decisions and used outside resources to meet local needs:

> Shiloh determined its own fate by both mobilizing internal social and political resources and manipulating external agencies to advance local problems. The story of developmental change in Shiloh County thus sheds light on the nature of the systemic linkages—what Loomis (1960:33) considered the articulations that allow two social systems to be thought of as one unit—between local and extralocal institutions [Clinton, 1979a: 157].

Clinton's most important conclusion (well supported in this fine-tuned ethnography) is that while locally generated programs for development are effective and successful, programs of imposed innovation frequently have few if any lasting consequences—a conclusion others have also reached in evaluating imposed education programs (see Hansen & Orlich, 1980; Wolcott, 1977). The reasons why this is true form the bulk of Clinton's case study.

By comparison, William A. Firestone's *Great Expectations for Small Schools*, a study set in Butte-Angels Camp (pseudonym), South Dakota, differs from Clinton's in that it tells us more about the tension-filled relations between Washington, D.C. (NIE) and the rural site. Thus the Clinton and Firestone books complement each other quite nicely—the one focused on community issues, the other on organizational issues, respectively.

Like Clinton's, Firestone's book is an equally insightful analysis of the misdirection and faulty assumptions about change that drew a federal agency and a local community together in an equal partnership for change. It fits the genre of educational and organizational sociology literature such as Smith and Keith (1971) and Sproull, Weiner, and Wolff (1978).

Firestone's study is oriented around four assumptions about how people in the local community and at NIE thought about the ES program. These assumptions were

(1) that new projects can be designed through a rational process;
(2) that participation can routinely overcome the biggest barrier to planned change—staff resistance;
(3) that the federal government is a major catalyst for constructive change; and
(4) that comprehensive changes can be implemented in schools (1980:8).

The first two assumptions are commonly held by planners and educational change agents and frequently appear in policy. The third is widely held in the Washington bureaucracy. The fourth was the central theme of the ES program (1980: 8).

Firestone is convinced that each of these assumptions is misleading and only true under special conditions. He writes that "all of them mask the complexity of the change process in ways that lead to faulty decisions" (1980: 8). His book examines each assumption by drawing on data gathered in the often highly charged conflict atmosphere of interaction within the local school system and between the local project and federal agency personnel.

Firestone concludes about the first assumption that, far from being a rational process, planning for change is often irrational "advocacy process," crossing interorganizational boundaries and often led by individuals proficient in "grantsmanship" (1980: 173). A grantsman is characterized as an entrepreneur or gamesman, not unlike the political Wheeler described in Clinton's case study from Shiloh County.

The second assumption suggests that resistance is often viewed as the primary barrier to planned change and that participation can overcome it (1980: 174). Resistance came from all levels in Butte-Angles Camp— from teachers, administrators, and local residents. To reduce the ill effects of resistance, Firestone suggests several alternatives for planners to consider; for example, anticipating both technical and political barriers, avoiding areas of obvious conflict, and pursuing the relevant connection between innovations and the problems at hand.

The third assumption posits that government is a major catalyst for change but the facts of the case clearly challenge this idea. Firestone notes that

> the whole Experimental Schools Program raises serious questions about the extent to which the availability of funding will generate attempts at change and the ability of agencies to ensure that funds will be spent for constructive purposes. The fact that less than 5 percent of the districts eligible for the rural ES competition even applied for funding suggests that without the stick of regulation, the carrot of funding competitions will not motivate a great deal of activity [1980: 177].

In addition, conflicting agendas and an unstable administration within NIE—the ES program's host agency—as well as the great distance between Washington and the rural sites challenged the validity of this assumption.

There is evidence that besides the great physical distance between Washington and the sites, there was another sort of chasm to be breached. Washington's urban bureaucrats were (with some noteworthy exceptions) generally unfamiliar with the life-styles and educational philosophies of the residents of the rural project communities. The federal project officers and administrators sometimes used government jargon while many rural folk respected straight and uncluttered speech. Federal values and assumptions about the program differed from those held by many rural educators. And not only did the actors at each level interpret and promote change in different ways, but "federal and local units of practice also differ from one another, and hence manage change differently"—in other words, the federal perspective is national in scope while the local perspective is far more parochial and narrow (Cowden & Cohen 1979: 4–5). In my own case study, I cite these differences as evidence of a vast "cultural distance" between the "locals" and the "feds" (Messerschmidt, 1979a, 1979b). This cultural distance is clearly evident in the case of Butte-Angels Camp, in Shiloh county, and in most other rural sites as well.

The fourth assumption that Firestone addresses is that the schools could undergo comprehensive change. Given a tight funding timeline, however, that change had to be accomplished quite rapidly. Firestone calls this "multicomponent, one-shot [and] high-risk" approach "the alternative to grandeur" (1980: 179: after Smith & Keith, 1971). It simply did not work, in South Dakota or anywhere else.

(3) The National Experience: On the Funding Agency and the Institutional Context. Throughout the life of ESP a number of observers, both from within and outside of the program, scrutinized the funding agency and the institutional context at the national level. Publications on this topic began to appear as early as 1974 and culminated in the outspoken critiques of 1979 (which have already been mentioned). Many writings on the national experience reflect the political load as well as agency agendas and constraints that typically attend large, congressionally funded social programs.

The NIE, as the agency that administered the ES program, was a subject which Abt Associates' analysts had hoped to study as a distinct, eleventh site. They saw Washington as an important part of the context and wanted to fulfill the quest for holism by placing a researcher within the agency. That individual would be in a unique position to collect data about affairs at the top complimentary to those already being generated by ethnographers at the 10 rural sites at the bottom. They felt that many of the problems, tensions, and outright conflicts that were being documented early in the program at each of the rural sites could only be fully appreciated by knowing what was going on within the funding agency. Permission to do so was requested, but Abt Associates was never authorized to conduct research within NIE, the ultimate site.

Despite the restrictions, however, several descriptive and evaluating statements about the ES program in its NIE context were prepared by observers both within and outside of Abt Associates. In 1976–1977, the organizational sociologist Ronald G. Corwin was contracted by the firm to prepare a brief study of the role of ES project officers responsible for implementing federal policy and assigned to oversee the local efforts. It was they who worked the front lines for the agency, articulating between the agency and the rural ES sites and school administrators, and it was their impacts on local administrators and planners that set much of the tone for federal-local relations. Corwin describes three types of project officer role: adviser, monitor, and technical assistant specialist, each of which reflects different conditions, different personalities, and different assumptions about what had to be done. The study concludes with recommendations concerning the necessary conditions of federal assistance of this nature (1977: 87–99; see also Corwin, 1983).

Further insights into the agency context, its history and its operating strategies and structures are presented by Herriott (1979) and Firestone (1980), both of Abt Associates, and in a collection of articles edited by a former NIE employee, Raymond Coward (1977).

The summary comments of Firestone in his view from the field give some indication of the situation which rural schools faced when they dealt with NIE. Despite its mandate to help improve rural schooling, the ES program in Washington "quickly lost touch with its rural districts as it faced problems of its own" (1980: 3). ESP was originally placed within the Office of Education (USOE), but in 1972 the program was transferred to the new National Institute of Education. In the role of step-mother, NIE provided

> a much more hostile setting . . . By May 1976 ES/Washington was shut down, responsibility for administering its final contract was spread throughout NIE. In all, only $55 million of the $190 million originally envisioned for this innovative project was actually spent [Firestone, 1980: 3]

The most comprehensive and insightful case history of the NIE bureaucracy is by Sproull, Weiner, and Wolff, *Organizing an Anarchy: Belief, Bureaucracy, and Politics in the National Institute of Education* (1978). This work was prepared outside of Abt Associates' purview. It provides substantial new insight into the situation in which ESP found itself after 1972, and it helps explain what happened within the ES program (one of NIE's major research arms) to create the pervasive climate and the conclusions so commonly described as chaos and failure, respectively.

Briefly, Sproull, Weiner, and Wolff describe two sets of models of organizational behavior, one rational and the other irrational. They indicate that contrary to the rhetoric and the rational intent behind the establishment of NIE, the agency was throughout its formative years the epitomy of irrationality. They describe and analyze what they call the "belief structure" of NIE, the pervasive attitudes that guide decision-making behavior and action. The attitudes of NIE administrators were based on two axioms, one of progress and one of management (1978: 202ff.). Part of the axiom of progress is "a firm belief that R&D (research and development) should yield tangible 'improvements' in schooling within a few years" and that "education R&D should be able to develop a strong constituency among school practitioners" (1978: 203). But the authors conclude that the quest for strong practitioner support out there in the hinterland of American education was never satisfied.

According to the axiom of management there was in NIE "a persistent belief that the R&D process (could and should) be managed from the federal level" (1978: 202). Despite the rhetoric about partnership and local involvement, federal officials tended to orchestrate the action themselves from the top. The image that came down to the local districts was not at all the one that was anticipated after the initial announcement and competitive selection of project sites.

In the larger context of NIE, the ES program was simply one of the pawns—an inherited outcaste, mixed up in a reorganization effort that had been going on since the institute's inception as a research and development agency. In a period of 29 months—from June, 1972, to November, 1974,—NIE underwent four reorganizations and several directors. In the last reorganization, the original purpose of NIE and of the ES program as its research prototype seems to have been forgotten. In 1974, "*NIE, mandated to carry out research in education, eliminated its Office of Research*" (Sproull et al., 1978: 161, original emphasis; see also Miller, 1974; Phi Delta Kappan, 1974). By 1976, ESP itself was completely disassembled.

The NIE and ES program are not without other hard-line critics. Cowden and Cohen's observations have already been noted. Orlich (1978, 1979) and Hansen and Orlich (1980) tend toward more generalization and are more critical in their appraisals. After considerable reflection on federal R&D exercises, Orlich writes that "the evidence overwhelmingly suggests that federal social engineering in the area of educational R&D has been a failure" (1979: 7). Elsewhere, Orlich singles out Experimental Schools specifically and says that "the program is useless," and that "tragicomically, no major experimental conclusions may be drawn, save one. There is nothing too insignificant for the social engineers at USOE to fund as long as it's with the taxpayers' money" (1978: 19–20).

It is easy to agree with some of these critical assessments. ESP *was* poorly conceived and administered. It failed to change effectively or to improve schooling in rural or in urban America. The ethnographies document this. But they also tell us a great deal more, and therein lies their greatest contribution to knowledge. Within them are the answers to questions such as why and how ESP failed, what can be done, and where we can go from here.

To summarize the national experience, NIE was a part of a big bureaucracy torn asunder by contending constituencies and agencies that motivated the agents of its design and its destruction. The Sproull, Weiner, and Wolff study tells what happens when people try to organize and manage a loosely connected set of ambiguous goals with an unclear technology and fluid participants. It provides the contextual setting (as good ethnographies should) of a confused ES program that came across in rural America as "poorly designed and ineptly administered" (Messerschmidt, 1981b: 185-186). The ES program as NIE's stepchild was doomed by association.

CONCLUSIONS

The ESP experiment in funding change clearly failed, but the research about it was a great success. While comprehensive change was on overly ambitious and poorly conceived goal even under the best of circumstances, the ethnographic studies of its attempted implementation have enhanced our understanding of the problems and issues involved, both in the individual ES project and in the host agency, the National Institute of Education.

The availability of these primary studies should encourage new research. Some of the social and educational issues raised should allow for secondary analyses to begin based on a research rich in data and contextual insight. The ethnographic knowledge of what happened in this large social program should also assist policymakers to appreciate why and to learn from the mistakes and lessons therein.

The ethnographic efforts in ESP demonstrate precisely what Britan (1978, 1981) concludes ethnographic evaluation should be: contextual evaluation. Ethnography has the potential to provide "a wealth of information about program activities and initiatives—what [the program] was actually doing and how it was being done" (1978: 125). Although Britan writes from experience in a quite different setting (the National Bureau of Standards), he is correct in saying that to the degree that ethnographic efforts researching federal programs reach conclusions about organizational and environmental factors—that is, to the degree that they have contextualized the process—they are successful (1979: 125). By so doing, they provide the requisite social science knowledge on which to make the choice to abandon failure and to pursue success.

Harry Wolcott has characterized the ES rural research effort as somewhat of an "eye-opener" for educational ethnography. He estimates that in setting out to accomplish the rural ES research and evaluation, Abt Associated employed "enough fieldworkers over enough years to produce up to a half century of original on-site research" (1975: 110). The results of that effort are now available in a literature that reveals and reiterates considerable insight into human and organizational behavior in the areas of educational and developmental change, of rural American politics and community life, of problems inherent in the research enterprise itself, and of cultural interface between all parts of the system—the researchers, the contract firm, the locals, and the federal bureaucrats.

NOTES

1. Those publications that are not ethnographic and hence are not specifically reviewed here include a variety of cross-site and special studies from Abt Associates. See Abt et al., 1977, Abt et al., 1978; Abt & Magidson, 1980; Corwin, 1983; Corwin & Louis, 1982; Deal & Nutt, 1979; Fitzsimmons & Freedman, 1981; Louis & Corwin, 1982; and Rosenblum & Louis, 1981. See also Firestone & Herriott, 1982; and Herriott & Firestone, 1983.

A comprehensive bibliography, partially annotated, appears in Herriott (1980: 24–32). A complete set of final reports from the ES rural research conducted by Abt Associates Inc. as "Project Rural" is found in each of these six regional libraries: Gutman Library, Harvard University; Cubberly Library, Stanford University; Regenstein Library, University of Chicago; The Center for Educational Policy and Management Library, University of Oregon; and the University Library, University of Florida at Gainesville.

2. Robert E. Herriott was the Director of Abt Associates' "Project Rural"; and oversaw the rural ES program research, analyses, and write-ups.

3. I was joined for six months of the research on my site by anthropologist Marilyn C. Richen, PhD.

4. I was occasionally identified as the federal "observer," and as "agent," with the connotation of "spy" (Messerschmidt 1981b: 193). This sort of appellation is, apparently, not uncommon. David Serber, studying an insurance commission bureaucracy found a plaque on his office door one morning that read: "David Serber Outside Spy." It had been placed there by one of his anonymous informants (Serber, 1981: 86).

5. Their concern, I feel, is overstated. In my experience ethnographers tend to be quite sensitive about the potential danger of this kind of elitism; some, in fact, tend to fall into the opposite camp—of taking the local perspective too seriously, with too little objectivity.

REFERENCES

American Anthropological Association *Professional ethics.* Washington, DC: Author, 1971.

Abt, W. P., Bock, G., English, P., & Marx, T. J. *One year out: Reports of rural high school graduates.* Las Cruces, NM: ERIC/CRESS, 1977.

Abt, W. P., Cerva, T., & Marx, T. J. *Why so little change? The effects on pupils of the Rural Experimental Schools Program.* Cambridge, MA: Abt Associates Inc., 1978.

Abt, W. P. & Magidson, J. *Reforming schools: Problems in program implementation and evaluation.* Beverly Hills, Sage, 1980.

Britan, G. M. The Place of anthropology in program evaluation. *Anthropological Quarterly*, 1978, *51*(2), 119–128.

Britan, G. M. *Bureaucracy and innovation: An ethnography of policy change.* Beverly Hills: Sage, 1981.

Burns, A. F. An anthropologist at work: Field perspectives on applied ethnography and an independent research firm. *Anthropology and Education Quarterly*, 1975, *6*(4), 28–34.

Burns, A. F. On ethnographic process in anthropology and education, *Anthropology and Education Quarterly*, 1976, *7*(3). 23–33.

Burns, A. F. Cargo cult in a western town: A cultural approach to episodic change. *Rural Sociology*, 1978, *43*(2), 164–177.

Burns, A. F. *From rural school project to rural school problem.* Cambridge, Mass.: Abt Associates Inc., 1979.

Burns, A. F. Politics, pedagogy and culture in bilingual classrooms: a case study. *NABE Journal*, 1981, *6*(2), 35–51.

Burns, A. F. Feds, and locals: Stages of fieldwork in applied anthropology. In R, Lawless & M. Zamora (Eds.) *Fieldwork: The human experience.* New York: Gordon and Breach, 1982.

Clinton, C. A. The anthropologist as hired hand. *Human Organizations*, 1975, *34*(2), 197–204.

Clinton, C. A. On bargaining with the devil: Contract ethnography and accountability in fieldwork. *Anthropology and Education Quarterly*, 1976, *7*(2), 25–28.

Clinton, C. A. Shiloh: The little county that could—and did. *Rural Sociology*, 1978, *43*(2), 191–203.

Clinton, C. A. *Local success and federal failure: A study of community development and educational change in the rural south.* Cambridge, Mass.: Abt Associates, Inc., 1979.(a)

Clinton, C. A. Shiloh County: A matter of agendas, In R. E. Herriott & N. Gross (Eds.), *The dynamics of planned educational change.* Berkley, CA: McCutchan, 1979.(b)

Colfer, A. M. & Colfer C.J.P., *Life and learning in an American village.* Cambridge, Mass.: Abt Associates Inc., 1979.

Colfer, C. J. P. *Women's communication and family planning: The case of Bushler Bay.* Honolulu: East-West Communications Institute, 1977.

Colfer, C.J.P. *Ethnography, communication networks and planned change: A case study.* Honolulu: East-West Communications Institute, 1979.(a)

Colfer, C.J.P. Rights, responsibilities and reports: An ethical dilemma in contract research. In J. P. Spradley & M. Rynkiewich (Eds.), *Ethics and Anthropology: Dilemmas in fieldwork.* New York: John Wiley, 1979.(b)

Colfer, C.J.P. & A. M. Colfer Inside Bushler Bay: lifeways in counterpoint. *Rural Sociology*, 1978, *43*(2), 204–220.

Corwin, R. G. *Patterns of federal-local relationships in education: A case study of the Experimental Schools Program.* Cambridge, Mass.: Abt Associates Inc., 1977.

Corwin, R. G. *The entrepreneurial bureaucracy: Biographies of two federal programs in education.* Greenwich, Conn.: JAI Press, 1983.

Corwin, R. G. & Louis, K. S. Organizational contexts and knowledge use. *Administrative Science Quarterly*, 1982, *27*(4), 623–640.

Coward, R. T. (Ed.) *planned educational change: The Experimental Schools experience.* Washington, DC: National Institute of Education.

Cowden, P. & Cohen, D. K. *Divergent worlds of practice: The federal reform of local schools in the Experimental Schools Program.* Cambridge, Mass.: The Huron Institute, 1979.

Deal, T. E. & Nutt, S. C. *Promoting, guiding, and surviving change in small school districts.* Cambridge, Mass.: Abt Associates Inc., 1979.

Donnelly, W. T. Arcadia: Local initiatives and adaptation. In R. E. Herriott & N. Gross (Eds.), *The dynamics of planned educational change.* Berkeley: McCutchan, 1979.(a)

Donnelly, W. L. *Continuity and change in rural schooling.* Cambridge, MA: Abt Associates Inc., 1979.(b)

Feldman, K. D. Anthropology under contract: Two examples from Alaska. In D. A. Messerschmidt (Ed.), Anthropologists at home in North America. New York: Cambridge University Press, 1981.

Firestone, W. A. Education research in a "contract shop." *The Generator of Division G* (American Educational Research Association, 1975, Spring, 3–11,15.

Firestone, W. A. Butte-Angeles Camp: Conflict and transformation. In R. E. Herriott & N. Gross (Eds.) *The dynamics of planned educational change.* Berkeley: McCutchan, 1979.

Firestone, W. A. Great expectations for small schools: The limitations of federal programs. New York: Praeger, 1980.

Firestone, W. A. & Herriott, R. E. The formalization of qualitative research: An adaptation of "soft" science to the policy world. *Evaluation Review*, forthcoming.

Fitzsimmons, S. J. The anthropologist in a strange land. *Human Organization*, 1975, *34*(2), 183–196.

Fitzsimmons, S. J., Wolff, P. C. , & Freedman, A. (Eds.) *Rural America: A social and educational history of ten communities.* Cambridge, Mass.: Abt Associates Inc., 1975.

Fitzsimmons, S. J., & Freedman, A. *Rural community development: A program, policy and research model.* Cambridge, Mass.: Abt Books, 1981.

Hage, J. & Aiken, M. *Social change in complex organizations,* New York: Random House.

Hansen, R. A. & Orlich, D. C. A preliminary study of legislated innovations for higher education (or, do shotgun weddings really endure?). *Phi Delta Kappan*, 1980, February, 426.

Hennigh, L. The good life and the taxpayers' revolt. *Rural Sociology*, 1978, *43*(2), 178–190.(a)

Hennigh, L. *The overriding problem approach to federal aid to educational innovation.* Ph.D. dissertation, Washington State University, 1978,(b)

Hennigh, L. *Cooperation and conflict in long-term educational change.* Cambridge, Mass.: Abt Associates Inc., 1979.

Hennigh, L. The anthropologist as key informant: Community research in southwest Oregon. In D. A. Messerschmidt (Ed.), *Anthropologists at home in North America.* New York, Cambridge University Press, 1981.

Herriott, R. E. Ethnographic case studies in federally-funded multidisciplinary policy research: Some design and implementation issues. *Anthropology and Education Quarterly*, 1977, *9*(2), 106–115.

Herriott, R. E. The federal context: Planning, funding and monitering. In R. E. Herriott & N. Gross (Eds.), *The Dynamics of planned educational change.* Berkeley: McCutchan, 1979.

Herriott, R. E. *Federal inititatives and rural school improbement: Findings from the Experimental Schools Program.* Cambridge, Mass.: Abt Associates Inc,. 1980.

Herriott, R. E. Tensions in research design and implemntation: the Rural Experimental Schools Study. *American Behavioral Scientist*, 1982, *26*(1), 23–44.

Herriott, R. E. & Firestone, W. A. Multisite qualitative policy research: Optimizing description and generalizability. *Educational Researcher*, 1983, *12*(3), 14–19.

Herriott, R. E. & Gross, N. (Eds.) *The dynamics of planned educational change: Case studies and analyses.* Berkeley: McCutchan, 1979.

Hill, C. E. Anthropological studies in the American South: Review and directions. *current Anthropology*, 1977, *18*(2), 309–326.

Knapp, M. S. Ethnographic contributions to evaluation research: The Experimental Schools Program evaluation and some alternatives. In T. D. Cook & C. S. Reichardt (Eds.), *Qualitative and quantitative methods in evaluation research.* Beverly Hill: Sage, 1979.

Light, L. & Kleiber, N. Interactive research in a feminist setting: The Vancouver Women's Health Collective. In B. A. Messerschmidt (Ed.), *Anthropologists at home in North America.* New York: Cambridge University Press, 1981.

Loomis, C. P. *Social systems: Essays on their persistence and charge.* Princeton, NJ: Van Nostrand, 1960.

Louis, K. S. & Corwin, R. G. Policy research in a policy vacuum. In R. G. Corwin (Ed.) *Research in sociology of education and socialization, vol. 3.* Greenwich, Conn.: JAI Press, 1982.

Messerschmidt, D. A. *The local-federal interface in rural school improvement.* Cambridge, Mass.: Abt Associates Inc,. 1979.(a)

Messerschmidt, D. A. River District: A search for unity amidst diversity. In R. E. Herriott & N. Gross (Eds.) *The dynamics of planned educational change.* Berkley: McCutchan, 1979.(b)

Messerschmidt, D. A. (Ed.) *Anthropolgists at home in North America: Methods and issues in the study of one's own society.* New York: Cambridge University Press, 1981.(a)

Messerschmidt, D. A. Constraints on government research: The anthropologist in a rural school district. In D. A. Messerschmidt (Ed.) *Anthropologists at home in North America.* New York: Cambridge University Press, 1981.(b)

Messerschmidt, D. A. On anthropology "at home." In D. A. Messerschmidt (Ed.) *anthropologists at home in North America.* New York: Cambridge University Press, 1981.(c)

Messerschmidt, D. A. On indigenous anthropology: Some observations. *Current Anthropology*, 1982, *22*(2), 197–198.(d)

Miller, J. Scuttling education research. *Change*, 1974, November, 46–47.

Orlich, D. C. *American education: Innovation of the first kind.* 43rd Distinguished Faculty Invited Address, Washington State University, 1978.

Orlich, D. C. Federal educational policy: The paradox of innovation and centralization. *Educational Researching*, 1979, *8*(7), 4–9.

Phi Delta Kappan Why the debacle at NIE? Departing director answers. *Phi Delta Kappan*, 1974, November, 224.

Rosenblum, S & Louis, K. S. *Stability and change: Innovation in an educational context.* New York: Plenum, 1981.

Serber, D. The masking of social reality: Ethnographic fieldwork in the bureaucracy. In D. A. Messerschmidt (Ed.) *Anthropologists at home in North America.* New York: Cambridge University Press, 1981.

Smith L. M. & Keith, P. M. *Anatomy of educational innovation: An organizational analysis of an elementary school.* New York: John Wiley, 1971.

Sproull, L., Weiner, S. & Wolff, D. *Organizing an anarchy: Belief, bureaucracy, and politics in the National Institute of Education.* Chicago: University of Chicago Press, 1978.

Stannard, C. I. *Problem of project direction and coordination.* Cambridge, Mass.: Abt Associates, Inc., 1979.

Wacaster, C. T. Jackson county: Local norms, federal initiatives, and administrator performance. In R. E. Herriott & N. Gross (Eds.), The dynamics of planned educational change. Berkeley: McCutchan, 1979.

Wacaster, C. T. & Firestone, W. A. The promise and problems of long-term continuous fieldwork. *Human Organization,* 1978, *37*(2), 269–275.

Wolcott, H. F. Introduction to ethnography of schooling. *Human Organization,* 1975, *34*(2), 109–110.

Wolcott, H. F. *Teachers versus technocrats: An educational innovation in anthropological perspective,* Eugene, OR: Center for Educational Policy and Management, University of Oregon, 1977.

Wolcott, H. F. (Ed.) Small town America in ethnographic perspective. *Rural Sociology,* 1978, *43*(2), 159–220.

6

Multimethod Policy Research
A Case Study of Structure and Flexibility

ALLEN G. SMITH
ALBERT E. ROBBINS

A t its best, policy research is a matter of trade-offs and compromises. Because they address the sometimes ambitious questions of decision makers rather than of academicians, policy researchers frequently find themselves at the fringes of existing social science methodology—adapting, combining, and improvising as they go. The study of Parental Involvement in Federal Education Programs illustrates such a situation. Funded to investigate a much discussed but elusive phenomenon within a distressingly short time frame, the System Development Corporation (SDC) devised methods that blended techniques from ethnographic and survey research traditions.

Much has been written recently about the advantages of case study or ethnographic methods for studying policy issues of implementation and change in schools (e.g., Cook & Reichardt, 1979; LeCompte & Goetz, 1982; Patton, 1980; Smith & Louis, 1982; Weiss & Rein, 1972). Because they characteristically include extended on-site observations, case studies tend to be more holistic, more flexible to emergent issues, and more sensitive to causal processes than traditional survey techniques (Lewis, 1982; Fetterman, 1982a). But case studies have important drawbacks as well. They are expensive to produce. Their very flexibility can make them idiosyncratic and irrelevant to particular policy questions. They produce findings of unknown generalizability. And, finished case studies tend to be lengthy, detailed, and cumbersome to read. As some have noted (e.g., Mulhauser, 1975), few policymakers

AUTHORS' NOTE: Like every other phase in the Study of Parental Involvement, reflecting on methodology has been a team effort. We would like to acknowledge the important contributions of several colleagues to this chapter: J. Ward Keesling, Ralph Melaragno, Hilda Borko, and Peggy Lyons.

are willing to invest the time needed to digest a case study when its generalizability and pertinence to immediate issues are uncertain.

The Study of Parental Involvement sought to capitalize on the strengths of both case study and survey approaches. Our purpose in this article is to discuss our experiences with that integration, particularly as they relate to some practical and philosophical issues common to multisite qualitative research.

BACKGROUND AND CONTEXT FOR THE STUDY

Almost all federal educational programs since the 1960s have required some parental involvement. Despite this pervasive emphasis, little has been known about the extent to which parents really do participate, about the nature and causes of that participation, or about its effects on children, parents, and the schools. Consequently, in 1978 the Department of Education issued a Request for Proposals calling for a study of just these issues in four federal programs: ESEA Title I, the Emergency School Aid Act, ESEA Title VII Bilingual, and Follow Through.

In its response to the request, the SDC proposed a design consisting of two sequential substudies. The first, known as the Federal Program Survey (Keesling, 1980), was intended to collect standardized, quantified, descriptive parental involvement data from a nationally representative sample of districts and schools participating in one or more of the four programs. The survey was based on a conceptual framework developed early in the study from the available literature, interviews with policymakers, and advice from two advisory panels. Questionnaires were mailed to one district-level representative, who responded on behalf of the district and selected elementary schools (286 districts and 869 schools). Data were then collected from respondents by telephone, yielding a response rate of 96%. Both the district and the school survey asked for descriptive information about the organization of the local project's parental involvement program, about the extent of parents' participation in the school, and about funding arrangements.

The second substudy—and focus of this article—was the Site Study (Cadena-Munoz & Keesling, 1981; Keesling et al., 1981; Melaragno, Keesling, et al., 1981; Melaragno, Lyons, et al., 1981; Robbins & Dingler, 1981; Smith & Nerenberg, 1981). This study was an intensive on-site investigation of parental involvement at 57 local projects selected from the larger Federal Programs Survey sample to illustrate parental involvement activities under a variety of conditions (reported high versus low involvement; rural versus urban, etc.). The Site Study was intended to provide detailed information about the nature, contributing factors, and effects of parental involvement in various contexts. This detailed information was important for two reasons. First, little was known about parental involvement in schools; the Department of Education and SDC believed that the intensive site study would yield more detailed insights into a little understood subject. Second, the Site Study would provide strategies and examples that could be included in a handbook for local schools interested in fostering greater parental involvement (Lyons et al., 1982).

These two substudies had to be completed from design through reports in less than 24 months—quite a short time frame for a study as ambitious as this.

SITE STUDY METHODOLOGY[1]

The Site Study was expected to provide a detailed picture of the nature, causes, and consequences of parental involvement in four federal education programs with quite different mandates and regulations. This meant that (1) a large number of local projects in each program had to be studied if we were to produce findings that could address the question of program differences; (2) a substantial on-site component was necessary to observe and interview the many actors involved in parent programs locally; and (3) procedures had to be developed to dramatically speed up the normally slow pace of field research in order to meet the stringent reporting deadlines. In response we developed a three-pronged data-collection approach at approximately 15 sites per program, an approach that included local field researchers closely supervised by senior SDC staff and guided by detailed "analysis packets" in their data-collection efforts.

THE LOCAL FIELD RESEARCHER

The original RFP assumed that site study data would be collected by SDC personnel with appropriate professional training. Although the study staff initially favored this approach, we became convinced that it had several severe shortcomings for studying parental involvement phenomena. First, interviews alone would be unlikely to yield the necessary information about dynamics and causal processes in parental involvement programs; we needed to actually observe key events. Since these events occurred intermittently, it seemed impractical to rely on site visits for their observation. Second, although we were confident that professional administrators could be interviewed successfully by outsiders, we were more skeptical about the prospects of parents speaking candidly to visiting social scientists from Southern California. Finally, there was going to be a great deal of data collected at each site in order to obtain a detailed understanding of projects' strategies and activities, and the more subtle or controversial aspects of the program as perceived by various actors.

Although in principle it would have been possible to have senior study staff members stay on site long enough to establish rapport and collect the data, this approach would have been time consuming and costly. We decided instead to hire local data collectors—although they would perhaps be less experienced as social scientists—and train them to collect the information we needed. At the time we felt that "locals" would (1) have more knowledge of the local culture and actors than would outside social scientists; (2) would be able to remain on site after the data collection, thus giving us a backup during the analysis period; (3) would be cheaper (our budget permitted 16-18 weeks of local data collectors' time, as compared to only 2-3 weeks of SDC staff time); and (4) would allow greater coverage of intermittent events, since they could work part time.

This approach to collecting data would not be without costs, we knew. Instead of five or ten core staff gathering and processing information at all sites, there would be almost 60. Coordination would be a problem, as would quality control. Further, we were sacrificing direct contact by senior staff with sites; some mechanism had to be developed to keep staff informed about developments and emerging issues at those sites. These were disadvantages, but we felt that the other features of our approach would compensate.

Field researchers were recruited at professional meetings and by sending announcements and job descriptions to social science departments in colleges and universities near each community to be studied. In come cases, particularly for the more rural sites where no qualified candidates could be located, local project directors were asked to identify potential field researchers. All candidates were interviewed by SDC staff. We sought candidates with some training in a social science, training in or experience with qualitative research, experience working with the public and in schools, and at least three years' residency in the target community. The resulting group of 57 field researchers was something of a mixed bag. About half met all the criteria, and several had Ph.D.s with experience directly pertinent to our needs. About a fourth barely met our minimum criteria. Another fourth, generally in rural sites with no local university, did not fit the criteria in important respects. We hired these latter field researchers with some trepidation, gambling that training, the analysis packets, and staff supervision could compensate for any weakness.

The field researchers were assembled for nine days of intensive training, where they were introduced to the goals and overall design of the study and trained in the use of the materials that would organize their work on site—the analysis packets. Through role playing, school visits, and individual exercises, field researchers were given hands-on experience collecting and reporting data under conditions similar to those they would encounter in the field, with SDC senior staff providing feedback.

THE ANALYSIS PACKETS

The decision to use locally hired field researchers forced us to confront the issues of how to guide and coordinate these separate data collection efforts without becoming too rigid. Our solution was to design a set of between 40 and 60 "analysis packets" for each field researcher, which defined the areas of research interest, outlined specific information needs in those areas, and recommended likely sources for that information. The packets were derived from the study's policy and research questions, from a conceptualization of parental involvement developed from the literature, and from discussions with knowledgeable practitioners, educators, and congressional staff.

Three types of analysis packets were developed. For some areas of the conceptual framework we could be quite specific about our information needs, even to the point of prescribing specific questions (called "constant" questions) that should be asked. In other areas we could only outline in general terms the topics that should be explored in interviews. For these we developed "orienting" packets that described issues and topics without prescribing specific interview or observation questions. Finally, for topics about which almost nothing was known prior to the study, a third type of packet, known as "exploratory," was developed. These packets alerted the researcher to explore the area further so that important issues could be identified. The analysis packets were not intended to be interview or observation instruments, rather they were used by the field researcher to plan field work.

The results from interviews, observations, and document analyses were transmitted to SDC in several forms, including taped interviews and field notes dictated by the field researcher, open-ended questionnaires, where the researcher served as respondent to the constant questions, and annotated documents from the site.

THE SITE COORDINATOR

The methodological glue that held this dispersed data collection effort together was the site coordinator. Site coordinators were core study staff who were assigned from four to eight field researchers, for whom they were to function as confidants/supervisors. Each site coordinator followed the course of the data collection through regular telephone contacts, a single site visit, and by studying the data provided by their field researchers. Site coordinators were, in turn, organized into four committees, each comprised of all site coordinators working on the study of a particular program. Through this mechanism, issues that emerged at one site could be considered in the context of all sites.

DATA REDUCTION AND ANALYSIS

Analysis of the site study data began with the start of data collection. Field researchers and their site coordinators were expected to be analyzing the information from their sites as it was collected, and upon concluding that a finding or issue at one site might be of more general importance in the study, a site coordinator was to alert colleagues on the committee for that particular program. The program committee could then modify the lines of inquiry described in the analysis packets to investigate emerging hypotheses and communicate these changes to their field researches in their regular telephone contacts.

Following the 16 weeks of data collection, analysis continued through a six-step process:

Step 1: Summary Protocols. Guided by the site coordinators, each field researcher summarized the site results in a series of taped "summary protocols," each of which was a well-documented analytic essay on a specific topic (such as "Advisory Council Involvement in Decisionmaking"). Together with the completed constant questions, these represented the field researcher's best effort to make sense of parental involvement at the site.

Step 2: Detailed Outlines and Roadmaps. Next, senior staff at SDC developed a detailed outline of the anticipated final report for each of the four programs studied. This reconfigured the basic topics from the analysis packets on the basis of field experience. Outlines were accompanied by "roadmaps" that suggested where in field researchers' summary protocols and constant question answers an analyst would most likely find the information needed to address a given topic in the detailed outline.

Step 3: Site Syntheses. Site coordinators followed the roadmap to summarize and organize the data from each site according to the outline. This reorganization and further summarization of data resulted in 57 "site syntheses," which became the foundation for all subsequent analytic steps. These syntheses resembled case studies in their length and scope, but were written solely to facilitate cross-site analyses and not to present a case in pleasing narrative form. To keep track of these suspected cross- or within-site patterns and other questions, comments, and notes, each site coordinator/analyst maintained an "insight journal."

Step 4: Construction of Analysis Tables. At this point, the program committees were supplemented by "analysis committees" that cut across the four programs (LeCompte & Goetz, 1982). These committees further distilled information from site syntheses onto a series of "analysis tables," each corresponding to a major section of the detailed report outline.

To summarize, the progression from Step 1 to Step 4 did two things to the data. First, the data were reduced considerably. A single analysis packet topic may have been addressed in Step 1 in a ten-page summary protocol. This same information might then have been summarized on one page in the site synthesis (Step 3), and reduced to a few short phrases in an analysis table cell (Step 4). Second, the analysis tables arrayed the reduced data in a way that allowed us to look back and forth across sites' data and thus facilitated identification of patterns across sites.

Step 5: Cross-Site Analysis. Because the four programs studied had quite different goals and regulations relating to parental involvement, all cross-site analyses were done within programs. However, to ensure cross-fertilization, analysts from the four programs met regularly in analysis committees to discuss and defend their findings. Cross-site analysis was done by comparing and contrasting rows in the various analysis tables. Generally speaking, each of these rows corresponded to a research question or subquestion for the study (e.g., What is the nature of parental participation in projects' decisionmaking? What factors contribute to or inhibit that involvement? What impact does that involvement have on parents, students, and the schools?). Each cell entry summarized a site's answer to the question. Through comparison of these entries, general categories of answers emerged that could be applied to all sites.

In effect, then, cross-site analysis of the site study data was essentially a process of pattern recognition. From the raw descriptive information about sites, categories were constructed that could be applied to all sites. These categorizations could then result in counts of sites within categories. Because samples were selected purposively, we could impose no hard and fast rule as to what constituted a strong pattern in the data. Something found at only three sites could be important if those three sites were known to share features (e.g., size or SES) that distinguished them from the others.

Step 6: Integration of Site and Federal Programs Survey Findings. Integration of findings from the Federal Programs Survey and the Site Study was not attempted until after Step 5. For the most part, this integration was informal; where the two substudies addressed comparable issues, the findings were compared and contrasted.

SOME REFLECTIONS
ON THE METHODOLOGY

ON THE USE OF LOCAL FIELD
RESEARCHERS TO COLLECT DATA

The key reason for using local field researchers was that it was the most cost-effective way to achieve extended data collection at each site. A secondary, but nonetheless important, motivation was the desire to have data collectors who were familiar with the communities and cultures they studied. In retrospect, the approach worked well. At most sites and local field researcher, guided by the analysis packets and site coordinators, gave flexibility and depth to the data collection. Because they were on site for 16-18 weeks, field researchers were able to have multiple interviews with a variety of individuals, to observe critical project events, and perhaps most important, modify their data-collection activities based on those interviews and observations. Field researchers could schedule interviews at the convenience of respondents and take the time needed to cultivate trust and rapport with parents who would otherwise have been reluctant to talk.

There were some problems, though. At rural sites especially, we were sometimes able to locate only marginally qualified candidates for the position, while at other sites we were able to hire experienced Ph.D. social scientists. Despite attempts to compensate for this variation in background skills, some field researchers at both ends of the experience spectrum were never able to produce what we needed for the cross-site analysis.

This raises the question of what makes a good field researcher. We found that a combination of seven attributes generally characterized the best researchers: good interviewing and observing skills, ability to critically analyze information, interest in the study, time to devote to the work, willingness to take outside direction, ability to observe without judging or intervening, and good interpersonal skills. There are several obvious omissions from this list. One is advanced academic training in a social science. The best field researchers did tend to have social science training, but those with Ph.D.s did not always fare well as field researchers. In part this was because the job was part-time and some had other jobs that sapped time and enthusiasm from this study. More important, though, was the peculiar nature of the field researchers' job itself—a cross between standardized data collection and full-scale ethnography. A field researcher had to be resourceful and analytic but could not be completely independent. Experienced Ph.D. social scientists were not always willing to make this accommodation.

Another omission from the list of desired attributes in field researchers is membership in the culture being studied. All of the field researchers in the study lived in the communities they studied, but not all were indigenous. Many were transplants from other states, or residents of geographically close but culturally remote suburbs. There were cases where a field researcher's membership in the local culture helped him or her gain access within the site; there were also cases where a culturally indigenous field researcher was blinded to important site issues. In general we relearned what anthropologists have known for years: Rapport with potential informants is more a function of time spent on site and of interpersonal skills than it is of cultural identity. Field researchers with the seven qualities listed earlier did well regardless of their cultural backgrounds.

In retrospect, the criteria and procedures that were used to select field researchers for this study were basically sound. In the future, though, we would try to better describe our requirements to candidates and clarify that as field researchers they would be neither data collectors nor ethnographers, but something in between. Several of our less fortunate hiring decisions could have been avoided if this had been made clear at the outset.

In the future we would also be less insistent about hiring local residents at all sites. For cost reasons, local field researchers would be used wherever appropriate, but we would be more willing to import outside researchers at sites where no qualified candidates could be found locally.

ON THE DILEMMA BETWEEN
STRUCTURE AND FLEXIBILITY

Although derived in large part from ethnographic traditions, multi-site qualitative research like this cannot afford to be radically inductive. There are specific policy questions to be addressed and not enough time or resources to investigate everything that could profitably be studied. Therefore, decisions as to what kinds of information are most important must be made before researchers are placed in sites.

There are tradeoffs here as well. Structure is needed if comparable data are going to be collected from the different sites, but too much structure defeats the very purpose for which qualitative methodologies were chosen in the first place. Flexibility must be built into the data collection if unexpected nuances and emergent issues are to be captured.

Probably any study that tries to use qualitative data from multiple sites encounters competing demands for structure and flexibility, but this tension was especially acute for us because of the decision to use local field researchers. This meant that day-to-day research decisions were in the hands of 57 very different people who were all somewhat removed from the policy issues and considerations framing the study. Further, since each field researcher only studied a single site, he or she did not have the benefit of the cross-site perspective that would have existed had core staff done the data collection.

Our solution to this problem was to design a data-collection strategy that provided each researcher with as much structure as possible while building in mechanisms that would ensure adequate flexibility. The structure came from the analysis packets that listed topics, information sources, and even questions and probes. Flexibility was also built into the packets: For most topics the field researchers decided whom to interview and how to frame the question. Also, the analysis packets allowed considerable latitude in deciding how much emphasis to place on each topic and how best to pursue it.

But it was the site coordinator who was to strike the balance between the structure imposed in the analysis packet and the flexibility needed for an exploratory study. Each site coordinator was to have a sense of the bigger picture and intervene wherever necessary to modify the structure imposed by the packets. Through the committee structure they were given the means to turn emergent site findings into cross-site data-collection topics. These mechanisms worked rather well and yielded a body of data that was both detailed and comparable across sites. In retrospect, though, we probably erred on the side of too much structure, for several reasons. First, we overestimated what field researchers could do in the time available. Field researchers had their hands full addressing the minimal set of issues in the analysis packets; they had little time to explore new issues. Second, we overestimated how much a site coordinator could do in the time available. Site coordinators had too many sites and too many other study responsibilities (such as planning the analysis) to keep up completely with the day-to-day activities of their field researchers. Finally, we told field researchers to begin with the structured constant question in their analysis packets, thinking that these would ease the less-experienced field researchers into the data collection. These took longer than expected to complete, leaving relatively little time for the more open-ended analysis packets.

Based on this experience, we would do several things differently in the future. First, we would either truncate the analysis packets or allow more time for the data collection. Second, we would not insist that field researchers begin with the constant questions; starting with them did not seem to make matters easier for field researchers and consumed too much time. Third, we would structure the work so that site coordinators were free to concentrate exclusively on their sites during the data collection. Finally, we would schedule the data collection in two phases with a one- or two-week break in the middle for site coordinators to meet and reflect on emerging findings and issues, and for field researchers to consolidate their data and plan their next steps.

ON DATA QUALITY CONTROL

The concepts of reliability and validity are really proxies for the quality and "believability" of the data that are collected in a study. A potential weakness of the site study methodology is that it does not lend itself to conventional assessments of data quality. The features that make the approach appealing—extended data collections, flexibility to emergent site issues, rich descriptive reports, and the like—rule out traditional psychometric techniques. For example, it is hard to imagine how one could practically measure interobserver reliability without imposing harsh burdens on respondents and the study's budget. Although difficult to measure, data quality was nonetheless an important concern. Our mechanisms were nonstatistical and imprecise, but in the final analysis, the credibility of our conclusions rests on their adequacy.

There were six major mechanisms used in the study to ensure data quality:

(1) Training. Each field researcher went through an initial nine-day training and a two-day follow-up session.

(2) The analysis packets. Each field researcher had a standard set of issues and topics to explore.

(3) The data-reporting procedures. Field researchers were expected to provide the site coordinator with taped summaries of interviews, with both researcher questions and respondent answers clearly noted. This gave the site coordinators a raw data base that was relatively free of field researchers' biases and interpretations.

(4) Triangulation of data. Field researchers were encouraged to challenge their data constantly by asking: (1) Are interviews and reports consistent with observations and documents? (2) Are reports consistent across respondents? (3) Are observed events and behaviors consistent over time? The analysis packets singled out particularly complex or controversial topics on which field researchers had to triangulate (Webb et al., 1966).

(5) The Site Coordinator. The site coordinator was supposed to be constantly looking over the field researchers' shoulders, questioning and challenging the data as they were collected.

(6) Systematic analysis procedures. Analysts were organized into committees that were expected to challenge the findings and inferences derived by each analyst from site data.

These procedures sought to make the data collection, reporting, and analysis more public—to force field researchers and site coordinators to expose their raw data and inferences from those data to the scrutiny of others (Wolcott, 1975). This worked to a large extent, and we have considerable confidence in the findings reported. But the procedures did not work flawlessly, again largely because of time. Triangulation, consultation, and public defense of findings take longer than solitary research, and the time frame for the Site Study made consistent application of these procedures difficult.

The main difficulties lay with triangulation and the site coordinators' roles. When faced with crushing deadlines for collecting data, tradeoffs had to be made between triangulation and gathering additional data. Generally, we opted for new data, which meant that the quality control would suffer. We have already mentioned that site coordinators were overburdened. Another contributing factor was that fully half of the site coordinators were themselves new to the study and, through the first half of the data collection, these coordinators had their hands full simply keeping up with the analysis packets and research issues, let alone contributing to the efforts of their field researchers.

In retrospect, it was a mistake to assume that experienced social scientists could readily act as site coordinators. But the site coordinator role was as uncharacteristic of traditional social science research as was the role of field researcher. In future studies we would spread the study over a longer period, identify site coordinators earlier, and spend more time training the coordinators to supervise their field researchers.

ON ANALYZING QUALITATIVE DATA

Despite a long ethnographic tradition, there is surprisingly little guidance in the literature for analyzing qualitative data within sites, and almost no precedents for cross-site analysis. We, like most of the other research teams in this volume, had to feel our own way through our data.

The analytic procedure described earlier is, we think, a reasonably effective and efficient approach to making sense of descriptive information from multiple sites. That procedure has several characteristics:

(1)   A cross-site emphasis. No one, save a few graduate students, can read and fully digest 57 individual case studies, no matter how well written. Therefore, every step in the analysis was designed with discovery of cross-site patterns as the paramount objective.

(2)   Concurrent analysis and data collection. Transformation and analysis of site-level data began with the first interview and continued throughout the data collection. Early analysis of data is critical in a study like this if it is to be sensitive to emerging site issues.

(3)   A strong emphasis on data reduction and organization. Even in traditional single-site ethnography one can quickly become buried under a mass of descriptive data. An academic ethnographer may have time to savor those data, but we did not; ways had to be found to efficiently reduce and array the data for cross-site analysis.

(4)   "Working backwards." We have made the point before that this was not an inductive study. The analysis was guided by some clear ideas about the desired structure and contents of the final reports. These were revised regularly, but having them meant we were better able to organize our efforts.

(5)   Flexible rules regarding significance. We believed at the outset, and continue to believe, that there is no simple way to determine the significance of patterns found across sites in qualitative analyses. A finding from a small number of sites sharing similar conditions can be of great significance to policymakers.

(6)   Informal, as opposed to statistical, pattern recognition. Quantification was central to the analysis in the sense that sites were categorized on various dimensions and counted, so statements could be made about the number of sites that shared a characteristic or causal sequence. However, the small and purposively selected samples made statistical analysis impossible.

(7)   Public defense of all conclusions. All analyses were conducted in the context of a committee. Colleagues were expected to challenge each other's conclusions and suggest alternative hypotheses or inferences.

In practice, the analytic procedures used in the site study seem to have been well-adapted to the purposes and constraints of the study. However, there were two issues that plagued study staff. The first, more a nuisance than a real methodological problem, was the collaborative nature of the analysis. Coordination and collaboration among ten analysts from very different disciplines, while stimulating, can also be cumbersome. Rules of evidence had to be forged on a case-by-case basis, a process that took many hours of frequently heated discussion. Collegial democracy is time consuming, and the time required increases geometrically with the number of participants. There is probably a limit to how many site coordinators/analysts can be involved in a study like this before other less democratic procedures are required.

A second problem in the analysis was that of missing and uneven data. A difficulty in qualitative data collections is that one cannot always tell whether a certain event or phenomenon is not reported for a site because it did not occur or because the field researcher neglected to ask about it. As elaborated earlier, much of the data collection was designed to minimize these problems, and field reseachers did remain on site through the analysis and could answer analyst's questions or gather new data. Despite these measures, though, some important gaps in the data did occur.

Finally, a danger in this analysis approach is that important data will be lost in the zeal to reduce the amount of information to be analyzed. Again, steps were taken to guard against this problem: Each reduction was done carefully after a consensus had been reached by the analysts as to which types of data to capture in a reduction; and analysts could always retrace their steps to retrieve information from sites' larger data bases. Despite these safeguards, though, some important information may have been lost in the reductions.

ON THE SEQUENCING AND INTEGRATION OF QUALITATIVE AND SURVEY DATA

The sequencing of the two substudies was unconventional but, we thought, necessary under the circumstances. Very little was known in the Department of Education about the nature or extent of parental involvement in local projects; some better information was needed to select the best mix of sites for close scrutiny in the Site Study. Consequently, SDC proposed that the expensive collection of site data be preceded by a survey to discover the national complexion of the phenomenon to be studied. This information was then used to select fifteen sites from each program for further study.

The Federal Programs Survey was also intended to provide data from a nationally representative population to which the Site Study findings could eventually be compared for purposes of generalization. This integration of results from the two studies was done qualitatively, as part of the reporting of Site Study findings. Whenever a major or secondary finding was described from the Site Study data, that finding was compared with findings in the same area from the Federal Programs Survey.

This integration was frequently difficult, though, and to a large extent the two substudies remained distinct research efforts. One reason for this difficulty of integration was a general tendency among survey respondents to overreport parental involvement. Project directors read their regulations, know what their parental involvement programs are supposed to look like, and consciously or unconsciously translate that ideal into survey responses. Further, there is room for legitimate differences in interpretation of questions. Subtle distinctions are possible in an intensive site study but difficult to build into a survey.

The survey was also limited in the topics that it could address, concentrating primarily on descriptions of the organization of parental involvement components, the number of parents who participate in each area, and sites' funding of those activities. Questions of contributory factors or impact were largely omitted. This meant that there are many site study data points for which there were no comparable survey data, and no comparisons could be made.

These problems were largely independent of the sequence in which the two substudies were carried out. Both the survey and the Site Study analysis packets were based on an elaborate conceptualization or parental involvement—a conceptualization that was not radically altered even by the Site Study. A survey designed on the basis of site study findings would have yielded data only moderately more comparable, and those data would still have been limited to a few topical areas and would have been as vulnerable to overreporting as the Federal Programs Survey.

Had we to do the study over again, we would still opt for an initial survey preceding the Site Study to guide us in selecting study sites. However, we would also like to have another broad data collection following the site study to validate those findings against a larger sample of projects. Recognizing that mailed or telephone surveys would be inadequate for this validation (for the reasons mentioned earlier), we would propose a series of one- or two-day visits, during which a variety of parents and staff would be interviewed using instruments and questions suggested by the site study findings. The results from these visits could then be processed for statistical analysis. While more expensive than surveys, this approach to validation would not be prohibitively expensive, since the data collection could be done by junior staff members or former field researchers.

ON REPORTING THE RESULTS
FROM QUALITATIVE RESEARCH

The Study of Parental Involvement had three principal audiences: Congress (or more accurately congressional staff assistants), decision makers in the four federal programs, and local project directors and staff interested in increasing parental involvement in their schools. None of these had the time to wade through a mass of descriptive information. Communication overload is a serious concern (Fetterman,

1982b). Ways had to be found to present the major findings for these busy audiences while still preserving some of the richness of description that made multisite qualitative methods so attractive in the first place. We now believe that there is no issue more important than the design and format of reports, and we have learned some valuable lessons about how to do it.

Plan for the Skimming Reader

Although we would all like for readers to delight as we did in the richness of our data, this will rarely happen. The question is not whether a reader will skim, but whether the report writers will be able to control the conclusions that a skimming reader will draw. Two devices of report organization make findings more accessible to those who skim: (1) summarize the major findings for each section at the beginning of the section; and (2), use headings that encapsulate the information that follows, instead of simply labeling it. For example, instead of "Parent Attendance Patterns," a heading might read "Few Parents Attended PAC Meetings."

It is possible to meet the needs of different audiences in one report. Although we designed our reports to accommodate the skimming reader, we also recognized that our three audiences had different needs for detail. The Congressional audience, we assumed, would be interested only in the major findings from the study—the two or three major conclusions in each area. The audiences in program offices also wanted major findings, but would be interested in the secondary findings, that contributed to those conclusions. Finally, the local project audience (and all audiences to some extent) would be interested in the specifics of parental involvement practice at study sites. To accommodate these three levels of need, we used three methods of presentation in our reports in conjunction with summaries of major findings and descriptive headings: First, the text focused on major and secondary findings only. Second, illustrative vignettes (mini-case studies of particular phenomena) accompanied the test as figures. Finally, each section contained tables that summarized that data from each site, organized by variables addressed in the study. Thus, a skimming reader could scan a report to learn the major findings from the study, while a reader interested in details could read vignettes or study the tables.

CONCLUSIONS

Was it worth it? Did the results from the Site Study justify the expense of intensive data collection? Although these questions must ultimately be answered by those who commissioned the study, we believe the Site Study yielded two valuable outcomes. First, the study produced a rich, detailed, and comprehensive picture of the nature, causes, and consequences of parental involvement in federal education programs. (It also generated another product with potential for a lasting contribution to education: a handbook of successful parental involvement strategies written for local schools.) Second, the study will help advance the state of the art in policy research.

We began this article with an assertion that policy research is at best a matter of compromises, and that the Study of Parental Involvement was no exception. Although sometimes painful, these compromises were, we think, productive. The methodology that finally resulted in the Site Study produced results that would have been unobtainable through other, more traditional approaches. Because we were improvising, though, the methods did not work flawlessly. We learned valuable lessons at each step along the way—lessons that can be applied in future research by us or by others.

NOTE

1. The design, methods, instruments, and analyses of the Site Study are described in Lee et al. (1981).

REFERENCES

Cadena-Munoz, R. & Keesling, J. W. *Parents and federal education programs, vol. 4:* Title VII. Santa Monica, CA: System Development Corporation, 1981.

Cook, T. D. & Reichardt, C. S. (Eds.) *Qualitative and quantitative methods in evaluation research.* Beverly Hills: Sage, 1979.

Fetterman, D. M. Ethnography in educational research: The dynamics of diffusion. *Educational Researcher.* March, 1982, pp. 17-22.(a)

Fetterman, D. M. Ibsen's baths: Reactivity and insensitivity (a misapplication of the treatment-control design in a national evaluation). *Educational Evaluation and Policy Analysis,* 1982, *4*(3), 261-279.(b)

Keesling, J. W. *Parents and federal education Programs: Some preliminary findings from the study of parental involvement.* Santa Monica, CA: System Development Corporation, 1980.

Keesling, J. W. Melaragno, R. J., Robbins, A., & Smith, A. G. *Parents and federal education programs, vol. 2: Summary of program-specific findings.* Santa Monica, CA: System Development Corporation, 1981.

LeCompte, M. D. & Goetz J. P. Problems of reliability and validity in ethnographic research. *Review of Educational Research,* 1982 *52,* pp. 31-61.

Lee, D., Keesling, J. W. & Melaragno, R. J. *Parents and federal education programs, vol. 7: Methodologies employed in the study of parental involvement.* Santa Monica, CA: System Development Corporation, 1981.

Louis, K. S. Multisite/multimethod studies: An introduction. *American Behavioral Scientist,* 1982, *26,* p. 1.

Lyons, M., Robbins, A., and Smith, A. *Involving parents: A handbook for participation in schools.* Santa Monica, CA: System Development Corporation, 1982.

Melaragno, R. J., Keesling, J. W., Lyons, M., Robbins, A., & Smith, A. *Parents and federal education programs, vol. 1: The nature, causes, and consequences of parental involvement in federal education programs.* Santa Monica: System Development Corporation, 1981.

Melaragno, R. J., Lyons, M., & Sparks, M. *Parents and federal education programs, vol. 6: Title I.* Santa Monica, CA: System Development Corporation, 1981.

Mulhauser, F. Ethnography and policy-making: The case of education. *Human Organization,* 1975, *34,* p. 3.

Patton, M. Q. (1980). *Qualitative evaluation methods.* Beverly Hills: Sage, 1980.

Robbins, A. E., & Dingler, D. *Parents and federal education programs, vol. 3: ESAA.* Santa Monica, CA: System Development Corporation, 1981.

Smith, A. G., & Louis, K. S. Multimethod policy research: Issues and applications. *American Behavioral Scientist,* 1982, *26,* p. 1.

Smith, A. G., & Nerenberg, S. *Parents and federal education programs, vol. 5: Follow through.* Santa Monica, CA: System Development Corporation, 1981.

Webb, E., Campbell, D., Schwartz, R., & Sechrest, L. *Unobtrusive measures: Nonreactive research in the social sciences.* Chicago: Rand McNally, 1966.

Weiss, R. S. & Rein, M. The evaluation of broad-aim programs: Difficulties in experimental design and an alternative. In C. H. Weiss (Ed.) *Evaluation action programs: Readings in social action and education.* Boston: Allyn and Bacon.

Wolcott, H. F. Criteria for an ethnographic approach to research in schools. *Human Organization,* 1975; *34,* pp. 111-127.

7

Ethnography as Evaluation
Hearing-Impaired Students in the Mainstream

MARTHA K. HEMWALL

There has been a growing concern with special education in the
United States. Approximately 5 to 10 million children are
handicapped, but one-eighth of these children have not been in school
and 50 percent have not received adequate special services (Gliedman &
Roth, 1980: 1-6, 173). In the past two decades the quality and
effectiveness of the special education programs have been questioned,
and legal cases addressing this social problem have increased. In 1972
alone, four landmark cases were decided. Pennsylvania Association for
Retarded Citizens (PARC) v. the Commonwealth of Pennsylvania,
Mills v. the Board of Education for the District of Columbia, Larry P.
v. Riles, and Diana v. the State Board of Education of California, all
helped to guarantee the rights of handicapped students to equal
educational opportunities.

The Education for All Handicapped Children Act of 1975 (P.L. 94-
142)[1] was passed by Congress in response to this growing public
concern with the educational rights of the handicapped. P.L. 94-142 is
extremely detailed and tries to guarantee equal educational opportunity
for the handicapped by calling for "the least restrictive environment"[2]
and listing a "normal" class placement as the most preferred educational situation. This legislation, as a consequence, renewed interest in
integrating handicapped children into regular schools,[3] an educational
approach termed "mainstreaming" in the United States.

Despite the effort to establish mainstreaming as an effective educational strategy, problems have developed. The sudden influx of special
students into regular classrooms has triggered emotional debates over
the value of this type of educational program. There is no apparent
agreement on whether experiences in a regular school are more
important educationally than full-time participation in a program
specifically designed for the students' special educational needs. The

controversy has been particularly intense in deaf education; the special language problems of hearing-impaired children complicate the already complex issues raised by mainstreaming (Brill, 1975; Greenberg & Doolittle, 1977; Large, 1980).

The present chapter is based on research that was designed to evaluate a particular mainstreaming program by providing an understanding of everyday mainstreaming experiences. This chapter discusses the use of ethnographic data in understanding the dynamics of mainstreaming hearing-impaired students. It also weighs the benefits and drawbacks of qualitative research in educational evaluations.

HISTORY AND RESEARCH

In the past, several attempts to integrate hearing-impaired students into regular schools have been made. Inadequate documentation makes a detailed historical analysis difficult. However, the available information suggests that these integration efforts were relatively short-lived and met with little success.

J. Gordon (1885) reviewed nineteenth-century efforts to educate the deaf in public schools. In 1821 in Bavaria, the first recorded attempts were made. Integration was seen primarily as a cost-cutting measure although the hearing-impaired students were given some tutorial support. This experiment eventually failed; the results had been slight and the hearing-impaired students were perceived as a detriment to the hearing students' education. Integration efforts were eventually abandoned. Of the hearing-impaired children 40 percent were educated in public schools in 1871, but not one child remained in the program by 1881.

Similar experiments were undertaken in other areas of central and northern Europe and had similar results. Gordon specifically reported on the work of Blanchet in France. Blanchet had proposed integration in 1836; two programs were operating by 1848. These programs grew in popularity until 1858. The French Ministry of Education withdrew its support in 1859, and by 1882 only a few students remained in the public system.

Shortly after the revolution, the Soviet Union instituted mainstreaming programs for the hearing-impaired. The results were so limited that these programs were dropped. Separate educational institutions for the deaf were created in which the curriculum was specifically designed for the hearing-impaired students (Moores, 1978).

This history indicates a very limited success with the use of mainstreaming as an educational strategy for hearing-impaired children. However very little is known about why the integration of hearing-impaired students has been so difficult. While the social research on the deaf community has been increasing in recent years (Baker & Battison, 1980; Covington, 1980; Erting, 1978; Higgins, 1980; Meadow, 1968, 1972; Padden & Markowicz, 1975; Stokoe, 1976) the mainstreaming of hearing-impaired students has rarely been addressed. The material that is available consists primarily of opinions or practical advice. Recent studies make an attempt to avoid the central arguments that have created past controversies, to accept the inevitability of mainstreaming as mandated by P.L. 94-142, and to offer constructive approaches to designing such educational opportunities (for example, see Birch, 1975; Nix, 1976; Yater, 1977).

Milo Bishop, who helped to develop a mainstreaming program at the National Technical Institute for the Deaf (NTID), also edited an introductory collection of practical articles. However, Bishop briefly becomes more analytical in his introduction and offers the insight that mainstreaming has long been considered a goal in itself. He argues that until mainstreaming is perceived as a means rather than an end, its success will always be questionable (1979:33-47).

More substantive analyses are limited in number. Donald Large, an attorney, discusses the implications of P.L. 94-142 for hearing-impaired students in a law review article, "Special Problems of the Deaf under the Education for All Handicapped Children Act of 1975" (1980). He thoroughly weighs the pros and cons of mainstreaming hearing-impaired children and imbeds these considerations in an in-depth historical review.

The National Swedish Board of Education published a monograph, "Research and Development Concerning Integration of Handicapped Pupils into the Ordinary School System" (1980). The monograph includes articles that analyze the social and academic implications of mainstreaming four different types of handicapped children. The article on integration of hearing-impaired students is particularly useful (Nörden & Ang, 1980). Not only are the authors careful in defining their terms, they confront the psychological and social implications of integration. Among these issues they discuss the environmental pressures these children experience to act "as if" they were "normal," communication's role in developing meaningful relationships, and the effects of deafness on social development.

THE STUDY

This chapter is based on ethnographic data collected during the first year of a two-year study of a mainstreaming program, Project Alternatives. This program had been a recent addition to the special services offered by Hathaway School for the Deaf, a state school on the Eastern seaboard.[4]

Project Alternatives was in its third year of operation when this present research began in the fall of 1979. The program involved 25 students from a Hathaway student population of approximately 160. This mainstreaming program was considered innovative for two reasons; it provided for the part-time placement of students, and it attempted to provide a full range of supportive services including tutoring and sign interpreters in the classroom. Neither of these characteristics was common in the majority of mainstreaming programs in the United States.

Despite the program's innovative nature, the students in Project Alternatives were not experiencing particularly smooth transitions to the hearing schools and the program was in a turmoil. Hathaway was able to hire an evaluator for Project Alternatives through a broadly defined HEW grant already operating within its structure. It was in this capacity that I conducted my research. I was asked to evaluate the program in two ways: (1) to assess how either Project Alternatives or Hathaway could better prepare the students for the mainstreaming experience, socially and academically; and (2) to gather information about the needs of the teachers, students, and the schools into which the students were mainstreamed in order to help Project Alternatives staff create a more effective program.

I gathered my data using the traditional anthropological tools of participant-observation and unstructured interviewing. I selected seven students of both junior high and high school age who were representative of the Project Alternatives students. These students were mainstreamed part-time in either academic or vocational placements. I regularly observed the students in both their Hathaway and mainstream classes. I conducted unstructured interviews with all their teachers as well as the administrators in each school. I periodically helped to tutor the students, and I talked with their parents. I worked closely with Project Alternatives staff as well, participating in meetings, planning sessions, and workshops.

In general, the ethnographic data suggested that everyone involved in mainstreaming—students, teachers, administrators, and even parents—were preoccupied with the possibility of failure and the related pressure to succeed. A mainstreamed student could not just choose to fail academically or socially; the implications of failure were deeper. Each person perceived such a failure as a reflection on his or her abilities. The regular school did not ensure an optimal environment and the school board would not be pleased; the sign interpreter did not cover the class material clearly enough; the teachers were not adjusting properly, not putting enough effort into the class, or were not sensitive to the students' needs; the mainstreaming program was poorly designed or made a mistake in a placement for the student; the parents were not providing adequate support at home. The pressures were an enormous burden on everyone in the program, including the students, however, little help was offered in coping with this perceived pressure to succeed.

The data also illustrated how the social and academic aspects of mainstreaming are interwoven and cannot be separated easily. To prepare a student for mainstreaming requires methods of improving academic skills but must also be accompanied by an understanding of the social context in which she or he operates.

The data offered specific insights as well. It suggested that the nonactive involvement of the mainstreamed students was created, to a certain extent, by their own need for certain academic and social skills. In addition, the data indicated that the presence of the hearing-impaired students caused enough discomfort to create inconsistency in the treatment of mainstreamed students in the classrooms, ineffective modes of communication between these students and their teachers and peers, and the occurrence of certain types of dependency relationships. These problems served to reinforce the apparent passivity of the mainstreamed students.

The ethnographic data, then, was able to offer insights into both general and specific areas of difficulty. Ethnographic details helped Hathaway and the staff of Project Alternatives circumvent the fear of failure and focus on solutions to achieving success in the mainstream.

BARRIERS TO MEANINGFUL INTEGRATION

A variety of problems confronted those involved in the mainstreaming program. Many of these difficulties caused the mainstreamed students to be set apart as different and as someone requiring help.

Receiving special treatment was a regular facet of the mainstreamed students' life in the regular schools. Some special considerations seemed justified and others did not. The mainstreamed students were given preferential seating assignments so they could watch their sign interpreter, who was seated in the front of the room. The mainstreamed students were allowed to take textbooks home from class but other students were not. The mainstreamed students used notes from other students and did not have to take notes themselves. Sometimes a mainstreamed student was late to class but did not receive a detention, which was always given to the other students when they were late. Sometimes mainstreamed students were allowed to repeat orally given tests because of their difficulty with verbal language, but other students were not allowed to retake these tests unless they had been absent.

The quiet demeanor and behavior of the hearing-impaired students further differentiated them. Despite the general activity around them, the mainstreamed students rarely engaged actively in either the information or the class. The apparent passivity of the mainstreamed students was striking. During classes they sat with their hands folded on their desks, books under their chairs, and watched their sign interpreter quietly. This behavior was in contrast to most other students who were copying from the board, taking notes on lectures, asking the teacher to repeat information, raising their hands, and asking questions. I questioned some of the hearing-impaired students about their lack of involvement. One replied, "Oh, we have a hearing notetaker in class who does that for us [gets the information]. We can't take notes. We're deaf." Another student pointed out, "If we have questions we can just ask our tutor or our interpreter later on. Its easier—we understand better. I guess the class isn't that important."

The special accommodations made for the mainstreamed students coupled with their lack of involvement in the class appeared to be reinforced by the teachers in the regular schools. The teachers expressed tremendous discomfort about the presence of the hearing-impaired students. Their anxiety seemed to center around two aspects of mainstreaming: (1) disciplining the students, and (2) communicating with the students.

The teachers uniformly found it difficult to discipline the mainstreamed students in the same way they would their hearing students. One example helps to illustrate this hesitation.

Three junior high school boys were mainstreamed together in a half-time placement. Although regularly uninvolved in the class, these three were not usually passive. In fact, they were unusually confident for hearing-impaired students. One time, the boys pushed in front of the other students in order to be first to experiment with a new learning device the teacher had shown the class. The teacher made no comment about this aggression. Instead of crouching around the demonstration with the rest of the class when the others took their turns, they pulled up their desks together on the outside of the circle and began to talk among themselves. This behavior also went uncorrected. When the teacher began discussing the lesson as the demonstrations continued, the boys became more unruly. The teacher still did not comment so the interpreter began to reverse interpret[5] everything the boys were saying to each other in sign language. When the boys realized what the interpreter was doing, one turned around and snapped, "Well, I don't care." Finally, the teacher said, "Well, I do!"

The hesitation to discipline the mainstreamed students was experienced by all the teachers in the regular schools. It served to reinforce both the students' lack of motivation to participate as well as their status as somehow "different." When the issue was discussed with the teachers, their responses reflected how uncomfortable they felt about teaching the hearing-impaired students. In theme, their responses were consistent:

> I didn't know if they understood what I said.
>
> I know they are in a terribly hard situation.
>
> It's better for the interpreter to do these things because she understands them better.
>
> Because they're deaf.
>
> I feel sorry for them, I can't discipline them.

In other words, the teachers had not yet been able to achieve an understanding of the mainstreamed students as people, as adolescent kids like their other students. Instead, they perceived them as persons who were deaf, whose hearing-impairment superseded other personal characteristics. The only exception was a physical education teacher who had lived with a profoundly deaf roommate in college. This teacher seemed more relaxed, but was aware of the difficulties that other teachers were having with the hearing-impaired students. She used this example:

> I think handicapped kids run the gamut like hearing kids—some brats, some good kids, some smart, some slow. I think some of the other teachers don't realize this. One time I was in the boys gym class the three mainstreamed boys are in. Nathan was goofing off and egging some other kids on. I pointed this out to the teacher. I said, "Look, perhaps they [the hearing-impaired students] cause it sometimes and they're not always picked on." The teacher turned around in astonishment and said, "But he can't hear!" I told him, "That doesn't mean he can't be bratty."

The data suggested that, in large part, the teachers' discomfort with the hearing-impaired students was created by the difficulty they experienced in communicating with them. The tension about effective communication increased as the semester continued. The teachers gradually realized that the task of establishing an easy rapport with these students was more complicated than with the other students. The teachers were initially uncertain about their abilities to teach the students, and this uncertainty grew into frustration while they tried to communicate effectively. Often they were left wondering if they could ever develop a comfortable mode of communication with the mainstreamed student. Sometimes they just abandoned any effort to try to communicate, as the next example poignantly illustrates.

One day a shy hearing-impaired student, Ann, was sitting in her social studies class in her mainstream high school. Her teacher approached her desk, but then turned his head away from her to look at the interpreter, thus making lipreading impossible. He said, "Tell Ann that her assignment is due tomorrow." After the interpreter translated his statement, Ann nodded awkwardly but did not look at the teacher except for a brief glance. He went on to tell the interpreter other things for Ann to know. Ann's eyes were riveted on the interpreter. The teacher's eyes were riveted on the interpreter also. After he finished, Ann tried to get his attention, but he was already walking back to his desk. The interpreter encouraged Ann to go up to the teacher's desk and ask her question. She began to get up and follow the retreating teacher, but suddenly she stopped, plopped back into her seat, waved her hand in frustration, and said, "Forget it!" and went back to her homework.

Communication was considered a particularly difficult problem because it appeared essential to the success sought by both the teachers and the students. For some teachers the unusual sound of the deaf student's voice created stress. For others it was having to use an intermediary such as an interpreter. For still others, the fact that the students could not easily understand what they said was most discouraging. "It's hard," one teacher said simply, "to not be able to banter and still establish a relationship."

Communication seemed to be a significant barrier to interaction between the hearing-impaired students and their hearing peers as well. While the hearing students appeared to be fascinated by the interpreter and some expressed varying degrees of interest in sign language, few understood that this sign language used in the classroom was based on English nor did they understand how they could actually approach the mainstreamed students. For example, a student once told a Project Alternatives staff member that she did not feel she could talk with the mainstreamed student in her class:

Student: I want to talk to her but I can't because I don't know her language.

Staff member: What language do you think she speaks?

Student: Sign language.

Staff member: No, she speaks English just like you.[6]

A commonly observed method of coping with the uncertainty was to develop a relationship of dependency. During the research, a variety of dependency relationships developed among the mainstreamed students, their hearing peers, the teachers, and the interpreters. That students in a new environment or teachers facing new experiences would seek out others to help them cope with uncertainty is understandable. The critical issue was neither the need for the relationships nor whether they were sincere. Rather the difficulties arose because the relationships often became crutches and/or prevented more meaningful integration in the mainstream classes. The following examples illustrate a few of the common ways in which such relationships manifested themselves.

Between Mainstreamed Students. Susan and Ann were two high school students who were mainstreamed together. During the year it became apparent that Ann would not approach anyone in her mainstream situation, neither teachers or peers. The way she survived was to use Susan to ask all her questions, to get her homework assignments and books, and to interact with other students if they were working on group projects. Apparently Susan felt uncomfortable about these duties but did not assert herself because she felt they were in the experience together and she wanted to maintain a good relationship with her only hearing-impaired companion in the mainstream.

Between a Mainstreamed Student and Her Interpreter. After a long period of being antagonistic to her interpreter, Dorie finally began to be friendly. This new acceptance pleased the interpreter tremendously who responded by trying to develop a friendship with Dorie even though this was an inappropriate role for an interpreter. Dorie then began to engage her interpreter in discussions using sign language, about topics like her extracurricular activities and the weather *while* the class was in session. Other serious ramifications of this relationship were apparent by the end of the school year. When Dorie informed the Project Alternatives staff which classes she wanted to take the next fall, a staff member questioned her about the reasons for her unusual choices. Finally Dorie admitted that the classes were her interpreter's choices. Her interpreter was convinced that certain classes would be more interesting than others and Dorie wanted to keep her happy so she would remain her interpreter.

Between Teacher and Interpreter. One day an English teacher was explaining iambic pentameter during a unit on poetry. Because the concept depended on understanding rhythm and beat, the teacher was concerned that his mainstreamed student would not be able to learn iambic pentameter. Instead of talking about the difficulty with the student or a Project Alternatives staff member, he asked the interpreter for advice. Although the interpreter had no background in deaf education, she responded that hearing impairment would prevent the student from grasping this rhythmic concept. This misinformation had to be corrected later by a Project Alternatives staff member. While upset with the interpreter's interference, the staff member also recognized the intense pressure often applied on interpreters to fill this kind of support role for the teachers. The interpreters were guided by a professional code of ethics that forbade them any interaction except direct interpreting, but if they chose to strictly follow this code the teachers usually became frustrated and sometimes quite angry.

These relationships of dependency could not be construed negatively except insofar as they were barriers to more effective mainstreaming experiences. Both academic and social independence and confidence needed to be nurtured in the mainstreaming experience, and these kinds of relationships did not appear to contribute positively toward this goal for anyone. Instead, the relationship appeared to further segregate the students.

The special treatment accorded the mainstreamed students, their relatively passive classroom behavior, and the resulting dependency relationships had academic and social ramifications. Academically, the lack of involvement and responsibility expected of these students in the regular schools affected their abilities to process information and to retain or retrieve information on their own. Basic skills of critical listening, selection, seeing causality, making inferences, composing and reconstructing information, were not being effectively developed or maintained.[7]

The issue of academic development is crucial if it is assumed that the mainstreamed student is not simply to be maintained at his or her current level of skills. In most cases, mainstreaming is not chosen as an educational strategy purely for its social benefits. Rather, the hearing classroom is considered an environment in which the student can be encouraged to develop skills and to enhance his or her general academic achievement.

However, these difficulties with the mainstreaming program had significant social consequences as well. Not only were academic skills not encouraged, but neither was the students' sense of independence and self-reliance fostered. Their quiet demeanor and behavior in the classroom was so different from the average student that they were immediately set apart from the class. The special treatment accorded them was noticed by their hearing peers especially. During their interviews, the teachers stressed this aspect as a major barrier to more meaningful integration.

My experiences indicated that the hearing peers were indeed confused about the motivations of the hearing-impaired students. One time while I observed a class from a seat in the back of the room, two students leaned over and pointed out the hearing-impaired students' lack of activity—they were neither taking notes nor were they referring to their books. The students inquired of me in a whisper "Don't they know that a test is coming soon? Why don't they care?" Another day, a student in a different class, expressed his feelings more adamantly: "Aw, those guys just get away with murder!"

The research suggested, then, that the hearing-impaired students were perceived as different—as handicapped—which led to special treatment and low expectations for their performance. The students reacted by maintaining a passive classroom role which only reinforced their special status. The teachers' and peers' feelings of uncertainty and discomfort further reinforced the students' passivity. Dependency relationships were developed as a mechanism to cope with the difficulties but these relationships served only to erect further barriers to meaningful integration. The hearing-impaired students, then, both experienced and created barriers in the mainstream that limited the potential academic and social benefits of integration.

DISCUSSION AND RECOMMENDATIONS

Based on the ethnographic information I collected during my research, I presented a general evaluation of Project Alternatives and also made several specific recommendations.[8]

In an overview of the mainstreaming program, I stressed the overall goal toward which Project Alternatives seemed to be oriented-meaningful social and academic integration. In order to achieve this goal, two important aims had to be pursued; the ethnographic data suggested that these aims seemed to get lost at times in the everyday complexities of mainstreaming.

First, mainstreaming should strive to remove as many barriers as possible between hearing and hearing-impaired people. This aim appears to be based on common sense, but the ethnographic data shows that this aim was continually frustrated. Teachers' difficulties with discipline, the fact that hearing-impaired students lack or are not encouraged to use helpful academic skills, the special treatment of the mainstreamed students, the limited and awkward communication between the mainstreamed students and their teachers and peers, dependency relationships—all these problems affected the process of effectively integrating these students. These aspects either erected barriers or reinforced existing ones between the two groups by limiting interaction and setting apart the mainstreamed student as somehow different and needing help.

Second, mainstreaming should be designed to encourage self-confidence and personal responsibility among hearing-impaired students. Mainstreaming should not be so preoccupied with integration in any form as a goal that these qualities are sacrificed. The dependency relationships, the inconsistent discipline, and special "help" given the mainstreamed students which undermined their motivation to be actively involved in a class all aimed at successfully coping with the mainstreaming experience but at the expense of these important qualities. Most situations in the mainstream classes did not encourage students to take responsibility for their social and academic performance and behavior. Part of the learning experience should include recognition that the hearing world has excellent and poor teachers, friendly and mean peers, difficult and easy assignments. Learning to take the ups with the downs is an important lesson learned only through the personal experience of taking responsibility for one's self.

Unfortunately, none of these issues in mainstreaming hearing-impaired students has an easy solution. Nevertheless, specific recommendations were offered. These suggestions were aimed at removing the barriers and encouraging independence and self-confidence in order to create integration experiences that would be more meaningful for all those involved.

(1) Skills tutoring should be provided for the mainstreamed students. These sessions should not deal exclusively with the content matter of specific classes. Rather, they should focus on learning strategies in reading, writing, discourse as well as on study skills important to academic adjustment, including notetaking and test taking. In addition to giving them new academic tools with which to learn, such skills will help students gain confidence and help to remove barriers to their integration by encouraging more active behavior in classes. The personnel of the mainstreaming program, together with the teachers at Hathaway and the regular schools should establish the content of

possible tutorial programs. These skill tutorials should be evaluated as students move through the academic year.

(2) Support systems must be established as a consistent part of the mainstreaming program. For the students, a counseling session should be scheduled into the student's week. This regularity removes any possible stigma attached to such sessions when the student needs specific help. Because of the special understanding required of the hearing-impaired students, the ideal person would be a deaf adult who was previously mainstreamed. For the teachers, a special position should be created for a deaf educator to meet informally on a weekly basis with the teachers in the mainstream schools to discuss the student's progress and any problems. The teachers do not always have specific problems, but they do appear to need regular assurance that everything is under control. In fact, they all requested this kind of reassuring support.

(3) More informal academic and social experiences need to be scheduled for the mainstreamed students. Many times the more significant interaction with hearing peers and teachers was in physical education, art, or in classes which incorporated project periods and work in small groups. The more concern about the mainstreaming experience that a teacher expressed seemed inversely correlated to the amount of time the particular student had available for such contacts. Numerous teachers suggested this recommendation: They wanted to see more time available so that students could come to them with their questions rather than to their tutors. This would provide an opportunity to get better acquainted with the mainstreamed students.

(4) Separating the groups of hearing-impaired students would be more effective in striving towards the goals in mainstreaming. Most teachers as well as the parents of the students who were mainstreamed with other hearing-impaired peers asked for the group to be split apart. The students in these groups had become so dependent on each other that the groups isolated themselves, thus preventing further integration. Teachers sensed that many of the students, if mainstreamed individually, would have integrated more easily. Alhough a few of the teachers felt that these mainstreamed students "kept each other company and were less lonely" the ethnographic data seemed to support the more widespread opinion that such groups were not particularly effective for either of the two main goals necessary to meaningful integration.

(5) Intensive in-servicing and training should be available for everyone—hearing-impaired students, their families, hearing peers, teachers, and administrators. The sessions would present general knowledge about hearing impairment as well as provide more specific

information about the classroom environments, adjustments needed in the classroom, discipline expectations, realistic expectations for learning, and how to develop effective communication modes.[9]

(6) Special training for interpreters who wish to work in an educational setting should be provided. Interpreters are limited to a certain extent by their ethical code and frequently by a lack of training in deaf education. However, their position frequently becomes a difficult liason role, and they need special preparation for effectively dealing with the one-to-one relationships they will have with students and teachers.

These recomendations were based on the ethnographic data. As the observation and interview data accumulated, the necessary recommendations either became apparent and/or were explicit requests from teachers, students, or parents. Consequently, all the recommendations were anticipated and implemented as much as possible during the next school year.

Two recommendations proved difficult to implement. One problematic recommendation was the special training of interpreters. This training was not immediately possible because interpreters were hired by the state's Department of Education and they were not under the auspices of either Hathaway or Project Alternatives. However, the staff of Project Alternatives attempted to remedy the situation through regular personal contacts with the interpreters. They also planned an optional workshop on educational interpreting for the next year.

The need for more informal social and academic experiences remained problematic as well. The part-time structures of most placements required bus transportation, making adequate free time hard to schedule. As much as possible, students were scheduled into at least one nonacademic class such as physical education, homeroom, or art, although few of the students' schedules allowed time to initiate more contacts with their teachers or peers outside of formal classes.

The other recommendations were more easily implemented. Skills tutoring began immediately, and the staff involved the students in defining specific goals and planning timetables to achieve these goals. One skill, developing a personal system of note-taking, was earmarked as essential enough to be experimentally incorporated into the curriculum at Hathaway.

Project Alternatives also made a conscious effort to provide adequate support systems and in-servicing for the teachers and the students. A full day workshop on the special problems of mainstreaming hearing-impaired students was held to in-service the teachers and any other interested professionals in the hearing schools. In addition, the in-servicing of entire classes in the regular schools was planned. The time spent on in-servicing the peers seemed to be especially productive. In the class in which the student had asked what language the mainstreamed student spoke, for instance, a staff member decided to teach the finger spelling alphabet to the class to encourage more interaction. As the staff member explained, "in this case, the situation went from 'What language does she speak?' to the hearing-impaired student being in the middle of a group talking the next morning."

The staff tried to redesign their schedules to allow more regular contact with both the teachers and the students. They seemed to be able to divert small but important crises through these chats with the students. For example, one staff member offered to do a short in-servicing for one of Dorie's high school classes. She planned to talk about hearing impairment, sign language, and interpreters and to help the peers try to understand the purpose of mainstreaming. When she told Dorie about talking to her class, Dorie quickly responded, "I don't want to be there when you do it!" After the session, Dorie rushed up to the staff member to ask what happened:

> Dorie: What did you talk about?
> Staff member: Hearing aids, deafness, and that kind of thing.
> Dorie: Oh? Didn't you talk about me?
> Staff member: Not really. We just talked about sign language and what it's like to be deaf.
> Dorie: Oh. I would have gone to that, that would have been fun.

The staff member was able to discover that the purpose of in-servicing had been misunderstood by Dorie who believed that the class was going to "talk about her" and somehow analyze her as a person. This short discussion highlighted how regular chats might help to avert the anxieties even an otherwise bright and confident mainstreamed student could experience.

Good fortune had provided Hathaway with students from Gallaudet College, a college specifically designed for hearing-impaired students, who were completing practicums in counseling. This new resource allowed each mainstreamed student to have regularly scheduled counseling sessions. Hathaway also received money to hire another staff counselor which further strengthened this effort to provide a strong system of support for the students.

Project Alternatives, then, actively pursued the implementation of the recommendations resulting from the ethnographic evaluation. In the short time since these changes have been introduced, the staff claims the information and the recommendations from this evaluation have been useful. Long-term results are not yet possible to assess.

CONCLUSIONS

The evaluation and the recommendations presented to Project Alternatives were based on ethnographic data gathered through participant-observation and unstructured interviewing. These methods were different in important ways. In the first, I was observing and interpreting action and intent; in the second, I was receiving retrospective accounts people gave of their actions or situations and interpreting the accounts.

Anthropologists often juxtapose the resulting data in order to provide further insights into the research situation. I found this to be a particularly useful tool. For example, three junior high school boys were mainstreamed together. Their teachers claimed the three were doing well, that they worked hard and presented no problem in the class. Yet, when observations were made, it became apparent these students were indeed a disruption. Furthermore, the teachers were unable to be consistent in disciplining these hearing-impaired students, and the other students felt the hearing-impaired students were receiving special treatment. When I asked about these difficulties, the teachers admitted they felt sorry for the students, were uncomfortable communicating with them, and felt their deafness excused any of their problematic behavior.

In this example, the apparent contradictions between the observations and the interviews helped to elicit further information. As a result, a mainstreaming situation that had been initially perceived as successful was discovered to be immensely complicated.

There is no way to use retrospective accounts as an absolute key to interpreting behavior, nor is observed behavior an absolute key to interpreting retrospective accounts. However, looking at the relationship between people's accounts and their behavior (as the above example illustrates) can provide important information.

However this kind of educational evaluation is not without problems. I found three specific problems in using ethnography as my primary method: First, getting access to the classrooms to observe proved problematic. The teachers were uniformly hesitant to allow another adult into their classes to observe even though they had been assured that no direct evaluation of their teaching was being done. By their own admission, questionnaires or brief formal interviews were preferable and seemed controllable and finite; the relatively undefined but in-depth nature of ethnographic research was more threatening. Even after acquiring their permission, a certain suspicion lingered about my "real" purpose; I periodically had my notebook snatched from under my pen by teachers who were sure they would find me evaluating their personal abilities. The teachers' suspicions were eventually alleviated after many hours of personal contact in teachers' lounges, through other colleagues, and in classrooms.

Second, the results from ethnographic evaluation needed to be carefully formulated to avoid any unintended consequences. My task had been complicated by the potential for conflict between Hathaway's administration, which was not convinced mainstreaming was useful for the students, and the Project Alternatives staff which was fully committed to mainstreaming. In providing my evaluation, I felt I had to be careful not to heighten this already tense situation.

While this kind of political consideration often faces any evaluator, I would suggest that the use of ethnography complicates the dilemma. Ethnographic data is rich in detail about everyday activities and the people involved in these activities; the potential for the use of this detail in ways not intended by the evaluator is constantly present.

Third, the use of ethnography raised the question of how to adequately protect the informants. The informants—students, teachers, administrators, Project Alternatives staff members—were interconnected in complex political ways. I had to be aware of the possibility that data from the informants could jeopardize either their jobs or their reputations. The research situation was relatively small, and people could be easily identified through their job position alone. The juggling of these considerations with the need for the forthright answers required in an honest evaluation proved to be a formidable challenge.

Despite these problems, the use of ethnography proved to be an effective evaluatory methodology in important ways. This effectiveness became apparent shortly after I was hired. Hathaway had also contracted an educational research firm to evaluate Project Alternatives and to provide ways to predict success and failure in the mainstreaming program. This study took only a few days in the regular schools and included questionnaires, brief observation periods in a few classes, and short structured interviews with selected teachers. The report, meant to be primarily statistical, had difficulty establishing a level of significance on many questions because the teachers frequently chose to write long descriptive answers on the side of the questionnaire rather than to check a multiple choice answer. The Project Alternatives staff was provided with the actual questionnaires to read for themselves.

The staff showed me the final report and claimed my information was, on the whole, more useful. When I asked why, they pointed out they were better able to understand both the feelings and the needs of the teachers and students involved. In other words, the staff was able to grasp the usefulness of an anthropological perspective for understanding educational situations. This understanding of the everyday situations was helping them identify possible answers about how to proceed. In beginning to understand how the people involved were actually perceiving the mainstreaming experience, they were able to isolate critical variables and to redesign the program accordingly.

The nature of ethnographic data is such that it allowed the staff of Project Alternatives to be actively involved with assessing the information as it accumulated during the research. As noted earlier, many of the recommendations were anticipated or actually suggested while in conference with staff members during the research. They awaited the latest ethnographic tidbits from teachers, classes, and students with great anticipation and usually wanted to discuss the data as soon as possible. Ethnography helped them feel they could be and were directly engaged in the evaluation and the resulting recommendations. This active participation helped the evaluation to be effective.

The question remains, of course, whether this ethnographic evaluation and the resulting recommendations actually helped to improve Project Alternatives or helped the mainstreaming program achieve its goal of integrating hearing-impaired students in a meaningful way on a long-term basis. However, the closer qualitative examination of Project Alternatives raised important questions for the educators to consider as a method of continuing to improve the mainstreaming experience in the future. These questions, uncovered through the use of ethnographic data, were complex but central to the direction of Project Alternatives: What exactly does meaningful integration mean? Why should hearing-impaired students be integrated? Are the academic, social, and emotional goals clearly delineated for each student? The ambiguity surrounding these questions seemed to contribute to the perceived faltering of Project Alternatives. The difficulty created by these unanswered questions suggests such ambiguity may well have contributed to the problems mainstreaming programs have faced in the past.

This study illustrated that the use of ethnography as a tool for evaluation can provide an exceedingly rich and complex body of information. The important benefit provided by this richness of detail is that it helps to avoid oversimplified assessments and evaluations. As a consquence, ethnography can create the basis for more fair and useful recommendations.

NOTES

1. I will use P.L. 94-142 to refer to the legislation because this is commonly used among deaf educators.

2. The term "least restrictive environment" is borrowed from P.L. 94-142 and refers to the placement of a special education student into the most integrated or "regular" education situation she or he could handle.

3. The students in the mainstreaming program were integrated in both public and private schools. Therefore, I use the term "regular schools" to refer to any of the hearing educational institutions not specifically designed for special needs.

4. Project Alternatives and Hathaway, as are all the names of people and institutions in this paper, are pseudonyms. This technique is used to protect the identity of those who participated in the research.

5. Reverse interpreting is also part of the interpreter's job. Not only does the interpreter use sign language to translate the verbal language into signs for the hearing-impaired student, but is also supposed to verbally repeat the words of the hearing-impaired student when the student speaks or signs during the class.

6. Not all sign language systems are based on English. American Sign Language (ASL) the most common system, was developed from the French sign system which was brought to the United States by Thomas Gallaudet in the nineteenth century. ASL syntax is quite different from English. However, the sign system which is used in schools and classrooms and for academic work is usually one of the many forms of Signed English, and is based directly on English grammar and syntax.

7. Credit for the insights into academic skills should be given to the staff of the Language and Concept Development Project which was conducting ongoing research on this topic at Hathaway School for the Deaf.

8. The recommendations were initally published in a paper whose printing and dissemination was subsidized by an HEW grant to the Language and Concept Development Project.

9. The possible modes of communication include how to use an interpreter effectively, how to use other means to communicate such as writing, lipreading, and the sign alphabet, and the pacing of spoken discourse in the class.

REFERENCES

Baker, C. & Battison, R. *Sign language and the deaf community: Essays in honor of William C. Stokoe.* Silver Springs, Md.: National Association for the Deaf, 1980.

Birch, J.W. *Hearing-impaired students in the mainstream of education.* Reston, Va.: Council for Exceptional Children, 1975.

Bishop, M. *Mainstreaming: Practical ideas for educating hearing-impaired students.* Washington, D.C.: A. G. Bell, 1979.

Brill, R. Mainstreaming: Format or quality? *American Annals of the Deaf,* 1975, *120,* 377-381.

Covington, V. C. Problems of acculturation into the deaf community. *Sign Language Studies,* 1980, *28,* 267-285.

Erting, C. Language policy and deaf ethnicity in the United States. *Sign Language Studies,* 1978, *19,* 139-151.

Gliedman, J. & Roth, W. *The unexpected minority: Handicapped children in America.* New York: Harcourt Brace Jovanovitch.

Gordon, J. Hints to parents. *American Annals of the Deaf,* 1885, *30,* 241-250.

Greenberg, J. & Doolittle G. Can schools speak the language of the deaf? *New York Times Sunday Magazine,* December 11, 1977,

Higgins, P. C. *Outsiders in a hearing world: A sociology of deafness.* Beverly Hills: Sage, 1980.

Large, D. Special problems of the deaf under the Education for All Handicapped Children Act of 1975. *Washington University Law Quarterly,* 1980, *58,* 213-275.

Meadow, K. Early manual communication in relation to the deaf child's intellectual, social and communicative functioning. *American Annals of the Deaf,* 1968, *112,* 29-41.

Meadow, K. Sociolinguistics, sign language and the deaf subculture. In T. O'Rourke (Ed.), *Psycholinguistics and total communication: The state of the art.* Silver Springs, MD: National Association of the Deaf, 1972.

Moores, D. M. *Educating the deaf: Psychology, principles and practices.* Boston: Houghton Mifflin, 1978.

Nix, G. (Ed.) Mainstream education for hearing-impaired children and youth. New York: Grune and Stratton, 1976.

Norden, K. & Ang, T. School placement of deaf and hard of hearing children: What do we know about integration? In National Swedish Board of Education (Ed.), *Research and development concerning integration of handicapped pupils into the ordinary school system, part II.* Stockholm: Garnisonstryckeriet, 1980.

Padden, C. & Markowicz, H. *Crossing cultural group boundaries into the deaf Community.* Presented at the Conference on Culture and Communication, Temple University, Philadelphia, 1975.

Stokoe, W. C. An elite group in deaf society. *Sign Language Studies,* 1976, *12,* 189-210.

Yater, V. (Ed.) *Mainstreaming of children with a hearing loss.* Springfield, Ill.: Charles C. Thomas.

8

Evaluation, Ethnography, and the Concept of Culture

Disadvantaged Youth in an Israeli Town

HARVEY E. GOLDBERG

This chapter discusses disadvantaged youth in an Israeli development town, which we will call Greentown. Like other development towns, Greentown is located in a peripheral region of the country and inhabited, to a large extent, by immigrants from Middle Eastern countries and their descendants. The term "disadvantaged youth" refers to those (mostly male) youngsters who are detached from any formal framework of study or work. The data presented in this chapter were collected as part of an evaluation research project concerning a new program to educate or reeducate these youngsters. The project utilized an anthropological approach that attempted to view the educational program, called Youthtown, in a communitywide perspective.

After providing a brief account of Greentown and the Youthtown project, we shall discuss, at a general level, some implications of the concept of culture for evaluation studies. Three senses in the use of the term "culture" will be distinguished: the classic meaning; culture as emergent in the project; and culture as a reflective process in which ethnographic evaluation regards its overall situation within the project and the project's setting. These three senses are illustrated with reference to the Youthtown program. The conclusion suggests an approach of evaluation as social history with the examination of cultural assumptions informing that history.

AUTHOR'S NOTE: This research was funded in its first phase by the Avi Ha-Yishuv foundation and later by the Ford Israel Foundation. The work was carried out in the framework of the NCJW Research Institute for Innovation of Education, School of Education, Hebrew University of Jerusalem.

GREENTOWN AND THE YOUTHTOWN PROJECT

GREENTOWN AND ITS YOUTH

Greentown is an urban settlement in a fertile agricultural valley. We find there a reversal of the "typical" town and village situation. Before the establishment of the town, Jewish settlement in the valley consisted of *kibbutzim* settled by European Jews, which now are economically thriving. Here the people of the countryside look down upon the city because of the reputed provincialism and "undeveloped" conditions of its inhabitants. This is not only a cultural attitude but reflects the economic and political strengths prevailing when the town was founded. Not only were the kibbutzim an important source of employment but they were the first political patrons of the town. Before a town council was established in 1953, municipal affairs were run by the regional council of the area. Even after Greentown was given official autonomy, it was "looked after" by the kibbutzim (which had firm connections in the nation's political center) with one well-known member of the Labor Party (then MAPAI) who resided in a nearby kibbutz, "keeping an eye" on politics within the town. Currently, the central problem of Greentown is not poverty or unemployment but a lack of growth partly attributable to the dependent political condition of the city.

A description of the town in 1956 (Rosenfeld, 1958) indicates that 75 percent of the labor force had temporary employment, but this situation has changed considerably. A number of large-scale enterprises— notably textile factories—have been established, and the town hosts hundreds of Arab laborers daily in the building trade. Whereas earlier much of the available employment was unskilled work in the region's kibbutzim, unskilled work today accounts for 7 percent of the labor force and agricultural work for 7.7 percent (State of Israel, 1975: 223).

Despite the improved economic situation it is still the common assumption that one is dependent on the municipality to help get the things that one needs in life: a job, housing (about 80 percent of the inhabitants rent apartments from a government corporation), or an adequate education for one's children. These are also viewed as rights of the individual, and the politician who ignores them is not likely to stay in office long; but given the bureaucratic complexity of obtaining these goods and the necesity for someone to pull the strings, the municipality is clearly in a position to give or to withhold. The dominance of the municipality is also felt in the case of any local political or social initiative. In view of this situation, the combined goals of economic betterment for the severely disadvantaged youth of the town and the general development of a sense of autonomy and initiative were among the central goals of the Youthtown project.

The project was defined as an educational program to help rehabilitate disadvantaged youth. It was conceived of before the question of disadvantaged youth became a political issue in Israeli society, but its establishment coincided with certain political developments that must be taken into consideration when evaluating it. Thus, as discussed later the establishment of Youthtown followed in the wake of the media-oriented "Black Panther" movement in Israel and the formation of a much publicized government committee entitled the Prime Minister's Committee on Youth in Distress (State of Israel, 1973).

The planners set high goals for themselves, nothing less than "to help marginal youths integrate into society at the highest possible levels" and to "achieve social interaction between youths of different social backgrounds." This was to be accomplished by the establishment of a campus called Youthtown which would allow the combination of two approaches in working with disadvantaged youth. On the one hand, the autonomy of natural street groups would be preserved by providing each group with a room and other facilities on the campus, while on the other hand, the same campus could provide centralized services such as a branch of the youth labor bureau, counseling, remedial education and so forth. It was hoped that this approach would prove more effective than traditional street work in itself or the simple existence of official bureaus which had no mechanisms for "reaching out" to the youth in their natural setting.

The site selected for Youthtown was Greentown[1] in the Northern part of the country with a population of about 16,000. In 1974, 47 percent of the population of the town was aged 18 or below, and 12.2 percent were in the 15-19 age bracket. The town did not have a developed industrial base, so that it provided little opportunity for the most educated of its youngsters. Of the teenagers 51 percent were in some sort of vocational program. There were 48 youths (or 3.5 percent) who were neither working nor studying, and thus detached from any formal framework. It was these latter youths, many of whom had dropped out of school before completing 8 years, who were viewed as the special concern of the project.

AN OVERVIEW OF THE PROJECT AND ITS RESULTS

The administrative setting of the project was complex. It had been initially conceived within a university setting and received the support of a funding institution interested in educational projects. These two "institutions" selected Greentown as the site of the project without a detailed understanding of the situation of youth in the town. At the same time, the project required the cooperation of local municipal authorities. The on-the-ground plan that emerged involved an outside steering committee and professional guidance as well as a research project to chart the development of this "experimental" project.

The Youthtown project ran in this format for three years. During the three years of operation the project developed in a number of directions not envisioned by the planners. This holds true with regard to the administrative and political settings of the project within Greentown, the activities of youth within Youthtown itself, and the counselors employed within the program. These developments were monitored by the research more in the form of an on-going "social history" than as a "test" of whether the program was having the predicted results. Some of these developments will be briefly character-ized below (for fuller discussions and data see Goldberg, 1979, 1983) before going into a general consideration of ethnography, evaluation, and the concept of culture.

First of all, the project ran into administrative difficulties at the outset. While the local authorities could not directly oppose the introduction of a new educational project within the scheme of local services, they were wary that Youthtown might turn into some independent base of influence. Cooperation was therefore always present, but always limited and reserved. The distance of Greentown from the major cities in which the members of the steering committee lived and worked meant that these individuals did not have a full appreciation of the political/administrative difficulties originating out of this situation.

Secondly, the program assumed the ability to recruit counselors and a director who possessed a fair degree of sophistication with regard to youth work and an ability to appreciate the special innovative nature of the program. It turned out that personnel meeting these requirements were not readily available in the region, and the program as it actually was run had to adjust itself to this fact. Part of the program involved professional supervision of the counselors and this supervision turned out to be one of the most stable and beneficial aspects of the program. With a mixture of irony and truth it is possible to say that Youthtown had its most consistent meliorative effects on the staff of counselors rather than on the disadvantaged youths who constituted its stated object.

With regard to the youth itself it may be said that the program had both positive and negative outcomes; but most importantly for the present discussion, many of these results were different from those originally envisioned. First, the outcomes differed depending on the age of the youths, with the younger ones (about 12-14, most of whom were still "supposed to be" in school) reacting to the program differently from the older ones (15-17). The presence of a variety of groups on the same premises led to a heightened sense of territoriality, and a pattern of mutual raiding and theft that did not exist in the "natural" setting of Greentown. The program was unprepared for this crisis so that often the original plans broke down and a pattern of conventional streetwork with individuals emerged with regard to many of the youngsters. While this differed from the stated goals of the Youthtown program, it matched the expectations of many of the town's youth. The "success" of the program is therefore to be viewed in relation to a set of varying and sometimes contradictory purposes with which it was invested by different parties to the Youthtown project. Beyond the complex "results" of the Youthtown project, the evaluation research gives us the opportunity of considering some basic questions concerning evaluation research, ethnography, and the concept of culture.

IMPLICATIONS OF THE CULTURE CONCEPT FOR EVALUATION STUDIES

INTRODUCTION

The research that followed the course of the Youthtown project was defined as evaluation research—an attempt to assess the impact of an innovative intervention program on a population of disadvantaged youth. Evaluation studies, in their purest form, claim to be able to provide objective and reliable judgments of the effect of a program on a given population with respect to some stated goal. In reality, however, this claim is rarely validated. There are many reasons for this (Weiss, 1972; Gordon and Morse, 1975). The goals of a project may be unclear or may change over time; the population to be affected may not be defined with adequate clarity; the research design may not be prepared with sufficient rigor. These shortcomings have been discussed with reference to such fields as health, social work, education, and criminology.

Various writers have advocated that evaluation research pay greater attention to the *context* of specific intervention projects (Belshaw, 1966; Weiss and Rein, 1969; Alkin, 1975). The development and effects of a project may have to be understood in terms of administrative structure, mechanisms of funding, and processes of decision making as much as in terms of the application of a specific method or technique of intervention. This point of view calls for research that can illuminate administrative and community structures and processes, as well as for concepts and methods yielding precise quantitative judgments.

Anthropological field research, based on a tradition of work in communities, is a natural candidate for inclusion in this aspect of evaluation studies. In a recent publication on anthropological studies of schooling, many of the papers highlighted the broader context of the formal educational framework (e.g., Kileff, 1975; Colfer, 1975; Eddy, 1975; Everhart, 1975). It was for this reason too that an anthropologist initially was requested to conduct research on the Youthtown project, as it was understood that the project's integration into the town would be a crucial aspect of its development. As indicated above, this proved to be the case. However, in addition to the social field that must be taken into consideration in evaluation research, we also seek to explore the relevance of anthropological *theory* with its emphasis on *culture* for the evaluation of the Youthtown project and evaluation research in general.

Anthropological studies have highlighted two major dimensions of community life—the social or *organizational* ,on the one hand, and the cultural or *meaningful,* on the other. This chapter seeks to further develop the cultural point of view in the hope that future evaluation research will be more sensitive to the cultural dimensions of the phenomena it attempts to assess. We begin by citing some general characteristics of the concept of culture and its relation to ethnography.

THE CONCEPT OF CULTURE AND ETHNOGRAPHY

There is, it should be noted, a paradoxical side to the standard anthropological approach to culture. On the one hand, anthropological research has a strong *empiricist* bent, an emphasis on very detailed description of the facts. This stress on ethnographic fact-finding has been criticized by some as naively non-theoretical, even while energetic fieldworkers for their part have been eager to topple grand theories by reference to in-depth studies of single cultures. Whatever stand one takes on this matter, it is recognized that a commitment to detailed contextual field investigation—or what happens "on the ground"—has been a hallmark of anthropological research for more than half a century.

At the same time, the central concept used by anthropologists to throw light on empirical events—namely, the concept of culture[2]—is notorious for the problematics of its ontological status. Is culture coextensive with its external manifestations (behavior), or does it enjoy "transcendental" existence, developing and influencing action according to its own peculiar mechanisms? Is it to be found in the minds or personalities of individuals, or is its locus primarily in social settings, arising out of the dynamics of interaction? Is it a tightly woven entity, each of its strands closely bound up with the others, or is it formless and loose, easily shaped and modified by shifting situations? Whatever stance is taken on these matters, there is growing consensus that culture is that aspect of action concerned with meaning, embedded in symbols (Schneider, 1968; Geertz, 1973), and that cultural analysis involves the discovery and delineation of patterns of meaning which shape and give expression to social forms.

These two separate facets of anthropological work, while appearing paradoxical, are in fact complementary. It is precisely the ephemerality of cultural "substance" — the difficulty of "putting one's finger on it" — that makes thorough ethnographic detail necessary. The only possible way of illuminating a world of meaning that makes sense of the diverse situations in which people find themselves is to carefully make a record of those situations and of what is said and done in regard to them. The elusive concept of culture can only be justified through "thick description," the term borrowed by Geertz (1973) to characterize the anthropologist's craft, and it is through this that behavioral reality takes on significance in terms of a theory emphasizing the importance of symbolic (meaningful) forms.

This particular relationship between data and theory also has relevance for ethnography's potential contribution to evaluation research. It claims that any particular "slice" of observed social behavior may be tied into a cultural context in a variety of ways. Events in a family, for example, may be linked meaningfully to the realms of economics, religion, stratification, and so forth. Such a web of cultural connections may be less apparent to planners who wish to solve a problem "in the classroom" or "with street-corner youth" — focusing on a concrete institutional or social setting. The contribution of ethnography in such cases may not only be to provide technical skills of observation in a priori defined situations but to show how action in these specific settings is related both functionally and meaningfully to a broader social and cultural field. In order to do this, the anthropologist must approach a social situation without completely circumscribing the boundaries of the topic that he or she intends to study in advance. In this way he or she is in a position to unravel the intricate web of social factors and cultural forms that contribute to and constitute interaction in a concrete setting.

THREE USES OF THE TERM CULTURE

The term culture has been used here broadly, but it is also necessary to specify several senses of the term in their particular relevance to evaluation research. First of all, culture can refer to a given community's whole way of life as that way of life, including beliefs and practices, has continued over time. When different ways of life come into contact, the boundaries of cultures and the borders of communities characterized by those cultures may cease to be coterminous. Here it is necessary to sharpen the definition of culture and focus on shared meanings that become the basis of action in given settings. The degree of "sharedness" is, of course, variable and dependent upon the relative power of the individuals and groups acting in a social field among other things. The main point here is that the concept of culture no longer directs our attention to a *whole* way of life but to sets of meanings from each of the original cultures (or to some emergent combination of them) that become explicitly or implicitly relevant in defined social situations.

The specification of culture as meaning points to a third aspect of the concept—that of self-regard or reflexivity. As has often been stressed, culture is both a "model of" and a "model for" social interaction (Parsons, 1968: 764; Geertz, 1966: 9) and these two sides of culture are not necessarily isomorphic. Varying images of social reality can be produced with reference to a group of people "looking at themselves" and alternative guidelines for future action may be drawn. Each of these aspects of the concept of culture has implications for evaluation research.

The first sense of the term culture may be called the *classic* meaning. Any program of intervention is directed toward a given population. It is of course desirable to have an understanding of the way of life of the population, an ethnographic appreciation of their culture. Second; it is now accepted that intervention programs do not appear on the scene as new and pure factors unrelated to a wider social context. These programs are formulated and administered by individuals and groups representing the more influential segments of a social field that wittingly and unwittingly impose new ways of thought and action on the more dependent segments. Thus there may be delineated a field of interaction reflecting the "classic" cultures of both administrators and clients but which takes the form of an emergent *culture of the project*. This consists of values and concepts that come to be taken for granted even if there is disagreement relative to them as the project develops— often in unforeseen directions.

Finally, it is critical to remember that anthropologists themselves are enmeshed in cultural process (Wagner, 1975; Rabinow, 1977; Bourdieu,

1978; Langness & Frank, 1981). The concepts they use with regard to their subject matter reflect a variety of influences just as do the cultural forms of the people they study. It is therefore particularly important that anthropological (i.e., anthropologists') concepts be exposed continually to the test of ethnography. This does not only mean the modification of ethnographic "facts" in the light of new empirical data, but it may entail a reassessment of basic premises of anthropological understanding. To give a controversial but instructive example, Dumont (1970) claims that the seemingly ordinary concept of "the individual" may hamper understanding of caste in Indian society. Thus in addition to introducing fine-grained ethnography to the tool-kit of evaluation researchers, anthropology's contribution to the evaluation of intervention programs may be to insist that those programs undergo continual self-testing of their basic understanding of the reality with which they are dealing. Moreover, in the context of a given program the social setting of evaluation research itself shapes knowledge about that program such that an evaluator's critique of his or her own efforts may be seen as a cultural process contributing to an understanding of the program as a whole. Here we may talk about the *culture of evaluation* as a critical self-reflective aspect of evaluation research. These points will be illustrated with reference to various aspects of the Youthtown project.

THE SENSES OF THE TERM CULTURE IN RELATION TO YOUTHTOWN

GOALS AND THE READING OF REALITY

It is common to first consider a program's goals in discussions of evaluation research because these appear to take logical precedence. It is best to evaluate a program in terms of some explicit aim that it sets for itself. After the goal has been made clear, discussions of the population, methods, and evaluation techniques naturally follow. The establishment of goals (which are specifications of a society's values) as a separate category distinct from existing reality has a time-honored place in the social sciences. It is our contention, however, that distinguishing between goals and reality is not always simple— particularly in cases where planners and clients do not come from an identical cultural universe. The setting of goals, on the part of some official agency, presupposes the existence of a certain reality in terms of how the problems of concern appear "on the ground." These implied presuppositions may or may not turn out to be valid. It is likely that many of the instances of "changing goals" in intervention programs—a situation that bedevils evaluation research—stem from an altered perception of social reality on the part of the planners as a program progresses.

It therefore would appear reasonable to have adequate ethnographic coverage of a given social field *before* program goals are established. This would seem to be particularly valuable for those cases in which, for some reason or another, planners *believe* they know what the reality is as compared to cases where there are salient cultural differences separating planners and clients. It is this type of misjudgment—of assuming adequate knowledge of a social situation when in fact much more needs to be known—that appears to have been made with regard to youth in Greentown.

We may consider this point further after relating an incident concerning the Israeli Black Panther movement, mentioned above. By coincidence (i.e., with no connection to the Youthtown project) the author was present at a Panther rally in the summer of 1971. In the course of a speech, one of the Panther leaders said that some people have asked, Why do you call your movement the Black Panthers? Saying that they understood the reasons for the protest and sympathized with them, they still found the name "Black Panthers" objectionable. The answer given by the speaker was "We called ourselves the Black Panthers in order to sting the government in the ass." The Mayor of Jerusalem is reported to have said that had the Panthers hired all the experts of Madison Avenue, they couldn't have picked a better name.

The power of this name, of course, comes from the association with the Black Panther organization in the United States, symbolizing radical alienation from "the establishment" and implacable hatred between blacks and whites. That this image did not fit the Israeli situation is shown by the short-lived history of the Israeli Panthers and by the fact that many of the leaders were coopted easily into existing political frameworks. Since the early 1970s several of the former Panthers have been elected to the Knesset (Parliament). What interests us here, however, is not only the accuracy in comparison of one movement and another but the process by which Israeli society is viewed through *imported* terms and concepts.

The use of the name "Black Panthers" in the Israeli context raises the question of how members of that society view *themselves* and the problem of the disadvantaged. Is the phenomenon of disadvantaged youth small in scope, growing out of the past (the mass immigration from Middle Eastern countries in the 1950s) and temporary in duration? Or, on the contrary, is it widespread, rooted in the present sociopolitical configuration, and becoming more permanent—unless far-reaching measures are taken to change the situation? The Panther movement forced the government, press, and society to face these questions which previously had not been prominent in the public consciousness. It may thus be said that the advent of the Panthers helped crystallize the notion of disadvantaged youth which then emerged as part of Israeli culture at large. Hitherto confined to a limited body of social workers, sociologists, criminologists, and the like, "disadvantaged youth" became a cultural concept relevant to the society's image of itself. While the imported Black Panther image was generally rejected as inappropriate to the Israeli setting, the growing awareness of the country's social problems required that some name, and thereby recognition, be given to the situation. These changes in public self awareness are clearly part of the "culture of the project."

The problem of how to define the reality of "Youth in Distress," as the question was officially designated, is not only reflected in general categorizations such as "disadvantaged youth" but also applies to more specific notions such as "street gangs." Thus the question of how best to define a situation also must be faced by social science researchers called in to study it. Science, at the same time that it claims to provide accurate reflections of reality, is also a cultural process and is therefore also subject to a variety of influences. Thus scientific concepts can be diffused from one setting to a second and should be understood in their systematic relationship to other concepts, both scientific and nonscientific, in addition to establishing their link to empirical phenomena. Israeli social science, in striving to be cosmopolitan as science should be, is faced with a plurality of concepts and theories with which to categorize the happenings in its own back yard. Are the distressed youths of Israel's cities similar to the "fighting gangs" of New York (New York City Youth Board, 1960), the "unattached youth" of a seaside resort town in England (Morse, 1965), or the boys passing through "brief adolescence" in downtown Liverpool (Parker, 1976)? The title of Leissner's book, *Street Club Work in Tel Aviv and New York* (1969), implies that problems of lower class delinquency are the same the world over, and indeed this is a point he explicitly makes (p. ix). On the other hand, Leissner himself cites instances (pp. 226ff.) of differences between the situation in New York and Israel's largest metropolitan area. The plethora of terms in Hebrew to discuss this "problem"— marginal youth, detached youth, youth in distress, disadvantaged youth, street-corner youth, nonstudying and nonworking youth—itself suggests that there is insufficient information to substantively describe what these youth are about. In the absence of relevant ethnographic data, social scientists are left with imported concepts whose application to the Israeli reality is yet to be established. To a significant extent, problems of the Youthtown project and problems of the evaluation research grew out of such unclear application. In the section that follows, some of the differences between Greentown's disadvantaged youth and those of larger urban communities (including Tel Aviv) will be indicated.

THE ETHNOGRAPHIC SPECIFICITY
OF GREENTOWN'S YOUTH

First, we must consider the notion of "gang" or even "group." Organized groups per se of teenaged youth, did not appear to exist in the context of Greentown. Instead, youths formed themselves into small and fluid "associations." When group structure did solidify it was through contact with some existing formal agency, including Youthtown itself. The same may be said with regard to leadership. "Fighting gangs" and other adolescent groups often have been found to be characterized by a clear authoritarian structure. A clear leadership structure did emerge in the longer-lasting Youthtown groups, but there is no evidence that it existed in the fluid "cliques" on the streets.

A second difference between Greentown's disadvantaged youngsters and those of bigger cities was the characteristic type of crime. Juvenile crime above the level of petty thefts was not common in Greentown. The methods of theft were not sophisticated either. It was common for people to leave their cars unlocked in Greentown. One local resident, owner of a relatively expensive car, purchased a tape-deck to be installed in his automobile. At the same time he installed a car alarm as well. Once, when visiting relatives in a town outside of Tel Aviv, his car was broken into and the tape-deck stolen. This was done without setting off the alarm. I doubt that this skill existed among the teenagers of Greentown.

A similar contrast exists with respect to violence (Marx, 1976). While there was much rowdiness between the boys in Youthtown, this never reached the extent of physical injury. Fights among the youngsters using dangerous physical objects or weapons did not occur.

On the positive side, the internal workings of the groups in Youthtown appeared to reflect certain cultural traditions. Middle Eastern norms relating to home and hospitality were evident in the way the Youthtown youngsters treated guests in their rooms. Horowitz and Schwartz (1974), comparing black and Puerto Rican youths in the United States, have suggested that cultural variation is a significant dimension in shaping youth behavior. The data from Greentown support this view.

The Greentown youngsters also differ considerably from their counterparts in the big city with regard to what might be called "age-grade" based organization. Leissner (1969: appendix) depicts how in Tel Aviv there are delinquent groups of different average ages in contact with one another. There appear to exist mechanisms whereby some younger boys are recruited from one group to an older group, thereby ensuring a continual supply of members for the latter. While many of the younger boys of Youthtown looked up to and emulated some of the older ones, this was by no means an established mechanism ensuring the reproduction of a delinquent subculture. Rather the older age-grade appeared to be a period of "settling down" in comparison with the younger. As such its main influence was to bring the young men closer to inclusion in conventional working class society.

Most generally, the "alienation" of Greentown youth appeared to be less extreme than that of the street youths in the metropolitan areas. The Greentown youth do not constitute an established delinquent subculture opposed to the accepted norms of society. Neither are they severely "unattached" like the English youth who have a clear "we vs. they" attitude toward the world of adults (Morse, 1965: 76). The delinquent youth of Greentown normally live at home and, as has been emphasized, their delinquent activities are relatively mild. Their involvement in a network of peers has not come to totally overshadow ties to family or ties to work. Relations with parents are problematic and strained, but there are strong feeling of family involvement and differences often are eventually reconciled. Similarly, even though youngsters move from job to job and have difficulties in getting on with employers, there are few who have given up trying to find respectable work (thereby opting to support themselves by a life of crime). Most of the youngsters responded *rapidly* to the attention of counselors and the opportunity of work advancement. This was not because Youthtown had developed any new and highly effective method of reaching these young men. Rather, it shows that few (if any) were at a point where they had "turned their back on society," requiring a complete change of direction to bring about rehabilitation.

LACK OF CLARITY IN THE TERM "YOUTH"

Not only were the formulators of the project off-target with regard to the "distress" that characterized Greentown, but they did not have a clear picture of what "youth" meant to many people in the town. Here, the "culture of the project" could have benefited from a more sensitive understanding of the culture of Greentown in the classic sense. It is suggested that the notion of "adolescence" is a relatively new one for many of the townspeople, particularly those coming from the tradition-al sectors of North African society. This should be taken into account in considering the readiness of some youngsters to leave school at an early age. There have been various explanations given to this phenome-non by educators and social workers. One is that the families of early school-leavers do not value education. A second is that the children would continue in school, but are forced to work by difficult economic circumstances. Third, there is a labeling theory which claims that these youngsters have been exposed to subtle messages while growing up suggesting that they cannot succeed in school and are only fit to work at simple jobs. In addition to these explanations, a cultural dimension requires exploration. In traditional North Africa many youths of this age, in the absence of a concept of adolescence, were viewed as partially adult and capable of sharing in a family's economic responsibility. As such, the decision to work does not necessarily represent a failure to meet some standard but rather a normal and respected progression toward the world of adulthood (Goldberg, 1983).

It is thus argued that the establishment of Youthtown was predicated on a conception of disadvantaged youth appropriate to larger urban areas and did not take into account the concrete situation in Green-town. It is possible to argue that many of the differences between "big city" juvenile problems and those of Greentown are related to the city's size. The smallness of the town, both geographically and in terms of population, acts against the creation of a subculture sharply separated from general life of the town. From this point of view, the differences discussed would not reflect "real" (classic) cultural differences but only degrees of organizational complexity or scale. This argument has merit and further systematic comparative research would be required to assess the importance of the factor of scale on the phenomena under discussion. The point to be emphasized here is that the planners of the Youthtown project were prepared to see the "problems of disadvan-taged youth" as an undifferentiated category without the kind of detailed information that an ethnography of youth in a development town would have provided. This cultural "lumping" on the part of the planners meant that the project was not adequately aimed at the concrete situation in Greentown.

It should be emphasized that we do *not* mean that the individual planners were naive or uninformed enough to think that the Greentown youngsters were a replica of those found in hardened, big-city juvenile gangs. What we do claim is that the individual sophistication of the planners was not incorporated into the assumptions of the program, which was permitted to develop on the premise that the nature of the problem was known. Certain conceptions and assumptions had become part of the *culture of the project* (as viewed by planners) and formed the basis for discussion and decision with regard to it.

Why certain aspects of individual comprehension did not become part of the shared understanding is difficult to say precisely. One reason probably was that the members of the steering committee were all involved in other projects outside of Greentown and therefore gave only a limited amount of attention to it. It may be that such a basic rethinking would have implied far-reaching changes in the program that the committee was "unconsciously" not prepared to contemplate. In any event, it is clear that the individual intellectual openness of the members of the committee (which might have paid attention to the above-cited interpretation of youth in Greentown) did not find expression in the accepted assumptions on which the project continued to operate.

The fact that the project met with some successes did not stem from an accurate reading of the situation in the town and the establishment of a program appropriate to that situation. Rather, the successes are best seen as a mutual adjustment between certain aspects of the program, notably the activities of the counselors and certain features of the local setting (namely, a segment of the youth). These developments are only partially related to the officially formulated goals of the program and the implied perception of reality on the basis of which it was operating.

These general considerations point directly to the place of the evaluation in the Youthtown project. The evaluators were the only ones who had the "leisure" (in the sense of not being responsible for the project's success) and the perspective to introduce these questions to the discussion, to make them part of the cultural terms of the project. This opportunity—and responsibility—was not fully realized at the time. It appears now, in retrospect, that one of the tasks of evaluation studies is precisely to inject such "self-consciousness" on the part of the researchers into the social consciousness of the project with regard to its most basic goals and assumptions. We shall now see how a self-understanding of the "culture of the evaluation" and its dilemmas reflect dilemmas of the project as a whole. (cf. Goldberg, 1979).

CULTURE AND EVALUATION:
SELF-CRITICISM AS PROJECT CRITICISM

APPROPRIATENESS OF THE EVALUATION PLAN
TO THE PROJECT DESIGN

As discussed above, the question of goals is not easily separated from other aspects of the project. Ultimately, the goal of the program was to better the situation of disadvantaged youth by the application of an innovative methodology. There existed an assumption that Greentown was an appropriate place to try out this methodology both from the point of view of the population and the possibility of putting the methodology into practice. As stated, these assumptions did not hold up as expected. The knowledge concerning the youth population was not sufficiently detailed, and the implementation ran into problems both of finding adequate staff and of being met with coolness on the part of the municipality.

Given the appearance of these difficulties, the question arose (although it was never faced squarely) of which aspects of the project's goals should take precedence? Should the project proceed as an "experiment," remaining as faithful as possible to the original plan regardless of the outcome? Or, should it adopt a "cut and paste" attitude, adopting itself to the realities of Greentown so long as it appeared that some of the needs of some youths were being met? The former point of view was represented by the supervisor from Tel Aviv who believed that nothing *new* would be accomplished or learned if the project lapsed into conventional methods of dealing with youth. The latter point of view, however, implicitly gained the upper hand due as much to the real factors operating in the situation as to a conscious decision on the part of the project's initiators. The evaluators too, by carrying out a broad community-study style of ethnography, implicitly took the stance that the goals of the project were best met by adopting to the Greentown reality rather than closely following a predetermined blueprint.

An alternative type of research, insisting upon an experimental design, makes certain demands on how a program is implemented. Not only should there be a large enough population to ensure proper statistical inference and adequate controls, but the project should be free from influences that would significantly change the way it is run during the period of study. While Youthtown was thought of as "an experiment," it in no way approximated a form in which experimental study could have been carried out. From the outset, part of the project's aims was that the special sort of education offered should be integrated into the youth services already available in the town. As such, the philosophy of Youthtown might be considered "organic" as opposed to "total." In a "total institution" (Goffman, 1961)—one setting in which far-reaching changes in behavior may be brought about—most of the significant factors impinging on a population are subject to the control of the institution's directors. In such an instance, an experimental or quasi-experimental (Campbell & Stanley, 1963) design has justification because one factor may be varied while the others are held constant. Youthtown was neither such a total institution, nor was it a self-selected sect—one which voluntarily isolates itself from its surroundings (another known setting of behavioral change). The aim of the Youth-town project to fit into the context of Greentown meant that it exposed itself to all sorts of influences rooted in the local situation. The expectation, therefore, that the project could progress according to a predetermined design and very specific goals without modifying itself in terms of on-the-spot realities proved to be naive. From this point of view, even thinking about the project as "an experiment" (except as a figure of speech) was simply misleading. Similarly, to attempt experi-mental type research in such a situation would be inappropriate if not futile.

THE ACCEPTANCE OF UNEXAMINED ASSUMPTIONS

There is a second issue, common to both the culture of the evaluation and the culture of the project, which reflects a shared oversight. It appears in retrospect that there was a serious lack of attention paid to the *parents* of the youth. Although it was intended to collect some in-depth data on a number of families, this task did not emerge as carrying high priority and eventually was neglected. If the suggested interpretation of "youth" (as compared to adolescence) discussed above is correct, this was a serious flaw. If many of the youths dropping out of school are to be viewed in their striving to become adults, then a better substantive picture of what adulthood means to these youngsters is called for. Such a picture can only be based on more thorough ethnography of working class and lower class family life.

Here too, a shortcoming of the research reflects the wider situation. The way the problem (and suggested solutions to the problem) of disadvantaged youth is normally discussed in Israel ignores the parents except in negative terms. This is the explicit (or implicit) notion of "the generation of the wilderness," a slogan that characterized administra-tive attitudes toward immigrants in the 1950s. This idea assumed that not much could be done to resocialize the parents of immigrant youngsters, but that educational and social efforts should be concentrated on socializing the generation of the children to the life of the new society. This point of view was taken for granted by the Youthtown planners and by the researcher.

In this view, the family is assumed to constitute one of the sources of the problem and solutions are sought in special non-family-oriented programs such as Youthtown. The researchers unthinkingly accepted the assumptions of the planners. The intention to study the family was seen as something that an anthropological community study "ought to do" but was not considered directly relevant to the direction of development of the youth in the program. For this reason it was a task that was put aside for other kinds of data collection that seemed, at the time, more pressing. We presently suggest that understanding what adulthood means in settings viewed as disadvantaged be established as a research priority, and point out once again how self-criticism of the research yields a critique of the overall project.

CONCLUSION

This chapter has discussed cultural aspects of the Youthtown project and the research intended to assess its development and impact. The emphasis on culture, in our evaluation, has revealed that basic assumptions concerning social reality have to be made explicit in understanding the project in its various facets. The simple phrase "disadvantaged street-corner youth" carries with it a host of meanings whose correspondence to empirical reality should be tested and cannot be taken for granted. The notion of "disadvantaged youth" only recently became significant in the society's view of itself. There are different understandings of what "street-corner youth" are like, and much ethnographic research needs to be done in order to reveal the variety of forms of organization hidden by that expression. Even the term "youth" demands greater clarification in terms of specifying the ages of the individuals involved and describing which forms of behavior characterize them in different settings. Lack of attention to these questions was reflected in problems of planning and implementation of the Youthtown project. The success and shortcomings of Youthtown appeared to be as much a willy-nilly accommodation of the program to the constellation of forces at work in Greentown as the systematic application of an explicit plan of intervention within a known social arena.

It may be that this outcome reflected the specific conditions of the Youthtown project—a broadly conceived plan which attempted to implant and instituionalize an idea in a social and political milieu over which it had no control. On the other hand, it may be asked whether many other "experimental" programs that seek to be evaluated may not be viewed in the same way? If so, a broader approach to studies that attempt to evaluate such programs may be warranted.

An evaluation study often starts with the assumption that there is a general fit between intervention programs and the social fields within which they operate. The evaluation research therefore aims to make an assessment with regard to a specific technique or method, often comparing one type of intervention with another (or with nonintervention). In some instances, this assumption may be correct and it may be possible to make refined judgments based on sophisticated research designs. In other cases, however, the intervention program and the cultural concepts that inform it may be operating in terms that are significantly distinct from those of the social field it hopes to affect. In this case, an evaluation study will miss its mark if it does not call attention to the relevant discrepancies.

Government and volunteer agencies generate plans, mobilize resources, recruit personnel and implement projects in response to a vortex of social pressures. A precise understanding of the social setting that a project hopes to affect is only one factor such agencies take into consideration and may be secondary in importance. The "target" social setting, for its part, is shaped by other economic, political, and ideological currents and develops in accordance with its own dynamics. At certain points, an existing social field and a newly introduced program may touch each other and discover mutual relevance. The former utilizes the latter to its own purposes, while the latter identifies certain aspects of the former that make sense in terms of its stated goals of social change. With few exceptions, such as in the case of "total institutions," can one speak assuredly about the "effect" of a program on a given population. More appropriately, an approach to evaluation that frankly sees itself as a kind of social history and points to cultural assumptions guiding that history can help trace the course of events growing out of the interaction of these different planes of human endeavor.

NOTES

1. The ethnographic present is used referring to the period between November, 1973, through March, 1976.

2. For the purpose of this discussion only the notion of social structure, central to British social anthropology, is set aside.

REFERENCES

Alkin, M. C. Evaluation: Who needs it? Who cares? *Studies in Educational Evaluation*, 1975, *1*, 201–212.

Belshaw, C. Evaluation of technical assistance as a contribution to development. *International Development Review*, 1966, *8*(2), 2–6, 23.

Bourdieu, P. *Outline of a theory of practice*. Cambridge: Cambridge University Press, 1978.

Campbell, D. T. & Stanley, J. C. Experimental and quasi-experimental designs for research and teaching. In N. L. Gage (Ed.), *Handbook of Research and Teaching*. Chicago: Rand McNally, 1963.

Colfer, C.J.P. Bureaucrats, budgets, and the BIA: Segmentary opposition in a residential school. *Human Organization*, 1975, *34*(2), 149–156.

Dumont, L. The individual as an impediment to social comparison in Indian history. In *Religion, Politics and History in India*. Paris: Mouton, 1970.

Eddy, E. M. Educational innovation and desegregation: A case study of symbolic realignment. *Human Organization*, 1975, *34*(2), 163–172.

Everhart, R. B. Problems of doing fieldwork in educational evaluation. *Human Organization*, 1975, *34*(2), 205.

Geertz, C. Religion as a cultural system. In M. Banton (Ed.), *Anthropological approaches to the study of religion*. London: Tavistock, 1966.

Geertz, C. *Understanding cultures*. New York: Basic Books, 1973.

Goffman, E. *Asylums, essays on the social situation of mental patients and inmates*. Garden City, NY: Doubleday, 1961.

Goldberg, H. E. A program for disadvantaged youth in an Israeli development town: An evaluation. *Anthropology and Education Quarterly*, 1979, *10*, 121–142.

Goldberg, H. E. Disadvantaged youngsters and disparate definitions of youth in a development town in Israel. *Youth and Society*, 1983, *15*(2).

Gordon, G. & Morse, E. V. Evaluation research. *Annual Review of Sociology*, 1975, *1*, 339–362.

Horowitz, R. & Schwartz, G. Honor, normative ambiguity and gang violence. *American Sociological Review*, 1974, *39*, 238–251.

Kileff, C. The rebirth of a grandfather's spirit: Shumba's two worlds. *Human Organization*, 1975, *34*(2), 129–138.

Langness, L. L. & Frank, G. *Lives: An anthropological approach to biography*. Novata, CA: Chandler and Sharp, 1981.

Leissner, A. *Street Club Work in Tel Aviv and New York*. London: The National Children's Bureau, 1969.

Marx, E. *The social context of violent behaviour: A social anthropological study in an Israeli immigrant town*. London: Routledge & Kegan Paul, 1976.

Morse, M. *The unattached*. New York: Viking, 1965.

New York City Youth Board *Reaching the fighting gang*. New York: Author, 1960.

Parker, H. Boys will be men: Brief adolescence in a down-town neighborhood. In G. Mungham & G. Pearson (Eds.), *Working class youth culture*. London: Routledge & Kegan Paul, 1976.

Parsons, T. *The structure of social action, vol. II*. New York: The Free Press, 1937.

Rabinow, P. *Reflections of fieldwork in Morocco*. Berkeley: University of California Press, 1977.

Rosenfeld, H. Ir ho'olim Qiryat Shmonah. *Mibifnim*, 1958, *20*, 87–116.

Schneider, D. *American kinship: A cultural account*. Englewood Cliffs, NJ: Prentice-Hall, 1968.

State of Israel *Prime Minister's Commission for Children and Youth in Distress and summary of recommendations, publication 545.* Jerusalem: Szold Institute for Research in the Behavioral Sciences, 1973.

State of Israel *Ministry of Commerce and Industry: Development town survey, 4 (July-September).* Jerusalem: H. Smith Research Institute, 1975.

Wagner, R. *The invention of cultures.* Englewood Cliffs, NJ: Prentice-Hall, 1975.

Weiss, C. *Evaluation research: Methods for assessing program effectiveness.* Englewood Cliffs, NJ: Prentice-Hall, 1972.

Weiss, C. & Rein, M. The evaluation of broad-aim programs: A cautionary case and a moral. *Annals of the American Academy of Political and Social Science,* 1969, *385,* 133–142.

PART III

Theoretical and
Ethical Dilemmas

9

Ethnographers sans Ethnography
The Evaluation Compromise

HARRY F. WOLCOTT

Ethnography has at least two potential contributions to make to the practice of educational evaluation. The first of these has largely been realized: to help educators recognize the value of descriptive research conducted in natural settings rather than to rely so wholeheartedly on experimental research in contrived or controlled settings. If descriptive research—or "qualitative" research, as it is fortuitously called—is not about to unseat quantitative research as education's king of the mountain, it has at least earned a place as one of education's legitimate and important ways of knowing.

Anthropologists are not alone in adhering to a long tradition of descriptive research, but educators seem to have taken special pleasure in proclaiming that their embrace of descriptive research has added an anthropological dimension to their research repertoire. Although educator pronouncements sometimes imply a wholesale embrace of anthropology that includes all four major subfields of the discipline—physical anthropology, cultural anthropology, linguistics, archaeology—their fascination is limited essentially to cultural anthropology and, even more specifically, to that part of cultural anthropology that deals with ethnographic research. It is the work of the cultural anthropologist *as ethnographer* that has captured the educator imagination, including those educators whose special interests lie in evaluation. And thus, although it borders on being a contradiction in terms, we hear educators talk about "ethnographic evaluation."

AUTHOR'S NOTE: Appreciation is expressed to James R. Sanders, Associate Director of The Evaluation Center, Western Michigan University, who directed the *ThinkAbout* study, and to Saul Rockman, Director of Research at the Agency for Instructional Television, Bloomington, Indiana, for their support during the original project and critical reactions to early drafts for this retrospective examination of the project.

It is hardly surprising that ethnography has achieved its primary recognition among educators through serving evaluative interests (cf. Smith, 1982: 590). Evaluation is at once education's new source of rigor and its Achilles' heel, a perspective that requires objectives to be precisely stated so that accomplishments can be properly assessed. Evaluative concerns predominate in an educator language comprised of competencies, goals, objectives, tasks, and measured performance—from teacher evaluations of student assignments ("Is 8 out of 10 very good?") to administrator evaluations of teacher performance, school board evaluations of administrative performance, or voter approval of school boards, budgets, and programs. The ethos of evaluation hangs as a spectre over educator subculture, and one's status and power in the system is a function of who one evaluates and by whom one is in turn evaluated.

Ethnography could not help but get caught up in this educator preoccupation with evaluation. The term "ethnography"—virtually unknown in educator circles prior to the 1960s—has provided a new, convenient, and comprehensive label for referring to the people, processes, and products associated with this recently awakened interest in on-site, descriptive studies: Educational "ethnographers" pursue "ethnographic" research and produce "ethnography." As the intent of these inquiries has often, although not invariably, been evaluative, it was not too long before ethnography became linked to and even synonymous with evaluation, at least in the eyes of some practicing educators understandably skeptical of any researcher who claimed to be "observing but not evaluating" them. The title "ethnographic evaluator" well served a new breed of self-proclaimed experts ready to take project assignments or district-level employment. If the work of the ethnographic evaluator is not satisfyingly ethnographic to an old purist like myself who insists on cultural interpretation rather than fieldwork techniques as the ultimate criterion for doing ethnography, these people are nonetheless helping build the case for, and demonstrate the utility of, employing descriptive research in assessing educational efforts and outcomes.

Ethnography's other potential contribution to the practice of educational evaluation makes headway more slowly and less dramatically and, to some extent, makes headway at the cost of the first. That potential is to recognize that ethnography can serve as an *alternative to* rather than merely as an *alternative form of* evaluation. Ethnography viewed as an alternative to evaluation suggests a descriptive and interpretive activity whose purposes are to understand rather than to judge and to examine facets of human behavior as part of larger cultural systems.

The ethnographer views human events in broad social contexts and explores them for multiple meanings. In that regard, processes and circumstances surrounding a set of activities that constitute an evaluation event belong properly within the ethnographer's purview as part of the broad context in which educators work, for evaluation is fraught with different meanings to people in different positions within the educational system. Nevertheless, placing educational evaluation in a cultural perspective is not the critical issue in ethnography viewed as an *alternative* to evaluation. What is critical is to focus on classrooms and other educational settings as cultural scenes and on how the individuals directly or indirectly involved in those scenes make sense of and give meaning to what is going on. To the anthropologist, evaluation— whether formal or only implicit—is part of that total scene, not apart from it.

Traditionally, ethnographers have endeavored to defer judgment rather than to render it. In school research that does not prove easy to do, either professionally or personally. Most of us who do ethnography in educational settings have occupied other educator roles; all of us have spent untold numbers of years in schools. We "know" what school is like and what we like in schools. We know the school setting so well that, unknowingly, we become our own best informants. We forget to ask others how they make sense of what goes on because we already know what to make of it ourselves. Thus the recent and growing tendency to make evaluation of performance the "bottom line" in every school activity is augmented by personal experiences in a society that is at once proud of and perennially dissatisfied with its schools. In the 1970s it was *quality;* in the 1980s, it has become *cost,* but the underlying theme is the same: There is always room for improving schools. Evaluation provides the focus and the arena for action in the constant call for educational improvement and reform. Given the evaluative ethos dominant within the educational establishment and the critical stance that virtually everybody takes toward the public schools, I must concede that school ethnographers (at least those recruited from our own society) probably cannot divest themselves of evaluative tendencies any more than they can afford for practical reasons to exclude themselves from evaluative assignments if they wish to remain involved with education.

Under most circumstances, traditional ethnographers insist that their commitment is to understand the peoples with whom they study. Anthropologists have often viewed with alarm the efforts of members of other groups (missionaries, educators, developers, colonial and other dominant powers) to "improve" the lot of a people by reforming or modernizing them. Among our educator colleagues, by contrast, ethnographers are most often called upon to augment or at least to chronicle systematic efforts at directed change. In the recent past, ethnographers have occasionally had the opportunity to proceed in the traditional manner with rather basic descriptive studies; the climate of the 1960s and 1970s nurtured the work, and we have been accumulating a solid foundation of ethnographic research about schools (cf. Burnett, 1974; Herriott, 1982; Smith, 1979, 1982; Spindler, 1982; Wilcox, 1982; Wolcott, 1975). Today, opportunities are more likely to be associated with short-term efforts to evaluate and improve specific educational programs than with long-term efforts to understand entire educational systems. We have to take opportunities as they come and try to provide the help requested of us, even as we endeavor to help educators become better aware of the ethnographic potential for understanding rather than evaluating.

Still, I would insist that an explicit ethnographic orientation should be apparent in anything labeled "ethnography"—an orientation clearly reflecting a tradition committed to discovering how things are and how they got that way in contrast to educator preoccupation with how things ought to be and how to move them quickly in that direction. "Evaluation for improvement and change" is the educator ethos; ethnographers working in educational settings need to be aware of it, but they do not have to adopt it for their own. As ethnographers, their commitment is to examine behavior in the broad social context in which it occurs, while evaluators ordinarily concern themselves with specific educational programs or relatively brief moments in educator—and educatee—lives.

For ethnographers who might prefer to help educators better understand *how things are* but who find their opportunities in education limited to assignments in ethnographic evaluation oriented to *how things ought to be*, a workable arrangement may lie in an evaluative compromise that I will call "ethnographers sans ethnography." Accepting roles as ethnographers sans ethnography would allow ethnographers to exercise their traditional practice of describing and interpreting rather than judging, and of attending to broad contexts rather than to isolated elements. The trade-off is the recognition that they are not free to indulge themselves in the professional luxury of conducting full-blown ethnographic studies.

I think there is currently more tolerance in educational circles—and perhaps even more support—for old-fashioned, descriptive, nonjudgmental ethnographers and their ethnographies than we sometimes recognize. Ethnographers do not have to go to the extremes of abandoning their ethnographic orientation and becoming evaluators if they are willing not to go to the other extreme of insisting they will only do traditional ethnography.

Following another anthropological tradition, let me turn to case study material and firsthand experience to illustrate how an invitation to participate in what seemed at first blush an out-and-out program evaluation actually provided an opportunity to observe, interpret, and report in essentially nonjudgmental ways not inconsistent with the ethnographic tradition. The purpose of the project I am going to describe was to learn (monitor) what happened during the implementation of a newly produced series in instructional television intended for classroom use.

THE INTRODUCTION OF *THINKABOUT*

In the fall of 1979, the Agency for Instructional Television (AIT) distributed among the 38 consortium-member state and provincial educational agencies in the United States and Canada that had helped sponsor its production a new 60-program television series called *ThinkAbout*. The series was designed for in-class television viewing and was intended primarily for use in fifth and sixth grade classrooms.

Although each program was self-contained within a 15-minute time frame and viewers were never handicapped by having missed a previous program or being unable to view a subsequent one, the programs all reflected an underlying concern with situational "problem solving," most often in meeting and solving some problem in an out-of-school setting designed to appeal to 10-, 11-, and 12-year-olds. At the anticipated rate of telecasting two new programs each week, the series was planned to extend for 30 weeks of school. A teacher's guide was available to help teachers prepare their classes for each program and conduct a follow-up discussion. The guide also listed activities related to the topics of individual programs and to each of the 13 topical "clusters" (e.g., collecting information; finding patterns; judging information) that comprised the series.

The series had been in preparation since 1973 and the investment included the time and effort of hundreds of educators and millions of dollars ($3 million from consortium members, $1.4 million from the Corporation for Public Broadcasting, and another $200,000 from Exxon Educational Foundation to assist with dissemination activities). An early release hailed the project as "the most ambitious instructional television series developed for national use."

In conjunction with the introduction of the series and consistent with the evaluation ethos of the times, AIT also commissioned an ambitious independent study of the program's introduction and effects, hoping even to assess the extent to which the program might actually improve students' problem-solving skills. To carry out that independent study, AIT contracted with the Evaluation Center at Western Michigan University.

Encouraged by a broad charter to document what actually went on in classrooms where *ThinkAbout* was used, the strategy proposed by the staff at the Evaluation Center called for augmenting two standard inquiry approaches, the use of mailed questionnaires, and the use of before-and-after testing in both user and nonuser classrooms, by commissioning case studies to be conducted independently by experienced but uncommitted outside observers. And that is where I came in.

For me, the assignment sounded just right. The schedule was convenient, the money good, the opportunity to get back into classrooms to do some observing quite welcome. I accepted the offer to become one of three project consultants contracted as independent case-study researchers.

Project meetings and formalities were held to a minimum. I had a full school year in which to locate teacher-users and visit their classrooms. Interim reporting requirements were modest. With such ample advance notice, I was easily able to plan time to complete my final report by the due date the following summer.

Working relationships remained pleasant, and my final report was eagerly and graciously received at the end of the project year. To my surprise, the three independently researched case study reports not only were forwarded to the sponsor exactly as written (as we had been promised) but were subsequently lithographed and bound intact as three of the five separate volumes that constitute the complete report prepared by the Evaluation Center and distributed by the Agency for Instructional Television.[1]

My only other surprise in connection with the project came quite early, during the first few minutes of my initial telephone contact with the project director. He explained that this venture into qualitative-quantitative research was a first for him, and because he was familiar with my work he had contacted me. "We want an ethnographer," he explained, "but we don't want you to give us a full ethnography."

Those words have continued to ring in my ears and prompted my title for this chapter. But those words, too, had a context, and the director's full statement and intent are important for understanding the sense of purpose shared by him and by AIT's Director of Research:

In our initial telephone conversation I said, "We want an ethnographer, but we don't want you to give us a full ethnography. We want a case study, limited in setting, time, actors, and to selected issues, but still open-ended to add new insights." What I was trying to communicate was that we did not need a wide-scope study of the "culture" of a school building or school district or even a school classroom. We wanted a study directed toward our objectives rather than your theories of cultural transmission or some other interest of yours [James Sanders, personal communication, 1982].

As I listened to the explanations and the outline of the assignment, I felt that as an "experienced" ethnographer I could compromise without feeling compromised. I would endeavor to provide ethnography without giving them "an ethnography." That is, I would try to provide an ethnographer's way of viewing, with attention to cultural context, to multiple points of view, and to unintended and unanticipated consequences as well as to intended ones. Assuming that my major (and possibly only) audience was the producers, I felt I should also offer whatever suggestions I might have for them to "think about," just as they had attempted to do for their intended audiences.

One specific request made of the three of us contracted to do the independent studies was that we include observations in one or two classrooms in which we would make sustained visits. Originally I planned to build my report around that case or cases. But during the fieldwork I found it helpful—even critical—to talk to many educators, to visit several classrooms, and to interview a number of teachers about instructional television in general and *ThinkAbout* in particular. In writing my final report, I reversed my original plan: I organized the first and major part of my discussion around several pervasive issues, and included two brief classroom case studies as part two.

For my purposes here, I have drawn only indirectly upon the main body of the report as it was directed to issues of special interest to the producers. What I have selected for illustration is one of my two case studies, this one from the classroom of a sixth grade teacher whom I call George Walker. Although I have slightly edited and abridged the original report, I have endeavored to leave it essentially as submitted in order to illustrate what I consider a satisfactory resolution to the issue of ethnographers sans ethnography.

I hope—and believe—that the case study both demonstrates and attests to the value of looking "ethnographically" even when it is quite likely that the ethnographer may have felt somewhat constrained by imposed limits on setting, time, actors, and issues and that the sponsor may have felt comparable misgivings about ever having invited an ethnographer at all. Further, I hope—and believe—that the case study both demonstrates and attests to the value of *describing* what is going on and how people are making sense of it rather than of *judging* what is (or is not) going on and how it ought really to be done differently (and, by implication, better). I did not feel obliged to evaluate either *ThinkAbout* or George Walker's teaching in meeting my ethnographic commitments. Yet I think that even in this brief case study, based on relatively few visits to only one classroom and focused on (but not limited exclusively to) their viewing of a 15-minute television program twice a week during only a portion of the school year, there is much to be learned and the implications are satisfyingly broad. In the formal report I submitted to the Evaluation Center those implications were spelled out in the discussion that preceded the presentation of case data; here I will recap some of them in my concluding remarks.

THINKABOUT IN GEORGE WALKER'S SIXTH GRADE[2]

Twenty-two years have passed since I taught sixth grade; yet when I made my first visit to George Walker's class, I had the feeling that things have not changed much. I could have "taken over" at a moment's notice. I felt completely at home in the class and relatively unobtrusive. My first school visit was in mid November 1979; my last taped interview with George was made after the close of school in June, 1980.

The text materials the sixth graders were using had changed somewhat, though I was not sure they were much improved. A newly adopted social studies text on Latin America looked so familiar that I had to check the date of publication to see if perchance it was the very book I had used. George was teaching the same folk dances I had taught (from what sounded like the same recording) and had chosen some of the same stories to read to his class that I once read to mine.

We bore other similarities as well. I was about George's age when I taught my class. I don't remember having a beard then—but that was because the superintendent of schools told me when I got the job (it, too, was a small town, with a few large schools inside the city limits and a number of small rural schools spread out over a huge outlying community) that he "hoped" I was going to shave the beard before school opened. As was true of my interests in those days, George enjoyed hiking and camping, and he managed to weave those interests into his classroom program through a curriculum in Outdoor Education that included a one-week experience at camp for sixth graders during the school year.

Even the composition of our classes was similar. Among my otherwise white pupils I, too, had one boy of "slightly dark complexion" and one girl of Asian background (my pupil was Japanese-American; George's pupil had been born in Hong Kong). I too had a class of about 25 pupils, with just a few more boys than girls (George had 11 girls, 14 boys). There may have been fewer pupils from blue-collar homes in my class, but both classes had children whose fathers were doctors and each of us had one pupil related to a school board member. It's a small world.

Under current operating definitions both our classes were "self-contained," though in retrospect I think my class was more self-contained than George's. My pupils went as a class to other teachers for shop and for art but otherwise were with me all day, every day. George's class was instructed in music (by the high school music teacher), in interpersonal skills (by the counselor), and, in the school library, in library skills. In addition, pupils came and went throughout the day to a series of special programs (math, reading, counseling); three boys consistently missed the *ThinkAbout* program each Monday and Wednesday afternoon because of a special remedial math lab (though they often returned just in time to participate in a follow-up activity or written assignment).

George also had access to one hour of assistance each day from a classroom aide. Rather expectedly, he chose to have that help during Reading, the second major period in each morning's regular activities. The aide usually came to the classroom and assisted with one of the three reading groups by hearing them read orally, presenting new vocabulary, or helping them check or correct a reading assignment. If there was a backlog of papers to correct, George sometimes asked her to spend her time correcting papers and recording grades.

Somewhat to his surprise after teaching at Washington Elementary School for six years, George found himself the "senior" teacher on the faculty. The principal and media-specialist-cum-librarian had been at the school many years, and some teachers had taught in other schools in the district, but George had been at Washington the longest of any teacher. He was beginning to enjoy a security borne of longevity.

There were three teachers at each grade level, grades one through six. George was friendly with and helpful to the two female teachers who taught the other sixth grade classes. He reported that the three cooperated on organizational matters more than on curricular ones. Although they occasionally shared texts and worksheets, their interactions usually involved music or dance programs, cafeteria and playground deportment, or plans for the outdoor education program in which all three classrooms and teachers were involved. The sixth grade teacher in the adjacent classroom told me she had never heard of *ThinkAbout* and did not realize that George was using it with his classroom until she talked with me. I noticed that she was a frequent user of films and filmstrips; she said she had never used instructional television.

George's classroom was of standard width but was unusually long, and the extra space allowed for a large old sofa and easy chair at the back of the room, favorite spots for leisure reading. George frequently rearranged the seating pattern of the individual desks and chairs. The customary seating arrangement was some variation on a U-shape, open toward the chalkboard at the front of the classroom. When the room was so arranged, the children were often allowed to sit on a large rug in the center of the room while they listened to a story or watched a film, filmstrip, or television. Early in the year, when George's class watched *ThinkAbout* with a fifth grade class as guests in that classroom (before the teacher decided not to continue with the programs), I noticed that strict attention was paid to having pupils sit rather than lie on the carpet. Protocol was relaxed in their own classroom. The children usually sprawled on the carpet in what I took to be a "living sociogram" of the interpersonal dynamics of the class. (At sixth grade, of course, the proximity was boy-to-boy, girl-to-girl; although by the end of the term there were some budding romances, members of the two sexes ordinarily kept their distance.)

Three idiosyncracies that I observed give some hint to George's style with the class. First was his red kitchen stool, a perch from which he always read the after-lunch story and often conducted classroom discussions. George used the stool the way some teachers use the corner of their desks, to sit in a slightly higher, more commanding position. Since he frequently relocated his own desk in the classroom, the red stool solved the problem of where he would sit regardless of the furniture arrangement.

Second was the considerable use George made of the overhead projector. More than any teacher I can remember, George relied on the overhead projector as an instructional aid for introducing words, giving assignments, drawing diagrams (or projecting diagrams already drawn), and keeping track of ideas presented during discussions. The projector was always at the ready at the front of the classroom, and if the class was not already at work when it was switched on, it gave a signal that they soon would be. Windows did not extend the full length of the long classroom, so on even the brightest days the front of the classroom was sufficiently dark that the overhead projections, film images, or television were easily seen without the necessity of closing the blinds. A screen for the overhead projector was mounted permanently above the chalkboard, and the projector itself was on a mobile cart that could be quickly swung into position directly under it.

Third was George's use of a number of abbreviated commands (e.g., "10:06," "Clear desks") and classroom rituals for handling organizational routines. Like George, many teachers use variations on a point system—more often noting negative than positive points—but I have never seen a teacher keep a tally of such demerits on his sleeve. In George's class, if particular students seemed to be having particularly bad days (invariably the same students, invariably boys), he would put a piece of masking tape on his sleeve and keep track of points that could lead to having to spend time after school. Recording of demerits was public: "OK, Randy, that's two!"

Another set of rituals were those in which the entire class responded in unison in acknowledging announcements or action. For example, announcements made by pupils from other classes (e.g., "Our class is having a cupcake sale on Friday so be sure to bring your money") were acknowledged by a single clap of the hands given in unison by all members of the class at the direction of the teacher, "Let's give them a hand."

My request to have pupils write about how their home viewing and school viewing of television were alike and different inadvertently produced a minor classroom revolt that resulted in George's adding an extra assignment of arithmetic homework as well. By my next visit all was forgiven and students were even pressing me to learn whether some of their papers were going to be "sent to Michigan," but George felt that since my request caused the commotion in the first place, my complicity should not go unrecognized. I got the "watermelon treatment," a ritual that I assume was restricted to "insiders." Each pupil took an imaginary slice of watermelon and pretended to devour it in one giant sweep from left to right. And the seeds? They were directed at me, in what became one loud Bronx cheer. But, and this is important, that was the end of it! Annoyance voiced, issue closed.

The "watermelon treatment" reveals George's style with the class: a sense of humor, tight but not intrusive control, a teacher-directed class, with room for "kids to be kids." I felt that George had adequate control over the class in spite of their obvious high energy and that he enjoyed them. As he noted during the year, he "probably had the hardest class" (of the three sixth grades) but they were also "the neatest" (i.e., best). In an interview after the close of school in June, however, George expressed frustration in terms of his impact on the class and stated, "If

I had to teach a group of kids like that one, year after year, I just wouldn't stay in teaching." He explained:

> My ability to communicate with them was unsuccessful. I felt at the end of the year they were doing the very things they did at the beginning that I didn't like. I felt that as a teacher I had very little influence—less than in any year I've taught. . . . It sure is nice that it's over.

George's frustration relates to the class as a whole and to their collective impact on him: "They got me upset, got me mad. . . . There were times when I'd shout, 'Shut up! Put your heads down!' That happens every year, but not as often as it did this year." He added, "I've always thought of myself as being lenient and open. But at times this year I felt I was just the opposite of what I want to be as a teacher."

Frustrated as he may have been—or was he simply worn out at the end of the school year?—George was not gloomy in his assessment of the progress made by the children individually. He felt that some of the pupils had made as much or more progress as he had ever seen. All was not lost; he simply hoped that he would not have "another class like that one."

A DAY IN CLASS

Flexibility has been much touted in education in recent years. The implication has been that new, alternative arrangements to building design or classroom organization are the way to achieve it. My visits to Washington School reminded me of the remarkable flexibility inherent in the self-contained classroom. In George's class one could never be sure exactly what was coming next.

At the same time, the class was organized around a strict timetable of routines. I think the daily schedule reflected George's (and perhaps most elementary teachers') perception of the ideal classroom day: the morning is for basics, the afternoon is for "other things." Let me describe an actual and rather typical day: Wednesday, February 27, 1980.

School began at 8:30 a.m. at Washington Elementary School, but so many pupils arrived earlier via school bus that classes were virtually "in session" by the time the morning bell rang, especially if the weather was cold (by local standards) or rainy. That morning about half the children were already in the classroom (some working at their desks, some playing the two-player board game of Kalaha, two girls practicing a dance the class would be presenting later in the month), while others were in the halls or playing outside in gentle rain.

A set of math papers, corrected the evening before, had been distributed on each desk. The teacher was preparing math problems that could later be flashed on the screen with the overhead projector. Without spoken direction, class members quickly seated themselves after the bell. George gave an opportunity for pupils who wanted to share current events (on this day the news focused on results of the New Hampshire primary elections). Again without announcement, George turned on the overhead projector to project five multiplication problems. Pupils immediately began copying and solving the problems and then proceeded to work for the next 45 minutes on individual assignments in arithmetic while the teacher (and visitor) answered questions on a request basis. Students who finished their day's assignment in math could go to the back of the room to play Kalaha; by about 9:25 a.m. ten children were doing so.

Then it was time for the class's scheduled period in the multipurpose room to practice for a forthcoming dance program to be presented for parents. After about a twenty-minute dance period, George dismissed the class by stating the time ("10:06") when he expected all pupils to return to their desks, following a brief interval when they could use the toilets, get a drink, visit, and so on.

Pupils, teacher, and teacher's aide converged in the classroom and proceeded immediately to their Reading Period tasks. An abbreviated schedule written on the chalkboard divided the class into three groups and distributed them according to the three elements of George's reading program: "R" (recreational reading), "M" (meet with teacher or aide as a group), "D" (desk work, consisting either of reading a story in a reader or completing an assignment). There were five pupils in the top group ("We're doing seventh grade reading," the one boy in the group informed me); and ten pupils in each of the other two groups. A boy from the middle group assured me that although the top group had "the hardest" reading, his group was also doing "advanced" work. He referred to the third group, using a reader entitled *Easy Going*, as "the flunkies." A boy from the *Easy Going* group immediately came to ask me, "What did he just say about us?"

During the one hour reading period all children were scheduled into each of the three facets of the reading program. The end of the reading period was signalled by the instruction, "Pink sheets," a reminder to record the number of pages read during recreation reading time.

"Clear desks" was the next direction, the signal to begin the third and final leg of the morning's instructional journey. On alternative mornings the music teacher visited, so the third "hour" in the morning was not entirely under George's control. When it was, however, it was given to academic tasks, including the completion of work begun earlier in the morning. As one pupil explained, "What we do next depends on what he tells us to do."

On this day the class was directed to return to the five problems in multiplication assigned earlier. "Now we'll see who is ready for the seventh grade," George chided. He had them pass papers so each was corrected by a different classmate. At student direction he completed the problems, working them for all to see on the overhead projector. Scores were then reported orally and recorded.

With about 35 minutes to go before lunch, and with several threats that he might have everyone "take out your English books instead," George divided the class into five team to work together to try to figure out "which number comes next" by discerning the pattern in a series of numbers. He later said that he'd had the number game ready for several weeks and finally saw just the right opportunity to present it.

Hot lunch was served for the upper grades in the cafeteria/multipurpose room promptly at noon. Because of the rain, pupils returned immediately to the classroom after lunch, playing games under the supervision of a classroom aide to allow teachers their "duty-free" lunch break. With shepherding his class through the lunch line, eating his own lunch, and going to the staff room to make himself a cup of tea, the 40-minute lunch period passed quickly. As we headed back to a classroom of children who had already been confined for four hours (8:30-12:30) and still had three hours to go (12:30-3:30), George made one of the most important comments I recorded during the entire year's research:

> Now comes the part of the day I don't like. The afternoon drags on, and I'm tired. And by evening I am too tired to do a lot of preparation.

The highly structured, basics-oriented, purposive teacher of the morning seemed, by both his perception and mine, to be a different, more casual—but also more uncertain—teacher in the afternoon, a critical point to which I will return. But let me first continue with this detailed account of one particular day in George Walker's class.

The impending dance program was on several teachers' minds. No sooner had George returned to his classroom than he received a message that a teacher in another class "needed some girls" to serve as partners so that her class could practice their dances for the program. Unhesitatingly George sent the required number of volunteers; then he faced the question of what to do with the remainder of the class until the others returned. (Cagily, no girls volunteered until they had secured George's promise that he would not continue with the regular after-lunch story reading until they returned.) Deciding to capture the sudden burst of interest he had seen that day in playing Kalaha (before school, during math, and at lunchtime) he proceeded to the chalkboard, and, without comment, drew the playoff pattern for a tournament. Then he announced "A Big Event, The First Annual Kalaha Derby." He quickly had pupils draw starting partners and got the tournament going with the two Kalaha boards in the classroom. Amid excitement and laughter the tournament ran quickly but far exceeded the ten-minute maximum he declared at its outset. By about 1:05 the tournament had ended, the girls had returned from their dancing, and he began storytime, concluding his reading aloud to the class a short story, "The Most Dangerous Game."

I found variations in the duration of storytime to be an indicator of the teacher's and class's mood after lunch. Between an occasional impromptu discussion, inspired by events of the morning or during lunchtime, and occasional rapt attention to the story being read, the story-reading period sometimes lasted so long that there was no other formal activity between the end of lunch (12:40) and the beginning of *ThinkAbout* (1:30). On other days, in other moods, and capped by inattentive listening, the story period might be finished by 12:55. All quite different from the tight, purposeful scheduling of the morning's activities.

On this day, story-reading lasted till 1:25p.m., in part because George had gotten so far along in the story that he realized he had to conclude it. After sending a pupil to bring the television "cart" from another classroom, he invited a brief discussion about which of the stories he had recently read was the favorite.

Sensing that the class still had not settled down after the Kalaha tournament and interruption from dancing, George announced that at 1:45 p.m. (i.e., after *ThinkAbout*) he would need a "Noise Break," a totally quiet time while pupils worked individually at their desks. Having now committed himself to a Noise Break, it occurred to him to tie in whatever assignment he would give (at this point he hadn't invented it) with the program the children were about to watch. As he switched on the television set, he anticipated aloud the possibility that the program shown might be out of sequence, as had so often happened in previous weeks: "I don't know what the show will be about today . . . but I'll be giving you an assignment on this program."

The *ThinkAbout* program aired that day was the first program in a new cluster "Judging Information." George had told me earlier that he *hoped* the telecast program would begin the new cluster rather than go back to a "missed" program on Maps and Models. But, he added cheerily, "I can do 'Models' if that's what they show." When the title of the day's program did prove to be from the new cluster (Program 44, "Should I Believe It?") he gave a sigh of approval and commented to the class, "Ah, this is a good one."

The classroom audience for this day's program consisted of 10 girls, 11 boys, the teacher, and one observer (me). At lunchtime a boy who had been absent during the morning returned to school, so the headcount increased to 24 present of 25 enrolled; however, at 1:25 three boys left the room for their regular session of special help in math.

While the big black and white television set warmed up, George gave directions to establish which pupils could have first choice for places on the carpet (not that there was any shortage of space, only the perennial competition to see who can be first). Pupils ordinarily were free to sit (lie) wherever they wished on the carpet, remain at their desks, or sit in the easy chair or on the sofa at the back of the room. The carpeted area was the favorite of most pupils, and they seemed to attend more closely to their proximity to friends than to their proximity to the television. Teacher's Guide in hand, George sat at a student desk at the side of the room. Invariably he would need to adjust picture or sound during the program.

The Teacher's Guide for Program 44 listed two teaching points: "It is important to question information and its sources" and "When judging the reliability of a source, ask yourself: 'Should I believe it? Who says so? Who else says so?' " The "After the Program" suggestions direct the teacher to "Talk about . . . how to decide if you can believe an information source" and suggest some questions about the story and some ways for students to relate the issue of reliable information to their own lives.

But George didn't want a "talk about" activity. He needed a written assignment for pupils to do during his announced Noise Break. The lesson *he* made out of the telecast was a lesson on "sequencing." Sequencing was one of twenty-four different follow-up activities listed on a set of teacher-made wall charts permanently posted high along one wall of the classroom, activities that could be used as "instant assignments" in conjunction with almost any reading done in class. Sequencing was task #17: "Skim your story. Write the events in sequence."

Immediately after *ThinkAbout*, George turned off the television and a pupil stepped forward to roll the sturdy cart into the corridor so the next users of the set would not have to interrupt the class. George rolled the overhead projector into place, switched it on, and began to list the characters in the story, a visit by two aliens from outer space: Sue, Eustace, Roto, Nurk, Dr. Davis. "What about Hank?" queried a student. "Who's Hank?" asked the teacher. "The guy's father," came the response. Add Hank to the list. Under these names he added the two interpretations suggested in the story: "Aliens Invade" and "Friendly Aliens Scared Away." Then he announced the assignment:

> OK. I need a break. I think this [program] is worth discussing, but I'm going to give you a "put-it-down-on-paper" assignment for ten minutes. We'll discuss it afterwards. When you get your paper done, just take out your book and read.
>
> Your assignment is activity number 17 [referring to the wall chart of written activities]. Skim the program and write the events in sequence as to what happened. Instead of writing out whole sentences, just write down the events in sequence. What happened? White paper. Any questions? . . . This is called "Ten-Minute Noise Break."

The children turned immediately to the task, taking (their own) writing paper from their desks. They worked without discussion and without asking the teacher for word or spelling help. He stepped into the hall briefly, then returned to the classroom and did some minor straightening up. The mood was not punitive, it was simply a time for quiet, a teacher "Time Out." Except for the sound of the pencil sharpener, no one violated the silence.

Promptly at 2:00 p.m. George announced recess. Pupils grabbed jackets and lined up at the classroom door. The playground included a covered "shed" area, so although it was still raining lightly, everyone could go out-of-doors without having to stand in the rain. Most of the girls remained in the shed area with the teacher, while the boys played a game of Four Square outside. This was the regular afternoon recess period for George's class, but he had to supervise it himself because his class was the only one on the playground. With his shout of "O.K., that's it!" recess ended and pupils returned to class.

Wednesday was Library Day for George's class, when the media specialist presented a brief lesson on library use and then allowed time for book selection. Library period was 2:30 to 3:00 p.m. Settled in the classroom again at 2:20, only ten minutes remained for a quick review of the steps the pupils had identified in their analysis of the sequence of events in the ThinkAbout program. George listed the events on the overhead projector as pupils suggested them, guiding the discussion with comments like, "No, something happened before that," if he felt someone had skipped a step.

The emphasis was entirely on "What happened next?" the lesson George made of the program, rather than on the reliability of information sources, the lesson proposed in the Teacher's Guide.

During the discussion the teacher had the class examine how there were really *two* sequences of events, one leading to each of two different conclusions. The "star" of the program—invariably a young person just a bit older than the pupils watching it—needed to understand what people thought was happening as well as what was actually happening. As George noted in a hasty summary just prior to dismissing the class for the library, "That made the sequencing a little confused."

George led his pupils through the hall to the library and then headed to the staff room for a cup of tea. He returned to his classroom but kept an eye on the clock so that he would not be late meeting the class at the library door promptly at 3:00. At his direction the class returned to begin a new activity, social studies. ("So-so studies," a bright pupil mumbled for my benefit.) Today the class viewed a filmstrip describing the exploits of one of the Spanish explorers in Central America. From a pupil perspective the challenge of the activity seemed to lie in getting called on to read the captions.

At 3:25 George terminated the filmstrip lesson, reviewed names of pupils with homework assignments, distributed one handout, reminded everyone to "put up your chairs" (to make it easier for the custodian to clean) and dismissed pupils at the door. Students did not linger, though many said a ritual goodby as they exited and a few directed their goodby specifically to the teacher: "Goodbye Mr. Walker. See you tomorrow." In less than a minute the classroom was empty except for two boys detained after school for accumulating "too many marks" against them during the afternoon.

REPEAT PERFORMANCE:
ANOTHER AFTERNOON IN CLASS

I was visiting George's classroom when the same *ThinkAbout* program was repeated on a Monday afternoon a week and a half later. By this time the *ThinkAbout* sequence had become hopelessly garbled. Five days earlier George had prepared the class for the expected program by having them write out directions for how to tie your shoe, a suggested follow-up activity for another program. However, the program was not broadcast that week. As the television set was warming up, he mused, "The assignment I gave you last time about tying your shoes was for the wrong *ThinkAbout* program. Maybe today that is the program we will see." George was scanning his Teacher's Guide as the program began. From the curiously enthusiastic response of the pupils he knew that it was not the program he expected and that it was a repeat; he soon realized it was the program "Aliens Invade" seen earlier. "Oh, let's not watch it," he said in a somewhat teasing manner. The pupils groaned in protest, and he changed his tone: "Would you like to see it again?" The class cheered, and George commented, "All right! Don't say I never did anything for you."

Attention was as rapt as on the first viewing, for this program was lively, action-packed, filled with imagination and humor. There was quite a bit of laughter. The classroom mood was light. And instead of jumping to his feet to turn off the set and take charge at the end of the program, George left the set on. The next program on the public broadcast channel was "The Letter People." George asked the class if they wanted to continue watching, and got another affirmative response. But pupils were soon laughing at a story aimed at younger viewers in which Mr. "Y" was explaining what would make him the "happiest person in Letterland," and after four minutes George turned the set off, accompanied by only a ritual moan of dismay.

George asked whether the class felt they had learned any more by watching the repeat broadcast of *ThinkAbout* or whether they learned it all the first time. One boy who always had a ready comment volunteered that he had not realized the girl in the story wore braces the first time he viewed the program. The teacher jokingly responded: "Well, that's important. Anything else?" There were no other comments. "I guess you learned it all the first time," he concluded.

And now what? Ten minutes to go before recess; no new *ThinkAbout* material to discuss. "I'll have to give you something else," George announced, "but it will have to be a bit more instructional." Apparently he was still in a teasing mood, for he filled the next few minutes with one of his popular short "filler" activities, having the children guess artist and title from his personal collection of old 45 LP records. (George referred to this lightly as "Music Appreciation.") At 2:02 he took the class out for recess.

After recess the pupils returned to their classroom for their regular Monday afternoon session with the school counselor. On this day her lesson was to show and discuss the film, "The Shopping Bag Lady." (I noted that although the picture was large and in color, in contrast to the small black-and-white television screen, the counselor had trouble with both sound and frame while showing the film. The sound was so poor that she stopped the film to ask whether everyone was able to understand it. Prior to showing the film she asked if anyone had seen it before; 10 of the 22 children present had already seen it, but she proceeded with her lesson as planned, pausing only to add, "And if you've seen it before, see what else you can learn.")

George returned to the classroom at 3:01 and the counselor promptly departed for her last session of the afternoon. The final period of the day was devoted to social studies, students taking turns reading orally from a text about Latin America until it was time to prepare for the 3:30 dismissal.

During the afternoon visit I wrote in my notes:

> George's style seems to be to keep things moving. He's always got something he can pull out to fill the time, nothing ever takes too long, and there is not a lot of follow-up. Also, his own mood—or his reading of the mood of the class—seems to be a big influence on the activities he chooses.

A number of events that day suggest how George's mood affected his choice of activities. The day had gotten off to a slow start, with 70 minutes devoted to another rehearsal of the forthcoming dance program that involved six classrooms. "Reading" was, rather predictably, on schedule. The third period of the morning has been devoted to rewriting "on good paper" an assignment that had been drafted earlier. After lunch George was about to begin his daily story-reading, but he sensed that the pupils would not be receptive to his reading that day. Instead, he put them to work on an assignment doing individual worksheets that required them to pair off and record a number of measurements (in centimeters) of themselves, made with the help of their partners. That activity had continued until *ThinkAbout* time. It had gone slowly but well and had ended on a light note as some (carefully chosen) measurements were shared. Although he intended to make no instructional use of it, he allowed the class to watch a repeat *ThinkAbout* broadcast (conceivably he might have turned to the intended lesson on information sources, but apparently he was "through" with the program). In the same mood he let the class watch a few more minutes of "The Letter People" (on another day, in another mood, they once watched a soap opera when *ThinkAbout* repeated), and then let them play the music game.

I emphasize mood rather than moodiness or brooding; I think the pupils did not find George at all bewildering and they seemed quite used to a style in which they did not always know what was coming next. There was a certain spontaneity about the class, a sense of give and take. But these elements were much more apparent in the (long) afternoon, after the more serious and structured part of the day was past. *ThinkAbout* was subjected to that same "mood." The class watched most, but not all, of the programs during the year. Sometimes programs were discussed; sometimes not. Sometimes the lesson taught was the lesson suggested in the Guide; sometimes the follow-up activity had little to do with the program itself.

WHY *THINKABOUT*?

I think the basic problem George was trying to solve was how to make constructive use of the long afternoon period when his daily ration of ideas and energy ran low. He himself noted how differently he perceived his morning and afternoon programs:

Basically the morning subjects are Language Arts and Math. I guess because I've done them every year and they kind of stay the same, I feel more confident or competent in teaching those subjects. I think I'm more prepared and have more to fall back on. So we do those in the morning, and everything pretty much goes as planned. As long as I've got things planned, classes go pretty well. And in the morning, we do a lot of work in writing, math problems, and meeting in small groups.

In the afternoon it kind of shifts when we're in the science or social studies areas. This year we've spent most of the time as a large group. And I just don't feel as good teaching those subjects as I do the others. For one thing, the social studies textbook is new. *If ThinkAbout came in the morning, I probably wouldn't use it.* There's just so much under Language Arts and Math that you have to cover—passing district objectives, all the things you want to cover that the kids will be tested on—that you don't want to give up the morning as much as you would in the afternoon.

It's a lot easier to give and take in the afternoon. If kids miss a lesson in social studies or science, it's not going to hurt them at all. If they don't get their math one day, I almost always have to be sure they get it later.

ThinkAbout does also come on in the morning here. We did take one morning to watch it because I thought the program was worthwhile [Program 26, Cultural Patterns, which most of the class missed during the afternoon of a Christmas program], but we wouldn't watch it regularly if that was the only time the program came.

He reflected further upon his use of *ThinkAbout* during the first year:

I don't think of *ThinkAbout* as a specific skill or something that's listed under our objectives. I think there's room for things like this, but you have to really pick and choose.

At this point, I just think of *ThinkAbout* as a good resource. I haven't looked that much up or planned that much around the programs. If the program has pertained to what we are doing, then we go with it from there. It it doesn't, then we just watch it and enjoy it and talk about it a little if we want to.

PUPIL REACTIONS

I never felt successful in my efforts to elicit "spontaneous reactions" to *ThinkAbout* from pupils in George's class. They knew that my interests were related to the program and had made the assumption that I was somehow responsible for its production. If that made their candid assessments about the series difficult to obtain, I should note that it provided an otherwise satisfactory explanation for my presence in their classroom. I heard one pupil explain my presence to a boy in another class, "That's Harry. The *ThinkAbout* guy. Doing research." The more outgoing students approached me easily, asked for help with their assignments, brought me up to date on any recent events, and scanned my notes thoroughly. But my efforts to get them to analyze *ThinkAbout* never got beyond their individual review of the programs they "remembered," their "remembering" standing as an implicit measure of the programs deemed to be "best." In a general discussion at the conclusion of the entire series, the class gave *ThinkAbout* a global rating of "about 8" (on a scale I assumed to be from one to ten). At that time 5 of 18 students present said they felt the program was best suited for 6th graders; the other 13 felt it was most suitable for grade five.

The teacher asked pupils to do two written assignments for me during the spring. In one assignment I asked pupils to compare home viewing and school viewing. Excerpts from three papers provide some flavor of their responses:

Sixth grade girl: When I am at school I watch television with the class and Mr. Walker and Mr. Wolcott. On the rug I sit by Donna, Barbara, Alice, Tina, and Joanne. At home I watch television with my sister and my dad.

At school I watch television at 1:30. When I watch television at home I watch it at 4:30 and then between 8:00-10:00.

At school I watch television on the rug. At home I watch television in my room. We have two television sets, one in my room and one in the living room. I mostly watch television in my room. My sister and I were in the same room and then my dad made a new room and I moved into the room. My sister got the stereo and I got the television.

I watch *ThinkAbout* at school. I watch mostly comedies and movies at home. At school I watch television to learn. At home for something to do.

Sixth grade boy: At home I watch television with my mother, my father, my sister, and my brother. At school I watch it with Mr. Walker, Harry, and my class.

At home on school nights I watch television from 3:30 to 10:00. On weekends as long as I want. At school I watch television at 1:30.

At home I watch television in the living room. We have another one in my mom and dad's room but I never use it. At school I watch television at my desk.

At home I watch mostly comedy. At school I watch ThinkAbout.

At home on school nights I watch television about 7 1/2 hours, on weekends about 10 hours. At school 15 minutes.

At home some of my favorites are One in a Million, Star Trek, Happy Days, Laverne and Shirley, and Fantasy Island. At school there's only one show so I don't have a favorite.

At home I watch television because I like to and there's nothing else to do. At school I watch television because we have to.

In the fifth grade we watched a history show and book show called Cover to Cover.

Sixth grade boy: At home I watch television with my mom and dad. At school I watch television with Steve and Tom. Well, the hole class watches.

At home I watch television in the family room and on Saturday morn in my room. At school on the rug.

At home I watch after school and after dinner and Saturday in the morn and at night and on Sunday at night. At school I watch television at 1:30 Mon. and Wed.

At home I watch Flintstones, Happy Days, Brady Bunch, Mork and Mindy, Eight is Enough, Hulk, Dukes of Hazzard, Hogan's Heroes, Charley's Angels, and cartunes. At school I watch ThinkAbout.

At home on weekdays I watch about 5 hours, on weekends 4 hours. At school 15 min.

I watch television at home when I don't have nothing better to do. At school to learn.

CONSERVING ENERGY

Too quickly we may forget the sense of panic felt across the nation during 1979-1980 as fuel costs soared and fuel shortages loomed. Thermostats were turned down, tax breaks were given for improved home insulation, and a nation with a seemingly insatiable capacity for fuel consumption suddenly became energy conscious. The new realization was that each individual's efforts at conservation could (or at least might) make a difference. For the skeptical, rising costs that saw gasoline go from about $.99 to $1.25 a gallon helped bring the point home. Everyone started reexamining ways to save fuel/money. Even school boards.

In early spring, 1980, the school board of the district in which Washington School was located joined the national effort by attempting to economize on the district's huge transportation expenditure. Included in that reorganization was the "revolutionary" idea of having school close at the same time each day for *all* elementary school children, thereby eliminating the doubling back that brought buses to its eleven elementary schools at 2:30 each afternoon for the primary children and again at 3:30 for pupils in the intermediate grades. I describe the decision as revolutionary because on other grounds (lack of preparation time for intermediate-grade teachers, too long a day for pupils and teachers alike) the board for years had steadfastly refused to consider a shortened day. When, several years earlier, they had finally acceded to having intermediate-grade pupils dismissed early *one* afternoon a week—a Thursday afternoon early dismissal still in effect—they had done it begrudgingly, almost punitively. And now, for reasons entirely unrelated to pupil or teacher welfare, the decision was accomplished in a moment and effective immediately.

The decision resulted in the saving of teacher energy as well. With a 2:30 dismissal, George Walker's class no longer needed a 15-minute afternoon recess, but nonetheless his instructional time was reduced 45 minutes a day, almost 4 hours a week. I do not think it a coincidence that after the "big bus schedule change," George's class no longer viewed *ThinkAbout* on a regular basis. I rather wonder whether he would have watched the final programs at all had I not contacted him in April to ask if I might return once more to "see how the class was doing."

The bus schedule change provided about the nearest equivalent an observer has to a natural experiment. The fact that George's *Think-About* viewing came to a virtual standstill when the afternoon schedule was shortened certainly does not prove my notion that George experienced a resource shortage of his own during the long afternoons (a notion suggested in part by George's own perception of the "afternoon program"), but it does lend support to it. The school district's efforts to save energy inadvertently, and unintentionally, reduced a drain on teacher energy as well. That savings in energy may have resulted in less dependence on an outside resource like *Think-About*. With the shorter schedule, George had less worry about how to fill up the day and could concern himself with covering topics that needed to be covered.

CASE-STUDY SUMMARY

George Walker was open to exploring the possibilities of instructional television and was, I believe, consciously looking for "help" (in both the sense of assistance and the sense of direction) with his instructional program. As George candidly admitted, *ThinkAbout* offered "15 minutes twice a week that I didn't have to plan or teach." In that regard, it was an energy-saver and a welcome one. George felt no misgivings if the children enjoyed the program or found it entertaining. He did not insist that everything he did in class had to be "good" for his pupils.

And yet he felt that *ThinkAbout* was good for them. It was a source of specific ideas (brainstorming, giving reports, getting information, becoming conscious of patterns, improving one's memory, analyzing issues), it addressed the broad issue of problem-solving (which "tied in nicely with a unit on the scientific method" that he presented briefly but was also of interest throughout the year), and it addressed problems related to science and social studies, two curricular areas in which George felt somewhat inadequate and unprepared.

George was part of the *ThinkAbout* audience; my assessment was that more attention might be paid to teachers like him in that audience. He turned to the program for help and it helped him. It could have helped him even more if—either in the program or in a supportive network of other users—he had found ideas for his teaching methods, including how to use the *ThinkAbout* program itself. He explicitly stated that he would have liked to hear how other teachers were using the program. But he was the only teacher in his district using the series. On the one day in the year when the opportunity arose to attend a *ThinkAbout* workshop offered at the county media center, George was still saying goodby to his pupils in a classroom some 35 miles away when the meeting was convened.

George said he planned to use *ThinkAbout* again and felt that his familiarity with the program the first year would make it "more valuable" next year: "It's just like knowing a social studies book. You can pick and choose and you know where you are going with it. It will be much easier to tie in with what we are doing. And I don't think it will be at all dated."

The introduction of *ThinkAbout* helped George solve some resource problems. A new district-wide rescheduling provided at least a partial solution to his energy problem. If George uses *ThinkAbout* again it will be for the help he seeks in curricular areas. He is the ultimate judge. Only a month after the close of school, the question of whether his pupils had liked the series was only academic. Next September they will be in junior high school; George alone remained behind to repeat the sixth grade. If *ThinkAbout* turned him on last year, he will probably turn *ThinkAbout* on in the year ahead.

ETHNOGRAPHERS SANS ETHNOGRAPHY

Wish though I may that ethnography can someday achieve both separate and equal status with evaluation in the field of education, and steadfast in working toward that goal as I intend to remain, for practical reasons I believe that ethnography will make its major contribution through its applications as an adjunct to, rather than an alternative for, evaluation. Most frequently I think that contribution will be in modest case studies like this one of George Walker's sixth grade.

Wishful thinking aside, there is much to celebrate in the increasing receptivity of educational researchers and evaluators to case study data and naturalistic inquiry. To those of us long committed to ethnography in education, it was heady stuff to watch our popularity grow during the 1970s. We had trouble keeping sufficient perspective of our own to realize that the interest was not in ethnography per se but in descriptive, on-site research in general. I think the issue of whether or not someone is really following an ethnographic approach is, and will probably continue to be, of rather little consequence to most educators although it is of paramount interest to those of us who insist that ethnography presumes a commitment to cultural interpretation (cf. Spindler, 1982; Wolcott, 1980, 1982a, 1982b). But a willingness not only to consider but to insist on qualitative, descriptive data and along with this a willingness to trade off some of the seeming obsession for measurement with some consideration for context and meaning is becoming increasingly evident among educators, even those whose own forte is quantification.

That receptivity was already present among both the client-sponsor for the *ThinkAbout* research, the Agency for Instructional Television, and project staff at the Evaluation Center.[3] That the nuances and full potential of ethnography were not critical is apparent in their preference for commissioning an ethnographer but not ethnography. Nonetheless, *they contacted me*; my participation in the project was their idea, not my own. Furthermore, they had a clear idea of how a set of independently conducted case studies could augment other, more traditional ways of monitoring the introduction of an educational innovation.

The constraints they imposed were similar to those noted by others doing "contract ethnography": constraints of time, scope, detail, and interpretation. Admittedly, those constraints can "ruffle the fur" of any free-thinking ethnographer (cf. Clinton, 1975). Collectively they also have the effect of making the target of most evaluation efforts (or "monitor" studies) loom disproportionately large and significant. Given the opportunity to pursue a purer ethnographic approach, the two brief *ThinkAbout* segments viewed each week by George Walker's class unquestionably would have appeared less important in the total picture of life in that classroom. But that was part of the trade-off. It is not unseemly for people to ask an ethnographer to turn attention to what interests them, and it is not unseemly for ethnographers to provide a perspective on a particular program or problem. Even ethnographers, after all, must look at *something* rather than at *everything*.

The *ThinkAbout* project provides a reassuring illustration of how broadly the task of "evaluation" has come to be interpreted. As noted in the Executive Summary accompanying the Evaluation Center's final report, the project was not designed to assess the value of the *ThinkAbout* curriculum for its potential consumers: Consortium members who funded the development of the series had already committed themselves to the worth of the endeavor (Sanders & Sonnad, 1982: 2). The intent of the study—to see what could be learned about the initial use and impact of the series—was sufficiently broad to spark ethnographic interest. However, it quickly became apparent to those of us engaged in the case-study research that we would have precious little to say about "impact." We learned far more about classrooms and teachers than about students and their thinking or problem solving, and that is what we discussed in our reports.

The locus of the research setting tended to circumscribe what we learned. Directed as we were to classrooms and classroom (i.e., teacher) use of the program, our case studies are most revealing about those processes. They are a bit less revealing about instructional television per se, and reveal almost nothing of what is going on in the minds of the student viewers. As a fifth grader summarized all too neatly, "It's just television. It's an interesting way to get out of work in the afternoon." But that "morning versus afternoon" contrast proved a fascinating one for me as I discovered that instructional television tends to be regarded as an "afternoon" activity. George epitomized that view with his comment, "If *ThinkAbout* came in the morning, I probably wouldn't use it."

Drawing my summary comments essentially from the case study conducted in George's classroom, I think I can point to the kinds of observations one can expect from inviting an ethnographer's attention and perspective, even when underwriting an all-out ethnographic effort is clearly out of the question.

Ethnographers are always interested in context, and ultimately with the broad social context of "cultural" behavior. I could not help but draw upon that perspective in my portrayal of George's classroom. Although most of my classroom visits were conducted for only the brief period immediately preceding, during, and following the twice-weekly viewing of *ThinkAbout*, when the time came to decide how to tell the "story" of that classroom I turned to notes made on an occasion when I had spent the entire day with George and his class. In so doing, I hoped not only to convey a sense of the classroom but also to serve reminder that a twice-a-week viewing of a 15-minute television program is something less than the focal point of classroom life for children who are intensely involved with their teacher and classmates for a minimum of 35 hours a week. Much as the children seemed to enjoy the programs, I could not escape the feeling that the content was no match in importance to them for such matters as where they would be allowed to sit to view the program, who they would sit with, or what "work" they might otherwise have been assigned.

In broader context still, the tight and purposive activities of the morning—nicely distributed among the three Rs with Reading as the central organizing activity of the entire classroom schedule—contrasted sharply with the relatively easygoing pace of the afternoon. At times individuals, communities, even the whole nation seems to rise up in indignation at any hint of educational easygoingness, but after almost 30 years as an educator and an observer of educational processes, I am ready to suggest that the morning/afternoon contrast reflects rather well the combination of "certainty plus confusion" about what our society demands of, expects from, and condones in its schools.

Schools and communities alike seem to be in basic agreement about the basics. Teachers at every level transmit basic literacy skills with a rather keen sense of purpose. George's "morning program" reflected that certainty. His afternoon program represented its complement: What else are the schools supposed to do besides teach the basics? For some teachers, those we refer to as "naturals," that question poses the challenge and reward of teaching; for others, like George, it posed something of a threat. I pondered why George had begun using *ThinkAbout* when no other teacher in his building or school district (a unified district of about 200 teachers, 3000 students) used it. Energy-conscious as we had all become in those days, I saw an analogy between his use of a twice-weekly instructional interlude supplied by television and someone in need of a mid-afternoon snack as a physiological energy boost. George was looking for a boost to help him fill out his daily program. In *ThinkAbout*, he found it.

A question came to mind: What would happen if an agency like AIT were to target its efforts at teachers like George who willingly seek help rather than diffuse its efforts in an educational broadside addressed to an entire nation's fifth and sixth grade pupils and teachers? Pursuing that idea in the discussion contained in the first part of my report, I proposed a rudimentary taxonomy of teacher-users of classroom television. I suggested that the producers of any curriculum materials might take a close look at the kind of help their most-likely-users need. The typology that I proposed consisted of three major categories: *nonusers, casual users,* and *committed users.*[4]

The first category, nonusers, includes the huge residual group of teachers who do not have access to or necessarily even hear about a curricular innovation. For *ThinkAbout*, that group included entire states and provinces that were not consortium members as well as teachers within member states who simply were not reached by a rather intense promotional effort. A case in point: George's class watched the program twice a week; the teacher in the adjacent classroom told me she had never heard of it.

Another important group of nonusers includes teachers opposed to particular kinds of instructional aids. Films and television programs produced for classroom use seem especially likely to provoke strong opposition. Many teachers feel that children spend far too much out-of-school time as passive viewers and certainly do not need to watch TV in school as well. Program quality is not the issue with them. I would think that the developers of curricular materials would want to know more about the teachers most likely to adopt them rather than try to design materials to appeal to everyone.

Casual users proved an interesting group in the *ThinkAbout* research. It might be worthwhile to refine some subcategories to better identify variations among this type of user. I began to suspect, but could not adequately document in a project of only one year, that some teachers who spoke enthusiastically about *ThinkAbout* had probably been just as excited about something different the year before and have eagerly sought out new curricular packages in the years since. When implementation research focuses on programs rather than people, we identify such users as "early adopters"; we usually do not remain on the scene long enough to learn whether it may be innovation itself that attracts them.

Another kind of casual users are teachers who describe themselves — and probably think of themselves — as regular users but whose *actual* use is spotty at best. George himself became a casual user of the program after the school board shortened his classroom day, although he regarded himself as a regular user of the *ThinkAbout* series and as one of its staunch supporters. I met other teachers whose actual viewing of the program was sporadic but who regarded themselves as faithful viewers. These are the respondents who confound questionnaires and surveys when we rely on self-reporting to assess behavior.

Committed users, the third category in my taxonomy, includes teachers like George who seemed "committed" to giving the program an adequate trial. Admittedly, it was critical for the three of us contracted to do case studies to locate a few committed teachers, and it is possible that there were "observer effects" in all the classrooms where we were regular visitors. (One must remember that teaching can be a lonely business in terms of peer interaction and that some teachers enjoy having another adult in their class, especially someone present long enough to see the "ups" as well as "downs" and to get a sense of the full instructional program.)

Even in talking to teachers whom I did not visit regularly, I found that those who felt committed to the program were quite forgiving of problems reportedly driving other teachers up the walls. The technical quality of the series was high, yet never once during the year did I watch a live program on a color screen in a classroom. Each of the two classrooms where I did my most extensive observing relied on a poor picture from antiquated black-and-white TV sets with "rabbit ear" reception because each happened to be located in a section of the school that did not have a cable television hook-up.

Far more disconcerting than poor reception was a problem (at least in our state) of having programs appear out of sequence or being repeated. Teachers frequently prepared their classes for the wrong program. As the case study shows, George took the scheduling problems in stride — to such an extent that I wondered if he regarded television viewing as instructional time or simply as "time out." My tentative conclusion is that it was a bit of both. George regarded *ThinkAbout* as instructional and was prepared to defend it on that basis (e.g., to a principal "lukewarm" to the idea of classroom television or, had the issue been raised, to parents who might question its use), but once written into his plan for the day's events, the time was allocated to television per se. As George himself declared, "Not everything we do in class has to be instructive."

Finally, I want to note that repeated observations of many observers in many classrooms provide opportunities to reaffirm, refine, or refute the understandings and generalizations we seek regarding classroom behavior. Watching teachers use *ThinkAbout* left me with the strong impression—also noted by other observers in other classroom settings and pursuing other research objectives—that the teacher *is* the curriculum (cf. Janesick, 1978). Put another way, the teacher decides what the formal lesson will be and whether there is to be one at all, sometimes quite independently from the lesson apparent in the materials themselves. Usually I watched teachers pursue the tack suggested in the Teacher's Guide, but sometimes they let pupils determine the lesson or used the program content in a way quite different from the intended one. George's transformation of a program whose explicitly stated "teaching point" was on judging the reliability of information sources into an exercise on sequencing (because he needed a "Noise Break") illustrates teacher adaptation to suit teacher purposes.

Sometimes teachers neither made nor acknowledged any lesson at all. I recall viewing *ThinkAbout* on one occasion where the teacher later confessed that she did not prompt a follow-up discussion because she herself was uncertain about the "point" of the program. On another occasion, involving a story about a child from a broken home, a teacher turned the class's attention to other matters immediately after the program and explained privately that she felt the issues raised were "too sensitive" for several of her pupils in similar circumstances. One teacher who regularly used the program (the only "morning user" I found) *never* conducted discussion; the program ended just as recess began, and then her class proceeded to another teacher. Her assessment of *ThinkAbout* fit nicely into her style of using it: "It's so good that it doesn't need further discussion."

During the year when I conducted my observations, an enthusiastic media specialist in our State Department of Education predicted that within the next three years nearly 50 percent of all the fifth and sixth grade teachers in the state would be using *ThinkAbout*. I appreciated such enthusiasm although I'd be reluctant going back now to ask what really happened. But I did telephone George while writing up these reflections to ask what use he had made of *ThinkAbout* in the two years since I last visited his class. He told me he still used *ThinkAbout*—a little. He has never again viewed the programs on live broadcast, but on occasion he has ordered videotapes of certain programs from the county media center. He said he had used four or five tapes each year (he refers to them now as "movies" and requisitions them with his regular film order) and probably will continue to do so. He is selective in his requests, ordering particular programs because of the issues they raise, although he is never certain that he will receive the material on the week he orders it. He continues to rely on the original Teacher's Guide issued in 1979 during *ThinkAbout's* introduction. He wonders if it was ever revised.

CONCLUSION

I hardly expect to receive international acclaim for my brilliant contribution to school ethnography based on research like by study of *ThinkAbout* in George Walker's sixth grade class. The report does not read like an ethnography, although it certainly is the stuff out of which ethnography is made. But it does reflect an ethnographic perspective. I endeavored to describe rather than to judge, and to place what I reported in cultural context. It might have been ethnographically more satisfying to have spent a full year in George's classroom or to have watched *ThinkAbout* develop from inception to premier, but, quite frankly, neither of these options is closely related to my professional interest in cultural acquisition. Further, the *ThinkAbout* research would by then have been long concluded, and there is some question about how many people at AIT would have been interested in all I might have to say. For the purpose at hand, what was asked of us was appropriate and what we provided appeared to be well received.

Perhaps next time there will be opportunity for more time and depth, but even in these modest (though by no means inconsequential) studies it was possible to serve reminder to our client-sponsor that classrooms have contexts and teachers have agendas and that the materials they prepare for classroom settings are interpreted in terms of those contexts and agendas. A narrowly conceived evaluation design or impact study would have revealed too little; a full-blown ethnography would have attempted too much. Under such circumstances—and I would think they will continue to be the prevailing (though hopefully not the exclusive) ones—the compromise seems warranted: ethnographers sans ethnography.

NOTES

1. The complete report prepared by the Evaluation Center, copyrighted (1982) and distributed by the Agency for Instructional Television, Box A, Bloomington, Indiana 47402, consists of five volumes and two additional reports, a *Content Analysis* and an

Executive Summary. Volumes II, III, and IV listed below are the case study reports prepared by the outside observers. The full report title is *Research on the Introduction, Use, and Impact of the ThinkAbout Instructional Television Series.* These are the five volumes and locations of their authors:

Volume I: Technical Report. James R. Sanders and Subhash R. Sonnad, Evaluation Center, Western Michigan University.

Volume II: ThinkAbout: Teacher Use and Student Response in Three Classrooms. Marilyn R. Cohn, Graduate Institute of Education, Washington University, St. Louis.

Volume III: Toward a Clear Picture of ThinkAbout: An Account of Classroom Use. Sylvia Hart-Landsberg, Portland, Oregon.

Volume IV: A View of Viewers: Observations on the Response to and Classroom Use of ThinkAbout. Harry F. Wolcott, University of Oregon.

Volume V: Appendices to Technical Report.

2. Abridged from Harry F. Wolcott, "A View of Viewers: Observations on the Response to and Classroom Use of ThinkAbout, a Program Produced by the Agency for Instructional Television," pages 89-117. Copyright 1982 by the Agency for Instructional Television, Bloomington, Indiana. Used by permission.

3. AIT's Director of Research, Saul Rockman, notes that AIT had previously made use of case studies but had not given them such a prominent role and had not commissioned uninvolved outsiders to conduct them. As he noted lightheartedly in a letter written after the conclusion of our work, he felt he encountered even more objectivity on the part of the outside observers than may have been necessary. He described the three of us as "uncommitted, unfamiliar, and, in fact, completely uninterested in the use of television in the classroom." Nevertheless, he lauded the case-study effort, commended the insights he had gleaned, and lamented the difficulty of getting his associates to read our long final reports. He also noted that, in spite of our being "actively uninterested in seeing how the technology and the curriculum in this project might have a use in the classroom," we nonetheless seemed "too kind" when he wished we had at times been more critical.

4. Elsewhere I have developed a more elaborate typology of the teacher repertoire of behaviors for coping with change (Wolcott, 1977: 195-211). The authors of a more recent study identified five teacher types and assigned them the colloquial labels "omnivores, active consumers, passive consumers, the retrenched, and the withdrawn" (Joyce et al., 1982: 41). More systematic attention to differing styles of teacher adaptations and adoptions and to discerning likely from unlikely adopters seems warranted.

REFERENCES

Burnett, J. H. *Anthropology and education: An annotated bibliographic guide.* New Haven, Conn.: Human Relations Area Files Press, 1974.

Clinton, C. A. The anthropologist as hired hand. *Human Organization*, 1975, *34*(2), 197-204.

Herriott, R. E. Tensions in research design and implementation: The Rural Experimental Schools Study. *American Behavioral Scientist*, 1982, *26*(1), 23-44.

Janesick, V. J. *An ethnographic study of a teacher's classroom perspective: Implications for curriculum.,* East Lansing: Institute for Research on Teaching, Research Series 33, Michigan State University, 1978.

Joyce, B., Bush, R., & McKibbin, M. *Information and opinion from the California Staff Development Study; the January 1982 Report.* Palo Alto, CA: Booksend Laboratories, 1982. (mimeo)

Sanders, J. R. & Sonnad, S. R. *Executive summary: Research on the introduction, use, and impact of the ThinkAbout instructional television series.* Bloomington, IN: Agency for Instructional Television, 1982.

Smith, L. M. *An evolving logic of participant observation, educational ethnography, and other case studies: Review of research in education 6 (1978).* Washington, DC: American Educational Research Association, 1979.

Smith, L. M. Ethnography. In *Encyclopedia of educational research.* New York: Macmillan, 1982.

Spindler, G. D. (Ed.), *Doing the ethnography of schooling.* New York: Holt, Rinehart & Winston, 1982.

Wilcox, K. Ethnography as a methodology and its applications to the study of schooling: A review, In G. D. Spindler (Ed.), *Doing the ethnography of schooling.* New York: Holt, Rinehart & Winston, 1982.

Wolcott, H. F. (Ed.) Ethnography of schooling (special issue). *Human Organization,* 1975, *34*(2).

Wolcott, H. F. *Teachers versus technocrats: An educational innovation in anthropological perspective.* Eugene: Center for Educational Policy and Management, University of Oregon, 1977.

Wolcott, H. F. How to look like an anthropologist without being one. *Practicing Anthropology,* 1980, *3*(1), 6-7, 56-59.

Wolcott, H. F. Mirrors, models and monitors: Educator adaptations of the ethnographic innovation. In G.D. Spindler (Ed.), *Doing the ethnography of schooling.* New York: Holt, Rinehart & Winston, 1982a.

Wolcott, H. F. Differing styles of on-site research, or, "If it isn't ethnography, what is it?" *Review Journal of Philosophy and Social Science,* 1982, *7*(1,2): 154-169. (b)

10

Guilty Knowledge, Dirty Hands, and Other Ethical Dilemmas

The Hazards of Contract Research

DAVID M. FETTERMAN

Fieldworkers encounter many personal and professional hazards in contract research. A few of the situations which can prove hazardous include entrance into the field,[1] role conflicts, fieldwork in the inner city, ethnographic reports, and the dissemination of findings. Job stress and burnout pose additional problems. Urban fieldwork, in particular, forces an ethnographer to confront the realities of guilty knowledge (Polsky, 1967), or confidential knowledge of illegal activities; and dirty hands (Klockars, 1979), a situation from which one cannot emerge innocent of wrong doing (Klockars, 1979:271). As Klockars puts it,

> I personally have little use for the kind of moral study which seeks to understand how angels should behave in paradise and do not intend this analysis to be a contribution to that literature [1979:265].

Implicit in this discussion is that good fieldworkers are both "competent at their vocations and decent as human beings" (Klockars, 1979: 265). Moreover, as a colleague has expressed, a fieldworker can only "act morally and responsibly if one knows the situation and understands the actors". Ethical dilemmas generated in the day-to-day

AUTHOR'S NOTE: I am indebted to Michael H. Agar, Carl B. Klockars, and Ned Polsky for producing works that have greatly influenced my thoughts and actions in moral decision making in the field. I am also indebted to G.D. Spindler, G.K. Tallmadge, and D.S. Waxman for their assistance in the preparation of this chapter. The National Institute of Education, the State of California's Office of Planning and Educational Research, and Stanford University have provided generous support for the research projects referred to in this discussion. Appreciation is also extended to Corina and her two girls for their contribution to my fieldwork. The views expressed in this chapter are my own and do not necessarily reflect the policy of any given agency or institution.

interactions between sponsor, researcher, and informant warrant closer examination.

> When only outstanding and scandalous cases are defined as matters for ethical concern, then the daily perplexities, interactions, and decisions occurring in the field may well be perceived as merely 'personal.' Ethics then becomes an academic subject, consisting primarily of abstract concepts counterposed by shocking violations [Cassell, 1980: 42].

A review of these issues serves to guide researchers in this growing field. Moreover, it is hoped that this discussion will be reflexive, encouraging fieldworkers in various fields to reevaluate their own roles in the pursuit of research.

CONTEXT

The hazards discussed in this review were based on my experience as an ethnographer in a bay-area contract research corporation for the last four and a half years. This corporation is typical of many modern research corporations in that it is part of a corporate conglomerate of unrelated industries. The mechanics of daily routine are typical of most research corporations. The personnel in a research company respond to governmental requests for proposals, gather the appropriate expertise, and write proposals to compete with other firms for the same research contracts. (See Fetterman, 1982b, for a detailed description of research corporation life.)

Ethnographers are hired by research companies to provide a qualitative insight into proposed research and to fulfill research specifications required by the sponsor. Typically, ethnographers are hired to conduct fieldwork for a portion of the study. Participant-observation may range from five years to 100 hours on site—depending on the nature and priority of the task, and on the funding. (See Fetterman, 1982a, regarding the current role of ethnography in educational contract research.)

The ethical dilemmas explored in this discussion were based primarily on my experiences as a contract ethnographer in four separate evaluation studies: a study of alternative high school programs for dropouts, a study of gifted and talented education, a migrant education study, and an arts education contract.

ENTRANCE INTO THE FIELD

Entering the field of educational evaluation as an evaluator represents one of the first problems encountered by the ethnographer. The experience is similar to the hazards of entering the field in a foreign culture. The ethnographer must establish him- or herself in an unknown and potentially hostile environment. In contract research it is not uncommon for the ethnographer to participate in a series of harrowing interviews paralleling Clinton's description (1975). The next step in this initiation is the corporation's rites of passage. This can range from frustrating methodological discussions to a routine exchange of ritual insults regarding the difference in fields. The last stage, much like a conventional employment experience involves "proving oneself" in this precarious role as a competent researcher and employee by performing such functions as gathering reliable and valid data, working under pressure, and constructively working with colleagues.[2] This process is evidenced in a portion of an ethnographer's recommendation. According to the director,

> Stanley [pseudonym] was hired by ABC research corporation to work as an ethnographer . . . He entered a somewhat hostile environment in that most other members of the staff had rather strong quantitative biases and were suspicious of qualitative approaches. Despite this inauspicious set of circumstances, he quickly established himself as a valued member not only of the project team, but of the entire office. He became well liked on a personal basis and well respected as a professional [President, ABC Research Corporation, 1982].

Anthropologists must determine from the onset if their values and temperament are suited to weathering these preliminary challenges. The consequences of being ill prepared or personally unsuited for such a role can be devastating to the profession as well as for the individual.

These trivial but personally draining difficulties are overshadowed by the problems resulting from conflicting expectations with sponsors. Sponsors have become increasingly aware of the strengths and weaknesses of ethnography in evaluation. Many sponsors, however, have been lured by ethnography's reputation for "finding out what's going on" without understanding what it is or more to the point what it is not. For example, a request for proposal may specify the use of ethnography, the proposal may specify the use of ethnographic techniques, and upon award of the contract the project officer may expect a priori closed questionnaire-type interview protocols with statistical correlations. These expectations may represent useful approaches in other studies, however, these expectations do not meet the realities of ethnographic research. A sponsor's acceptance of a proposal is a binding contract and it marks the formal entrance of the fieldworker into evaluation. Ethnographers entering such an agreement must recognize that the two parties may have differing sets of responsibilities and expectations. It is both the ethnographer's and the sponsor's responsibility to resolve these conflicts in an manner that serves each parties pragmatic interests without compromising the methodological integrity of the agreement.

ROLE CONFLICTS

A major problem for the anthropologist in the field is being viewed stereotypically as an evaluator (Everhart, 1975; Colfer, 1976). The stereotypic concept of an evaluator as someone looking for problems or deficiencies effectively blocks many communication channels. As the ethnographer is interested in finding out how the system works from the insider's perspective, such barriers to communication must be broken down. The problem was illustrated dramatically during a site visit when personnel would not speak to the site visitors, believing them to be spies. Colfer (1976), Clinton (1976), and Thorne (1980) have reported similar experiences.

The anthropologist-evaluator is faced with more than the methodological dilemma of data collection in the field. The ethnographer must function as an intermediary between informants and sponsors, informants and the research corporation, and between informant and informant. One of the most serious ethical dilemmas that emerge from working in this setting is the development of conflicting roles and interests.

> Even in unusually benign instances the field researcher must be very sensitive in his presentation of self and management of social interactions. In most cases, though, the fieldworker encounters social complexities and problems at every turn, and successful role maintenance demands great presence of mind, flexibility, and luck [Pelto, 1970: 200].

Politics further compounds these role maintenance problems. The ethnographer is required to play many roles in the political context of contract research. These roles confer many responsibilities.

Conducting research in a recent national evaluation illustrated the complexity of these relationships and the diversity of roles required to function in this setting. The ethnographer conducted research in the street, the classroom, students', and community members' homes, public schools, the programs' local and national disseminating organizations, city governments, the research corporation, the governmental managing agency, and the sponsoring agency. Each of these levels have conflicting groups within each strata (e.g., student, teacher, and principal in the school level). Klockars (1977) explains in the following:

> The problem of conflicting role obligations in biomedical experimentation, where researcher-subject and physician patient

dilemmas arise, has been highly troublesome to attempts to develop ethics for biomedical research. However, such problems do not begin to approach the complexity of conflicts and reciprocal obligations and expectations characteristic of anthropological or life history fieldwork [p. 219].

It is difficult to maintain a rapport with rival groups unless one establishes oneself as an independent entity, one who is sensitive to each party's concerns and interested in collecting information from all sides. Taking sides (purposely or inadvertently) early in the research erects barriers to communication with rival groups (see Berreman, 1962). First and foremost, however, the anthropologist's responsibility lies with the informant at the center of the research task—in this case, the student. The anthropologist must respect the informant's rights and maintain an intricate web of obligations, including confidentiality and reciprocity. The anthropologist must maintain perspective within this convoluted structure and remember that the central informant's rights must take priority according to personal and professional ethical codes, if we are to continue to work with informants, as Mead (1969) said, "in an atmosphere of mutual trust and respect." In addition, this position serves to protect future anthropological endeavors.

This juggling act becomes more difficult with the addition of another party. The ethnographer is also responsible to the taxpayer. Supporting the federal or state bureaucracy (a representative of the taxpayer) is often an unpopular position. An "agency relationship with the state" is created when a researcher accepts governmental funds. The state assumes both legal and political liability for the actions of the researcher in this relationship. The researcher that enters into a binding contract, in return, has an obligation (contractual and ethical) to fulfill his or her commitment to the sponsor. This includes following the evaluation design of the study (unless amended or modified), pursuing research and presenting findings with the sponsor's interests guiding the research and being fiscally, administratively, and academically account-able to them. In a Weberian[3] sense, these relationships force one to conclude that "the occupational structure of modern science makes research, ethically speaking, a 'political vocation.'" (Klockars, 1979: 264).

In conventional ethnography, for example, it is not unusual to scratch one's line of inquiry and select another topic and mode of investigation based on informant's information. This usually occurs when the anthropologist is alerted that there is a more pressing or appropriate research concern in the area. In contract research, however, the sponsor and researcher establish the topic and mode of inquiry before entering the field and leave little room for alteration. This is not to say that the study design is cast in stone. Information gathered from field experiences is taken into consideration and may suggest alternative methods are required to answer the study's policy questions. Field information, no matter how compelling, however, is rarely considered sufficient to drop one's topic of investigation—political pressures are the most powerful force in this regard.

This is not a call for blind obedience or an abdication of one's responsibilities to ensure that research is conducted properly regardless of political pressures. Nor is this discussion aimed at absolving the researcher from a commitment to informants and colleagues. This discussion is presented to stress an obligation that receives little attention at best and outright condescension at worst.

FIELDWORK IN THE INNER CITY

Another problem for the anthropologist is urban fieldwork. Fieldwork in the inner city poses many challenges, both morally and physically. Powerlessness, political corruption, racial tensions, violent assault, and vandalism represent the backdrop of fieldwork in the inner city. The pressure of these daily activities alone generates considerable personal stress in an urban fieldworker. This stress can affect one's judgement regarding data collection and ethical decision making. When researchers are confronted with such activities as police corruption, large-scale drug transactions, burglary, and extortion, they are forced to make serious ethical decisions. These decisions can be guided by a cost or risk-benefit approach (Reynolds, 1979: 69-84), a respect for persons' ethic (Mead, 1969), or a simple pragmatic manner. A few cases drawn from my urban fieldwork as well as that of others are presented below. The examples are followed by a brief discussion of one or two of the plethora of ethical issues involved in each case.

GUILTY KNOWLEDGE:
THE FRONT

During the early period of fieldwork it is important to establish rapport with informants. This involves presenting oneself and one's aims in as honest and direct a manner as possible. In addition, it involves time. The ethnographer must spend time with people, participating in their daily activities, working with them, joking with them, and in some cases, participating in illegal activities. Evaluating a school for dropouts requires an intimate knowledge about dropouts and their activities. Often their activities lend themselves to extralegal and, periodically, illegal activities. In this regard, I would concur with Polsky's sobering position:

> If one is effectively to study adult criminals in their natural settings, he must make the moral decision that in some way he will break the law himself. He need not be a "participant" observer and commit the criminal acts under study, yet he has to witness such acts or be taken into confidence about them and not blow the whistle. That is, the investigator has to decide that when necessary he will "obstruct justice" or have "guilty knowledge" or be an accessory "before or after the fact, in the full legal sense of those terms" [1967: 139-140].

The following is a case in point.

I became close friends with one of the students participating in the school under study. When I first met him he divided his life into two worlds—school and the street. The latter dominated his interests and activities. He was proud of his ability to thrive in the street. He had "a reputation" and was respected in his community. One of the most important elements of cultural knowledge in the street is knowing where to "cop dope." Illegal drugs and various other commodities are exchanged in the inner city in places called "fronts." Fronts are stores that sell legitimate goods such as records, health foods, shirts, and so on as fronts for routine illegal drug transactions.

My friend introduced me to this element of street life with a "hands on" approach. He invited me out for a bite to eat after school. We walked down the main street of the inner city for a few blocks until he pointed to a health food store. He said he thought that I would want to eat there since I was from California. We entered the establishment and my friend asked the clerk to give me a Granola bar. I said thanks and I reached for the bar. The patron handed it to me with a smile and a small envelope underneath it. I looked down at a "nickel" bag of marijuana. My first reaction was "how am I going to look and how is ethnography going to look to my company if their ethnographer is busted for drug possession on one of his first site visits." My discomfort was compounded by two policemen walking by viewing the exchange. The policemen saw the transaction, smiled and continued walking. When I asked my friend why they didn't bust us he said, "they don't need the money right now." I asked him to clarify his response and he explained as follows:

> They only bust you if they need the money. They get paid off regular. But if they're hurtin' for money then well, that's another different story. They'll come right in and bust ya, take money out of the cash register and take your dope too. If they're on a run and they gotta show that they

mean business then they'll bust your ass. Otherwise they just look the other way.

My informant's words echoed William Foote Whyte's racketeer in his classic *Street Corner Society* (1943):

The cops are paid off. They call it the "union wage." The patrolman gets five dollars a month for every store on his beat that sells numbers. The plain clothes men get the same, but they can go anywhere in Cornerville [p. 123].

After being initiated by this brief encounter with criminal activities and official corruption, I continued to learn a great deal about the environmental pressures that affect the dropouts' behavior. My conclusions paralleled Whyte's when he reported the following:

Observation of the situation in Cornerville indicates that the primary function of the police department is not the enforcement of the law but the regulation of illegal activities [1943: 138].

Moreover, I was faced with a number of ethical dilemmas involving guilty knowledge (incriminating information made privy to the fieldworker) and dirty hands (a situation from which the fieldworker can not emerge "innocent of wrong doing") which required a series of immediate decisions. First, a researcher must decide whether the research merits involvement in criminal activities. Students of deviant behavior must discriminate among the range of activities involved and decide which specific activities justify their involvement. These preliminary considerations are routinely based on a utilitarian ethic:[4] Do the ends justify the means? For example, the "in the name of science" position would argue that the insights gained during this involvement contributed to knowledge which outweighs the short-term legal and moral transgressions. Soloway and Walters described a fieldwork episode in which one of them was made an unwitting party to the execution of an armed robbery (1977: 171-172). This behavior was considered too cavalier for some colleagues; however, his research was "breaking invaluable ethnographic ground" in the study of heroin addicts. The pursuit of research, however, is not above the law.[5] The researcher must be willing to suffer the consequences of such involvement. Personally, the researcher must balance the potential significance of the research against the severity of the criminal behavior involved. This is a useful guide in moral decision making. Alone, however, this overly rationalistic risk-benefit approach is at best off target when making moral decisions in the field.

A second question that emerges from this experience is, What is the researcher's civic responsibility after observing or inadvertantly being involved in criminal behavior? In this case, three illegal acts were involved: selling illegal drugs, buying illegal drugs, and police corruption. The researcher technically has a conflicting set of responsibilities to the student in this case. This student is a former dropout who has reentered "the system." Condoning his behavior in this case may represent a criminal type of benign neglect (see Yablonsky, 1965). Protecting the student from himself, however, is condescending at best and a breach of confidence at worst. Similarly, although the researcher has an obligation as a citizen to report illegal activities, informing on the drug dealer involved would have constituted a breach of confidence—and posed a considerable threat to one's plans for an extended longevity. Moreover, the researcher must acknowledge that like prohibition, the punishment may not fit the crime—thus a form of nonviolent civil disobedience may be appropriate. Fundamentally, however, the respect for persons position overrides all of these risk-benefit considerations. The respect for persons position is essentially a code which "holds that there are certain means which are deontologically repulsive and in se wrong"[6] (Klockars, 1979: 267). In this case, a breach of confidence would constitute "deontologically repulsive and in se wrong" means.

Finally, the third act—police corruption—is of some significance. The idea of tackling such a problem may appear insurmountable. In addition, like the other acts it is at least outside the scope of the work that must be accomplished in a short period of time. It is important to explore such important variables in the social equation; however, the researcher must maintain some boundaries on the research endeavor if the task is to be completed.

Risk-benefit analysis, respect for persons ethic, and basic pragmatism are all appropriate approaches that must be taken into consideration when making moral decisions during fieldwork. As Klockars has stated, however,

> the good end of the dirty means . . . is not the long-term good of science, nor the potential value of the particular research at hand, and certainly not the worldly benefits continuation of that research may have for the researcher's career. It is the immediate, morally unquestionable, and compelling good end of keeping one's promise to one's subjects. In particular, it is the keeping of that minimal promise which every fieldworker makes explicit or implies to deviant subjects in the process of gaining first-hand access to their deviance [1979: 275-276].

My response to this experience was not to intervene. I recorded the event in detail to provide background material regarding the various inner city pressures operating on the students. I chose this route because it was early in the research endeavor and much more information was needed to understand how the community operated and how my actions would affect all participants. In addition, a more active role would have constituted a breach of confidence—a confidence which in and of itself I was obligated to uphold. In turn, this breach whould have served as a barrier to all future communications. This parallels Pelto's (1970) position that

> any interference by the fieldworker [in this type of situation] would mean that he would have to violate the confidences of his informants, and this would seriously jeopardize his work [p. 222].

A description of police corruption, however, was printed in the report to provide the environmental context. The matter was also discussed with city officials on the researcher's own time. I temporarily separated research from activism. My reactions were based on timing, a trust, a professional responsibility to respect the environmental norms or rules and regulations until the dynamics were understood, and a responsibility to complete my objectives.[7] (See Beattie, 1965; Klochars, 1974; and Wax, 1971, for discussion of similar guilty knowledge experiences.)

DIRTY HANDS:
BURGLARY AND EXTORTION

Urban fieldwork requires both direct and indirect involvement with criminals. Polsky explained that

> in doing field research on criminals you damned well better *not* pretend to be "one of them" because they will test this claim out . . . [moreover,] before you tell a criminal who you are and make it stick, you have to know this yourself, know where you draw the line between you and him [1967: 124-125].

During one of my site visits to these alternative high schools for dropouts my car was burglarized and my clothes and notes stolen. The burglars then attempted to sell me my stolen possessions. In this case the line was easy to draw between the researcher and the criminal because the criminals were neither acquaintances nor participants in the study. They were simply criminals. This episode provided another case for intervention in the field (Gallin, 1959; Gallagher, 1964; Gearing, 1973; Holmberg, 1958; McCurdy, 1976; Spradley, 1976). The potential for producing deleterious results has been documented (Horowitz,

1965; Sahlins, 1967; Berreman, 1969; Holmberg, 1954). However, this instance illustrated how intervention with dirty hands can provide useful data for the research endeavor.

The event began at the end of a long day of interviewing at the school. I had just completed an extra interview to get ahead of my self-imposed timeline for the week and was satisfied with the week's work. I said goodbye to everyone for the day and walked down the block to my car. The window was broken, the battery removed, my suitcase and my briefcase stolen. My briefcase contained my notes and slides of my work for the two preceding weeks on site, as well as a completed paper to be presented at a professional meeting and a paper in progress.

I was stunned. Neighbors in the community who knew me came out of their houses to see the damage. One woman said her daughter had seen the burglars: two young men who had "been terrorizing the neighborhood for months." I asked for their names and Corina (pseudonym) declined to respond, explaining her situation:

> My kids, they go to that school. They would be put in danger. I try to run a good Christian home but I'm afraid of the revenge for my girls. They could get hurt by the other kids. You know.

I explained that I understood. I called for assistance from the neighborhood grocery store. No cab would come to the area so I had to wait for the tow truck to pick up the car and take me out of this part of the city. I stayed with the car to protect it from the car parts "vultures" until dark. Corina invited me into her house at dusk explaining, "It gets bad at night, especially since you're white and all. You'd be safer in here with us till the man comes." I immediately accepted her invitation and we talked about the community for a few hours. She explained how these "thugs" had held a gun to her friend's head and stolen her stereo:

> They had the gall to do that and tell her when she got another one they'd be back for that one. A year later, sure enough. She moved about a block away and they came back and stuck a gun to her head again and said it wouldn't be the last time.

Corina also told me about arson-for-hire in the neighborhood. She told me about the time she

> woke up to a phone call at two in the morning. The man over the phone said to be out of the house in 15 minutes because it was going to burn. That's what they do when it's arson, they call you just like that at two in the morning. I had my rollers on and I was in my bathrobe, that's all I had. I was on the second floor and my grandma she was on the third. I can still remember seein' the flames all around her in her wheelchair. I

tried to get her out but I couldn't. I had rheumatic fever, you know, so I'm weak. She was so heavy I just couldn't. I got my babies out but she was so heavy. I just watched her die. I still go to the county [psychiatrist] even now. I dream about it. It still frightens me. I couldn't save her.

Her moving story was cut short by the arrival of the tow truck. The burglary experience had already provided an opportunity to learn more about the community and develop a rapport with another member of the community. I met with Corina the next day to continue our talk about life in the inner city. She said she would be willing to serve as a mediator between the young men (burglars) and myself. She knew their mother from the PTA and agreed to meet with her to "rescue" my papers. Corina and her husband frequented one of the burglar's homes in an attempt to come to an agreement regarding my materials. During negotiations, however, one of the little girls in the burglar's home opened a curtain dividing the rooms and Corina's husband saw his color television set—stolen from them six months ago. They forgot about my problem and "blew up" at the mother for condoning this behavior. Needless to say neither their television or my materials were recovered. That evening, however, Corina volunteered to serve as a witness if I wanted to go to the police. I thanked her and told her I would have to ask a few other people in the community before contacting the police. I had been in the community off and on for over a year and a half, and feared police reprisals if the police were asked to become involved. I discussed the matter with neighbors, community action groups, members of clergy, and city officials directly associated with the community before taking any action. They unanimously agreed that "something must be done to stop these punks from having the run of the community." They suggested that I involve the police and I agreed. I contacted the police and their first response was "forget it . . . it will just end with a bullet anyway." I later learned that burglary was a low priority in an area where murder, rape, and arson were the norm. Later they said that if I felt it was necessary, I should pursue it myself.

One of the burglars then contacted Corina and told her he was willing "to negotiate" with me. I was told to wait in the school at night until he called. I observed much about night life in the inner city while I waited for his call. A crowd of young men drinking and smoking gathered outside the school, growing and dwindling in size and volume all night long. I had to check on my locked (replacement) car every 15 minutes to prevent it from being stripped to the frame. A well-dressed young man in a new Cadillac, however, did not have the same concerns.

He parked his car in the middle of the street with the motor running and the radio playing loudly, while he disappeared into the darkness of the school playground with a small box under his arm. He came back empty-handed 15 minutes later and drove away. No one had touched his car. Later I learned that he was known by everyone in the community and "no one crosses the man." I was introduced to him later in the study and learned that he ran the "underworld" portion of the community. This experience provided numerous insights into the students/dropouts in the community. The burglar finally called that night and offered to sell me my materials at 15 dollars per folder (20 folders). I agreed on a trial basis—one folder at a time. Corina served as "go between." The venture failed. The burglar took the money and kept the folder. We set up another series of phone negotiations to recover the goods, also unsuccessful. I eventually called them and told them I knew who they were and where they lived and if the materials were not returned in an hour I would call the police.

I waited for two hours—no response. I called the police and explained that I had decided to prosecute. They said they would not go in at night and would pursue the matter in the morning. Briefly, I had to orchestrate the entire event: secure the deposition from the witness, find the exact location of the burglars, and bring the police to the location. The burglars were arrested and prosecuted with the "blessing of the community." During the booking proceedings, when the police officers left the room for a minute, one of the burglars leaned over and whispered to me, "we've heard about what you're doin' and we know that you're tryin' to help the brother so we'll try to get the book stuff back to you after this is all over."

They later explained that they wanted to get busted:

> We're hot now, ya see. So if we just chill out for a month or two somebody else is in the spotlight, ya see. And then we can go along with our business with no more trouble. There's just a little too much heat on us right now, don't ya know.

I am still negotiating with them. I do not, however, anticipate recovering the goods.

This experience demonstrates that intervention can yield positive results and suggests what steps are required before such behavior is appropriate. "The dilemma of the fieldworker . . . is not *whether* to interfere in the local cultural scene, but *how much* to interfere" (Pelto, 1970: 223). This experience required intensive involvement. I had been in the field long enough to know the members of the community in depth. In addition, I understood most of the repercussions resulting from police involvement in community affairs. Moreover, I consulted with various members of the community (e.g., neighbors, clergy, city officials, etc.) before making a decision to intervene. I also took a series of time consuming and potentially hazardous steps toward resolving the matter by negotiating directly with the burglars. My final decision was my own; however it was influenced by these sources of information and approval in the community.

The decision to have the burglars arrested was required after discussing the matter with (and receiving the "go ahead" from) various community leaders—to fulfill my citizen-obligation as a special guest-member of the community. It may appear odd to sound apologetic for having burglars arrested; however, had the "hard core"[8] burglars been the focus of my study (with explicit or implicit trust established) these same actions would have been inappropriate, if not immoral. Pragmatically, I wanted my notes and slides back and I had taken all of the conceivable steps required short of this final decision. The risk-benefit approach was inconsequential at this point given that the portion of the community involved in the study had decided to risk any retaliation for the "greater good of the community." The respect for persons ethic was inappropriate to apply to the burglars given that no bond of trust had been established with them. The respect for persons ethic was applicable, however, to the traditional segment of the community given that a strong bond had been created with religious and social leaders, teachers, students, and various families in the community. The decision appeared logical and appropriate; however, there are "no hard and fast rules to be laid down [for these types of moral dilemmas in fieldwork]; these are matters of conscience rather than of science" (Beattie, 1965: 55).

At a recent professional meeting, I was asked whether I thought there was an ethical problem regarding the use of my uncensored fieldnotes by outsiders in this case. I explained as follows:

> If you had asked me what I thought if I had delivered uncoded, uncensored fieldnotes to the federal government I would agree there would have been a problem of breach of trust or confidence. However, the case of fieldnotes being stolen during fieldwork from a locked car is another matter. Given the fact that the notes were stolen, not deliberately disseminated, the fact that the burglars had no use for the materials (except extortion) and the lengths I went to retrieve the notes, I do not feel that an ethical dilemma exists regarding this facet of the incident.

The experience of being burglarized and extorted provided me with an insight into the turbulence that most of the neighbors experience daily. Moreover, deciding to take an activist role extended my understanding of the community simply by expanding my contact with the community. Intervention in this case provided a number of extremely important data bases which were tapped throughout the study. The staff and students in the school were upset about the experience and generously offered their assistance. A number of students with street contacts helped me to identify the location of the burglars. The positive reaction of the staff and students in the school to this dilemma served to strengthen rapport. The cost of these insights, however, was extremely high. The cost is human suffering, which "is the lowest price that decent human beings must be willing to pay in order that they stay competent at the vocations of policework and fieldwork" (Klockars, 1979: 277).

THE ETHNOGRAPHIC REPORT

Fieldwork conducted in highly political settings can be more dangerous than fieldwork in the streets of the inner city (Diamond, 1964; Peattie, 1968). One of the most common mediums for interaction in the political realm is the report. An ethnographic report rich in detail is potentially as dangerous as it may be helpful—depending upon how the material is presented and who uses the information. Tobin's Ph.D. dissertation, for example, "The Resettlement of the Enewetak People: A Study of a Displaced Community in the Marshall Islands" (1976), represents a classic case of misused information. Tobin's study was used by the Air Force as a resource document for preparing a misleading environmental impact statement regarding the Pacific Cratering Experiments (PACE) project. This area was the site of numerous nuclear tests. The PACE project planned to use this area for further high explosive testing and used parts of Tobin's work to support their position. Tobin responded with the following:

> I did not give you permission to do this and it is protected by copyright as clearly indicated in the early part of my dissertation. Parts of this work that would have helped the people of Eniwetok against the PACE program were not quoted in the draft environmental statement.

> I am biased against the PACE program as I have told Mr. _____ (the director of PACE) as I feel it is against the best interests of the Eniwetok people and it is against their expressed wishes [Department of the Air Force, 1973: 56].

The ethnographer's moral obligation, in this example, required a written response to protect the interests of the people of Enewetak and the use of his own publication.

Serious ethical dilemmas emerge, however, when one's role makes one privy to confidential information that requires exposure. Ibsen's *An Enemy of the People* (1959), Solzhenitsyn's *For the Good of the Cause* (1972), and Daniel Ellsberg's *Papers on the War* (Pentagon papers; 1972) dramatically illustrate this type of double bind. In one of my studies, this type of double bind was confronted on every level. A few of those encountered in the street have already been discussed. The school setting provided numerous cases. For example, substituting for a sick teacher presented no serious difficulty; however, substituting for a frequently tardy or alcoholic teacher presented a number of difficulties. Should the researcher condone such behavior and administrative laxness by substituting for the teacher and not reporting the incident in his or her report? Or, should the researcher simply look at the practical side—the students need a teacher for that period. From a research perspective, serving as a teacher-researcher provides an invaluable insight into the program. Moreover, the problem of managerial laxness can be demonstrated in other manners. In this case, a risk-benefit approach was extremely useful in moral decision making. The risks of reporting the incident for the individual teacher's reputation and the program's survival outweighed the benefits, given that the matter could be resolved with less drastic measures (informally bringing the problem to the attention of the school administrator). The matter would have required publication if administration had not resolved the problem immediately, because the risk to the student population (of dropping out again) and to the staff (lowering morale) would have been greater than the benefits of protecting one teacher and administrator's positions. Discretion, in any case, must be exercised in the case of reporting observed indiscretions. For example, reporting a rare occurrence such as a fight or an affair between a student and a staff member on school grounds can unfairly distort a picture of program operations. Moreover, the consequences of reporting such behavior "may not match the crime"—for example, the entire program could be closed down for such activities. (See Deloria, 1980, for discussion of larger social context of research and role of researcher.)

Another problem that must be confronted is the power of numerous vested interests. The pressures of various vested interest groups often impinge on the ethnographer's ability to produce a fair and balanced report of study findings. For example, in the study discussed above the staff wanted me to record and document the implementation difficulties in the report as a means of solving their programmatic problems. The disseminators, however, took a different position. They commented on a draft of one of the reports that the ethnographic study was "a scholarly approach," however, they were concerned with the presentation of the findings.

> Certainly, [the disseminating agency] has gleaned a great deal of knowledge during the demonstration which we are applying to future replication approaches. [The research corporation] has been very helpful in this regard. However, we are down to the wire in terms of the presentation of the final results to society at large. Certainly, [the disseminating agency] has a vested interest in the [program] being presented in the final reports in the best possible light. I am sure that others such as _____ , _____ [federal agencies], and [the research corporation] feel the same . . . [Program] expansion in the future faces an uncertain future in this age of shrinking financial resources and competitive and political realities, etc. We need to present the most accurate, fair, and balanced picture of the replication which, hopefully, proves that [the program] merits continuation and expansion. I trust that you will consider the same.

Their message was clear. I was sympathetic to the political realities; however, I was obligated to include some negative findings to present the most accurate picture of program operations. For example, along with numerous positive findings I included serious implementation problems such as high staff-turnover rates and managerial incompetence and/or lack of appropriate qualifications. These problems had a serious impact on program operations. The negative impact of the federal government and the evaluators was also discussed to provide a picture of the extrinsic forces that negatively affected the program and resulted in unfavorable site descriptions (Fetterman, 1981a, 1981c). This was an example of "studying up" in the stratification system (Nader, 1969). Ignoring these problems would have done little for knowledge development in the area of implementation and distorted the readers' view of program operations. This would have represented an abdication of my responsibility to the staff, taxpayers, and my colleagues. A basic misconception that was dispelled in this regard is that ethnographers are always coopted by their informants and always present the most positive side (their key informant's side). The duty of the ethnographer, like any scientist, is fundamentally to accurately record and report his or her observations and interpretations. In this case the observations were primarily positive, but the findings were not exclusively placed in a positive light.

DISSEMINATION OF FINDINGS

The dissemination of the draft report was also problematic. The code of ethics explains that the findings of research must be shared with clients and sponsors. This guide, however, does not prepare the researcher for dealing with many levels of administration and protocol. In the study under discussion, there was a rivalry between the parent organization disseminating the alternative high school program and some of the local affiliates directly responsible for managing the programs. The parent organization was the central conduit for draft reports. The evaluators were informed, however, that one site would not receive the draft for comments because they had new management and staff and would be demoralized by the descriptions of past strife. In addition, the new program would not have the background required to critique the work. The evaluators were also informed that another site would not receive the report, according to the parent organization, because they misused it the last time; they revealed portions of the confidential draft report to various sources out of context. In the first case, it was true that the report referred to the old staff and would not have been productive reading for the new staff. In the second case, the evaluators would have fed the fire of this rivalry if it were to circumvent the system of protocol by sending the drafts to the sites directly; however, they would not be fulfilling their obligation if they allowed the parent organization to control the distribution of the report.

A compromise was made. All the copies were sent to the parent organization to follow protocol and avoid charges of favoritism. A provision was made, however, that site comments would be requested directly by the evaluators by the end of the month. Any report lost in the mail would then be sent directly to the site by the evaluators. This placed a check on the distribution of the drafts without compromising the evaluator's role or neglecting the significance of protocol.

The presentation of findings to the public is a political activity. The manner in which research findings are presented influences how the information will be used or abused. The researcher who plays the role of politician while conducting and presenting findings, however, is likely to be used as a pawn by various vested interests. The dissemination of findings after the research has been conducted is a separate matter. The evaluators disseminated the generally positive findings to appropriate individuals in government and quasi-governmental institutions. Future funding for the program was dependent on the dissemination of the evaluation findings and the recommendations of various agencies. In addition, the evaluators prepared a Joint Dissemination Review Panel

Submission that was substantially based on the ethnographic findings to improve the program's credibility and potential to secure future funding. (This was accomplished in the face of significant resistance because it was politically hazardous to favor social programs during this period.) These actions were in accord with Mills' position:

> There is no necessity for working social scientists to allow the potential meaning of their work to be shaped by the "accidents" of its setting, or its use to be determined by the purposes of other men. It is quite within their powers to discuss its meanings and decide upon its uses as matters of their own policy [1959: 177].

The evaluators agreed that they had a moral responsibility to serve as an advocate for the program based on the research findings. James has stated it this way:

> Advocacy on behalf of social change is the final step in the use of ethnography. It is also the only reasonable justification for probing the life-styles of these human beings [1977: 198].

There is a difference between being an academic and an activist; however, academic study does not preclude advocacy. In fact, often anything less represents an abdication of one's responsibility as a social scientist. (See Berreman, 1968; and Gough, 1968.) It should be acknowledged, however, that the researcher functions as a public relations person or politician in this arena rather than as a researcher.

JOB STRESS AND BURNOUT

Finally, the ethnographic evaluator faces one of the most common but least discussed hazards in the profession—job stress and burnout. The job-related stress that an ethnographic evaluator or fieldworker experiences has been discussed throughout this review. Job burnout involves the complete loss of interest or motivation in pursuing the individual employment tasks required to satisfactorily function in one's role. This is often the result of prolonged exposure to the pressures of the job. This can severely cripple the most able researcher. Judgment, determination, and stamina (all critical qualities for a fieldworker) are all affected by job stress and burnout. Fieldwork in contract ethnography must be conducted at an accelerated pace in a much shorter period of time than traditional fieldwork. This is both physically and mentally demanding. Continuous immersion in the personal and professional problems of informants can be emotionally draining as well. Stories of arson for hire, a mother stabbing her daughter's boyfriend, an administrator harassing a staff member, graft, and racism are part of the everyday lives of many informants; however, this continual immersion into hundreds of individual lives can take its toll on the ethnographer. Wax (1971) provided a detailed picture in this regard of "shooting, beating, and murder" and the resultant turmoil she experienced in a Japanese-American relocation center. Kobben reported of his Surinam fieldwork that

> since an ethnographer studies people and not insects, his fieldwork also causes emotions in himself. Personally, I lived under great psychological stress and felt little of the proverbial peacefulness of "country life." Few books touch on the subject, but I know that the same is true of quite a number of other fieldworkers. Perhaps it is even a *sine qua non* for fieldwork [1967: 46].

The theory, research, and intervention practices related to job stress and burnout in human services occupations are discussed in detail in Cherniss (1980) and Paine (1982).

This experience is compounded by the father confessor or mea culpa compression effect. Contract research requires in-depth immersion in a site for short periods of time at regular intervals throughout the year. Informants realize the ethnographer will only be on site for a week or two and rush to communicate pressing problems. The nature of the visits structures the informant's response. An effort must be made to take this phenomenon into consideration—to balance one's perspective of the site's operations. Once a rapport is established with a few key informants and the ethnographer learns who must be listened to with a grain of salt this problem can be ameliorated.

The fieldwork experience is made more stressful by a demanding travel schedule. One to two week site visits throughout the country can keep a researcher away from home for over a month at a time. Life on the road has all the hazards faced by old-time salesmen: road food, empty motels, and the routine separation from your family—in this case every three months. Allan Holmberg (1969) provided vivid illustrations of the physically draining side of fieldwork. (Also see Wax, 1960: 175.) A few survival tips learned in the field to cope with this type of stress include maintaining regular contacts with the family, spending time with friends in the field in relaxing or entertaining settings, or meeting relatives or colleagues during weekends or "break periods" while on the road. Also, attending professional meetings during these free periods serves to recharge oneself while in the field. Pelto emphasizes the value of brief vacations during the fieldwork experience:

> A number of fieldworkers have noted that brief vacations away from the research community can be excellent tension relievers—for both

informants and researchers. After all, at least in small communities the ubiquitous presence of "the man with the notebook and a thousand questions" can be very taxing for the local inhabitants. They must surely wish that for once they could enact a small bit of local custom without having to explain it all to the anthropologist. A few days away—or even longer—in the city, at the beach, hiking in the mountains, or visiting a nearby game reservation—can give the fieldworker time to dissipate his anxieties and hostilities, get some needed physical rest, and perhaps restock his supplies. At the same time, the research community itself gets a rest. Often the return of the fieldworker after even a brief vacation is an occasion for a warm welcome, a reaffirmation of friendships. He may be treated like a returning relative, and a few slightly reluctant informants may have been opened up a bit in their willingness to give information [1970: 225].

One of the few redeeming virtues of this work life-style, aside from meeting new people, is that it enables you to step back from the field experience to gain perspective and then back in to test one's hypotheses throughout the year. This is an advantage over traditional fieldwork where it is much easier to go native or lose touch with the primary research task at hand.

CONCLUSION

Moral decision making is a tortuous process since each event is a convoluted and almost endless labyrinth of considerations and commitments. A simple shift in perspective or an unexpected twist of fate can alter one's entire set of responsibilities and obligations. Guilty knowledge and dirty hands are at the heart of the urban fieldwork experience. Recognition of this fact is essential if a fieldworker is to function effectively and morally. Awareness of the context of research can prevent paralysis as well as overzealousness in the field.

Ethical decisions in fieldwork must continuously be discussed and reviewed. This is not to suggest that we must institute sanctions against ethical wrong doing, for

> the cost of emphasizing punishment as a means of regulation and control of occupational deviance is that it suppresses the kind of candid moral discourse which is necessary to make genuine moral maturity possible [Klockars, 1979:279].

Fieldworkers will continue to encounter numerous personal and professional hazards in contract research. They may range from fieldwork conducted in an accelerated fashion to reporting in a highly political atmosphere. Many of these pressures affect one's judgment while in the field—whether in the streets of the inner city or in plush conference rooms with governmental officials in Washington, D.C. Ethnographers can adapt to most of these environmental pressures if they are aware of them.

> There have been few times in the past century when it has been so important for fieldworkers to involve themselves in processes of ethical decision making. As we do so, we are well advised to temper our instincts for self-preservation and self-determination with a realistic sense of the full range of contexts which impinge on contemporary research activities. Two seemingly opposite images come to mind. The first is an image of a world breathing down our necks, and the second is an image of a world ignoring us entirely [Chambers, 1980: 341]

Participation in the art of moral decision making may not prevent the world from "breathing down our necks" or from "ignoring us," but it will ensure that we do not forget our own multiple sets of responsibilities.

> To improve the level of fieldwork practice, investigators must examine the moral dilemmas particular to this type of research, discover the appropriate ethical principles, and learn how best to apply them. If it is not done, regulation will become an elaborate and expensive charade, useful only in assuaging the sensibilities of legislators, who can convince themselves that they did their best to legislate morality without ever having bothered to examine just what moral standards are appropriate to a particular scientific method [Cassell, 1980: 38].

This exploration into the hazards and ethical dilemmas that arise from urban fieldwork and contract research has attempted to examine the appropriateness of certain moral standards to the ethnographic method. It is hoped that this probing will be reflexive, stimulating other fieldworkers in anthropology and in other disciplines to examine themselves in their pursuit of knowledge.

NOTES

1. For further details regarding the role of the ethnographer in educational evaluation, see Britan (1977, 1978); Burns (1975, 1978); Clinton (1975, 1976); Colfer (1976); Coward (1976); Everhart (1975); Fetterman (1980, 1981a, 1981b, 1981c); Firestone (1975); Fitzsimmons (1975); Hall (1978); Hord (1978); Mulhauser (1975); and Wolcott (1980).

2. It should be emphasized that this involves working with colleagues from different disciplines and potentially conflicting paradigms in a multidisciplinary effort.

3. Weber's "Politics as a Vocation" is a study of the moral hazards of a political career. It emphasizes the use of morally dubious means in the attainment of "good ends." The parallel between the context of contemporary research and the political environment that Weber discussed highlights this moral hazard for contract research (Weber, 1946).

4. Weber's term was an "ethic of responsibility" (1946: 120).

5. In the Soloway and Walters case no law was broken, according to the Pennsylvania penal code (see Soloway and Walters, 1977: 172-174). The moral issue remains and in other states the legal status of the event might differ significantly. It is inappropriate, however, to second guess the legitimacy of a fieldworkers actions in hindsight. There are a multitude of factors influencing behavior in the field at any given moment. Moreover, serendipity more closely characterizes even the most diligent efforts at structuring ethnography. Soloway and Walter's case indirectly emphasize the unpredictability of fieldwork.

6. The respect for persons ethic is usually applied to situations in which a researcher is contemplating deceit in order to secure information from a subject. The respect for persons ethic can also be applied to situations in which the researcher considers breaching a trust. These two examples demonstrate the role of "different levels of analysis" in ethical decision making.

7. This experience differs from what Wax describes as "when the fieldworker's overblown sense of his ability to offend or injure his hosts may so paralize him that he cannot carry on his work" (1971: 274). This type of problem can occur at the early stages of fieldwork when the ethnographer is overly sensitive to informants (1971). Pauline Kael's solution, as noted in Wax (1971) is useful in this regard, "a mistake in judgment is not necessarily fatal, but that too much anxiety about judgment is." Nevertheless, although there are similarities of inaction the problem Wax describes is more of a methodological problem related to the early stages of fieldwork, while the problem discussed in this review is an ethical problem related to the respect for persons ethic in the process of conducting fieldwork.

8. In the study under discussion, most of the students involved in crime were involved in dope dealing, pimping, and petty theft—few were involved in "hard core" burglary. The "hard core" group was known in the community to have its own rules, sanctions, and social structure. This experience signalled to the "hard core" group what my role and position was regarding the burglary group in the community. The experience also provided an insight into who the program could and could not serve in the inner city.

REFERENCES

Beattie, J. *Understanding and African Kingdom: Banyoro.* New York: Holt, Rinehart & Winston, 1965.

Becker, H. S. Whose side are we on? *Social Problems,* 1976, *14*(3), 239-247.

Berreman, C. *Behind many masks.* Ithaca, NY: Society for Applied Anthropology, Monograph 4, 1962.

Berreman, C. Is anthropology alive? Social responsibility in social anthropology. *Current Anthropology,* 1968, 19, 391-396.

Berreman, G. Academic colonialism: Not so innocent abroad. *The Nation,* November 10, 1969.

Britan, G. M. *Public policy and innovation: An ethnographic evaluation of the experimental technology incentives program.* Washington, DC: National Academy of Sciences, 1977.

Britan, G. M. The place of anthropology in program evaluation. *Anthropological Quarterly,* 1978, *51*(2), 119-128.

Burns, A. An anthropologist at work. *Anthropology and Education Quarterly,* 1975, *6*(4), 28-34.

Burns, A. On the ethnographic process in anthropology and education. *Anthropology and Education Quarterly*, 1978, *9*(4), 18-34.

Cassell, J. Ethical principles for conducting fieldwork. *American Anthropologist*, 1980, *82*(1), 28-41.

Chambers, E. Fieldwork and the law: New contexts for ethical decision making. *Social Problems*, 1980, *27*(3), 330-341.

Cherniss, C. *Staff burnout: Job stress in the human services.* Beverly Hills: Sage Publications, 1980.

Clinton, C. A. The anthropologist as hired hand. *Human Organization*, 1975, *34*197-204.

Clinton, C. A. On bargaining with the devil: Contract ethnography and accountability in fieldwork. *Anthropology and Education Quarterly*, 1976, *8*, 25-29.

Colfer, C. J. Rights, responsibilities, and reports: An ethical dilemma in contract research. In M. A. Rynkiewich & J. P. Spradley (Eds.), *Ethics and anthropology.* New York: John Wiley, 1976.

Coward, R. The involvement of anthropologists in contract evaluations: The federal perspective. *Anthropology and Education Quarterly*, 1976, *7*, 12-16.

Deloria, V. Our new research society: Some warnings to social scientists. *Social Problems*, 1980, *27*(3), 265-271.

Department of the Air Force. Transcript of testimony. Environmental hearings "Project PACE." Office of the Judge Advocate Pacific Air Forces, Honolulu. Cited in Kiste, R., The people of Enewetak Atoll vs. the U.S. Department of Defense. In M. Rynkiewich & J. Spradley (Eds.), *Ethics and anthropology.* New York: John Wiley, 1976.

Diamond, S. Nigerian discovery: The politics of fieldwork. In Vidick, Bensman, & Stern (Eds.), *Reflections on community studies.* New York: John Wiley, 1964.

Ellsberg, D. *Papers on the war* (Pentagon papers). New York: Simon and Schuster, 1972.

Everhart, R. B. Problems of doing fieldwork in educational evaluation. *Human Organization*, 1975, *34*(3), 183-196.

Fetterman, D. M. Blaming the victim: The problem of evaluation design, federal involvement, and reinforcing world views in education. *Human Organization*, 1981, *40*, 67-77.

Fetterman, D. M. Ethnographic techniques in educational evaluation: An illustration. *Journal of Thought*, December 1980, pp.31-48.

Fetterman, D.M. Ethnography in Educational Research: The Dynamics of Diffusion. *Educational Researcher*, March 1982, pp. 17-29. (a)

Fetterman, D.M. Ibsen's Baths: Reactivity and Insensitivity (A Misapplication of the treatment-control design in a national evaluation). *Educational Evaluation and Policy Analysis*, 1982, *4*(3), 261-279. (b)

Fetterman, D. M. New perils for the contract ethnographer. *Anthropology and Education Quarterly*, March 1981, pp. 71-83. (a)

Fetterman, D. M. *Study of the Career Intern Program. Final Report—Task C: Program dynamics: Structure, function, and interrelationships.* Mountain View, Calif.: RMC Research Corporation, 1981. (b)

Firestone, W. A. Educational field research in a "contract shop." *American Educational Research Association, Division Generator*, 1975, *5*(3), 3-11.

Fitzsimmons, S. J. The anthropologist in a strange land. *Human Organization*, 1975, *34*(2), 183-196.

Gallagher, A., Jr. The role of the advocate and directed change. In W. C. Meierhenry (Ed.), *Media and educational innovations.* Lincoln: University of Nebraska Press, 1964.

Gallin, B. A case for intervention in the field. *Human Organization,* 1959, *18*(3), 140-144.

Gearing, F. The strategy of the Fox Project. In *To see ourselves: Anthropology and modern social issues.* Glenview, Ill.: Scott, Foresman, 1973.

Gough, K. World revolution and the science of man. In T. Roszak (Ed.), *The dissenting academy.* New York: Random House, 1968.

Gouldner, A.W. The sociologist as partisan: Sociology and the welfare state. *American Sociologist,* 1968, *3*(1), 103-116.

Hall, G. *Ethnographers and ethnographic data, an iceberg of the first order for the research manager.* Austin, TX: Research and Development Center for Teacher Education, University of Texas, 1978.

Holmberg, A. Adventures in culture change. In R. F. Spencer (Ed.), *Method and perspective in anthropology.* Minneapolis: University of Minnesota Press, 1954.

Holmberg, A. The research and development approach to the study of change. *Human Organization,* 1958, *17*(1), 12-16.

Holmberg, A. *Nomads of the long bow: The survivors of eastern Bolivia.* Garden City, NY: Doubleday, 1969.

Hord, S. *Under the eye of the ethnographer: Reactions and perceptions of the observed.* Austin, TX: Research and Development Center for Teacher Education, University of Texas, 1978.

Horowitz, J. The life and death of Project Camelot. *Trans-action,* December 1965.

Ibsen, H. An enemy of the people. In *Four great plays by Henrick Ibsen.* New York: E. P. Dutton, 1959.

James, J. Ethnography and social problems. In R.S. Weppner (Ed), *Street ethnography: Selected studies of crime and drug use in natural settings.* Beverly Hills: Sage, 1977.

Klockars, C.B. Field Ethics for the life history. In R.S. Weppner (Ed.), *Street ethnography: Selected studies of crime and drug use in natural settings.* Beverly Hills: Sage, 1977.

Klockars, C.B. Dirty hands and deviant subjects. In C.B. Klockars & F.W. O'Conner (Eds.) *Deviance and decency: The ethics of research with human subjects.* Beverly Hills: Sage, 1979.

Kobben, A. Participation and quantification: Fieldwork among the Dyuka. In D. G. Jongmans & P. Gutkind (Eds.), *Anthropologists in the field.* New York: Humanities Press, 1967.

Mead, M. Research with human beings: A model derived from anthropological field practice. In P. Freund (Ed.), *Experimentation with human subjects.* New York: Russell Sage Foundation, 1969, pp. 152-177.

McCurdy, D. The medicine man. In M. Rynkiewich & J. Spradley (Eds.), *Ethics and fieldwork: Dilemmas in fieldwork.* New York: John Wiley, 1976.

Mills, Ç. *The sociological imagination.* New York: Oxford University Press, 1959.

Mulhauser, F. Ethnography and policymaking: The case of education. *Human Organization,* 1975, *34*, 311.

Nader, T. Up the anthropologist perspectives gained from studying up. In D. Hymes (Ed.), *Reinventing anthropology.* New York: Vintage Press, 1969.

Paine, W.S. (Ed.) *Job stress and burnout: Research, theory, and intervention perspectives.* Beverly Hills: Sage, 1982.

Peattie, L. *The view from the barrio.* Ann Arbor: University of Michigan Press, 1968.

Pelto, P. *Anthropological research: The structure of inquiry.* New York: Harper & Row, 1970.

Polsky, N. *Hustlers, beats, and others.* Chicago: Aldine, 1967.

Reiman, J.H. Research subjects, political subjects, and human subjects. In C.B. Klockars & F.W. O'Connor (Eds.) *Deviance and decency: The ethics of research with human subjects.* Beverly Hills: Sage, 1979.

Reynolds, P.D. *Ethical dilemmas and social science research.* San Francisco: Jossey-Bass Publishers, 1979.

Sahlins, M. The established order: Do not fold, spindle, or mutilate. In J. Horowitz (Ed.), *The rise and fall of Project Camelot: Studies in the relationship between social science and practical politics.* Cambridge, MA: MIT Press, 1967.

Soloway, I., & Walters, J. Workin' the corner: The ethics and legality of ethnographic fieldwork among active heroin addicts. In R.S. Weppner (Ed.), *Street ethnography: Selected studies of crime and drug use in natural settings.* Beverly Hills: Sage, 1977.

Solyhenitsyn, A. *For the good of the cause* (D. Hoyd and M. Hayward, trans.). New York: Praeger, 1972.

Spradley, J. Trouble in the tank. In M. Rynkiewich & J. Spradley (Eds.), *Ethics and fieldwork: Dilemmas in fieldwork.* New York: John Wiley, 1976.

Thorne, B. "You still takin' notes?" Fieldwork and problems of informal consent. *Social Problems.* 1980, *27*(3), 284-297.

Tobin, J. A. The resettlement of the Enewetak people: A study of a displaced community in the Marshall Islands. Ph.D. dissertation, University of California, Berkeley.

Wax, R. *Doing fieldwork: Warnings and advice.* Chicago: University of Chicago Press, 1971.

Wax, R. Twelve years later: An analysis of field experience. In R. Adams & J. Preiss (Eds.), *Human organization research.* Homewood, IL: Dorsey, 1960.

Weber, M. *Max Weber's essays in Sociology* (II. Gerth and C.W. Mills, trans. and eds.). New York: Oxford University Press, 1946.

Whyte, W.F. *Street corner society: The social structure of an Italian slum.* Chicago: The University of Chicago Press, 1943.

Wolcott, H. Criteria for an ethnographic approach to research in schools. *Human Organization,* 1975, *34*(2), 111-127.

Wolcott, H. How to look like an anthropologist without really being one. *Practicing Anthropology,* 1980, *3*(2), 6-7, 56-59.

Yablonsky, L. Experiences with the criminal community. In A.W. Gouldner & S.M. Miller (Eds.), *Applied sociology.* New York: The Free Press, 1965.

Name Index

Abt, W. P., 109
Alkin, M., 98, 157
Alvarez, R., 27
American Anthropological Association
    Code of Ethics, 94
Anastasi, A., 47
Ang, T., 135
Apple, M. W., 38
Baker, C., 135
Barker, R. G., 49
Battison, R., 135
Beattie, J., 220, 224
Becker, H., 44, 85
Belshaw, C., 157
Berreman, C., 215, 221, 229
Biber, B., 48
Birch, J. W., 135
Birdwhistell, R., 50
Bishop, M., 135
Blumer, H., 69
Boaz, F., 21
Bock, G., 109
Borman, K., 51
Boruch, R. F., 30
Bourdieu, P., 160
Brenner, M. 25
Brill, R., 134
Britan, G. M., 25, 108, 232
Brock, J. A., 50
Burnett, 180
Burns, A., 25, 26, 42, 85, 93, 94, 100,
    101, 232
Cadena-Munoz, 116.
Campbell, D. T., 25, 40, 49, 51, 52,
    66, 67, 69, 83, 169
Carroll, T. C., 44
Carter, L. F., 65
Cassell, J., 26, 212, 232
Center for New Schools, 42

Cerva, T., 109
Chambers, E., 26, 232
Cherniss, C., 230
Clark, B. R., 63
Clinton, C. A., 25, 26, 79, 85, 89, 92,
    93, 100–104, 203, 213, 214, 232
Cohen, D. K., 65, 74, 89, 104, 107
Cohn, 209
Coleman, J. S., 68
Colfer, A. M., 85, 100, 101
Colfer, C. J., 25, 26, 85, 94, 95, 100,
    101, 158, 214, 232
Collier, J., 39, 48
Colson, E., 46
Comitas, F., 37
Cook, S. W., 67
Cook, T. D., 38, 64, 69, 82, 115
Cordray, D. S., 30
Corwin, R., 105, 106, 109
Coulthard, R., 51
Covington, V. C., 135
Coward, R., 25, 106, 232
Cowden, P., 74, 79, 89, 104, 107
Crain, R. L., 37
Cronbach, L. J., 25, 30, 64, 67, 82
Cusick, P. A., 63
Datta, L., 65
Dawson, J. A., 71, 79
Deal, T. E., 42, 109
Dean, J. P., 44, 46
Dean, L. R., 44
Deloria, V., 226
Denzin, N. K., 37, 39, 44, 45
DeSanctis, J. E., 74, 79
Denenberg, V., 21
Diamond, S., 225
Dingler, 116
Dolgin, J., 37
Donnelly, W. L., 85, 92, 100

Subject Index

About the Contributors

DAVID M. FETTERMAN, a senior member of Stanford University's administration, conducts qualitative formative evaluations and audits of the management process in university departments. Concurrently, Fetterman is a Guest Lecturer in the Anthropology Department. Formerly, he was a Senior Associate and Project Director at RMC Research Corporation where he conducted national and state-level ethnographic evaluations. Fetterman has published significant works in both educational and anthropological journals. Recently he was awarded the American Anthropological Associations's Praxis Publication Award and the Evaluation Research Society Award for his work in ethnographic educational evaluation.

WILLIAM A. FIRESTONE is a research associate and Director of Field Studies at Research for Better Schools. He formally was a member of the field research team for Abt Associates' Longitudinal Study of Educational Change in Rural America. Firestone is the author of *Great Expectations for Small Schools: The Limitations of Federal Projects.*

JUDITH P. GOETZ is an Associate Professor of Social Science Education in the School of Education at the University of Georgia. She has also taught at the junior high school level in Minnesota. She served as the Council on Anthropology and Education's Secretary-Treasurer and as Chair of the Committee on Women in Schools and Society.

HARVEY E. GOLDBERG is an Associate Professor in the Department of Sociology and Social Anthropology at Hebrew University of Jerusalem. Goldberg has taught at several universities, both American and British. He has received awards from the American Philosophical Society, the Social Science Research Council, and the Israeli Academy of Sciences for his research on Moslem-Jewish relations in North Africa. He is the author of *Cave-Dwellers and Citrus-Growers: A Jewish Community in Libya and Israel* and *Antropologia: Adam, Hevrah Vetarbut.* Goldberg has also been the special topic issue editor of *Ethnic*

Groups. Goldberg continues to be *Current Anthropology's* corresponding editor for Israel.

MARTHA K. HEMWALL is an Adjunct Instructor at the University of Wisconsin—Green Bay. She has worked with the Rhode Island School for the Deaf, and she was the ethnographer on the Language and Concept Development Project.

ROBERT E. HERRIOTT is a private research sociologist in Massachusetts. He was a Senior Associate at Abt Associates and Project Director of the Longitudinal Study of Educational Change in Rural America. Formerly, Herriott was a Professor of Sociology at Florida State University. He was also the Director of the University's Center for the Study of Education. He is the coauthor of *The Environment of Schooling: Formal Education as an Open Social System* and *The Dynamics of Planned Educational Change: Case Studies and Analyses.*

MARGARET D. LeCOMPTE is the Executive Director for Research and Evaluation at the Houston Independent School District. Formerly, she was Assistant Professor of Education at the University of Houston. She was also a Visiting Professor in Sociology at the University of North Dakota, Rice University, and the Universidad de Monterrey, Mexico. She is currently President-Elect of the Council on Anthropology and Education's Board of Directors. LeCompte also served on the Council as the Chair of the Committee on Women in Schools and Society. She is the author, with Judith Goetz, of *Tools and Techniques: Designing Ethnographic Research and Evaluation in Education.*

DONALD A. MESSERSCHMIDT is an Associate Professor at Washington State University. He was a member of the on-site research team for Abt Associates' Longitudinal Study of Educational Change in Rural America. Concurrently, Messerschmidt is conducting fieldwork in Kathmandu, Nepal, for AID. He was the editor of *Anthropologists at Home in North America: Methods and Issues in the Study of One's Own Society.*

ALBERT E. ROBBINS is a research scientist at System Development Corporation. He was Codirector of the Study of Parental Involvement. Formerly, he was a research associate at the Stanford Center for

Research and Development in Teaching. He was also a classroom teacher in the New Haven, Connecticut, public school system.

ALLEN G. SMITH is a research scientist at System Development Corporation. He was Codirector of the Study of Parental Involvement. Formerly, Smith coordinated the Implementation Study component of the National Evaluation of Project Developmental Continuity for High/Scope Educational Research Foundation. He was the coeditor of a special issue of the *American Behavioral Scientist.*

HARRY F. WOLCOTT is currently Professor of Education and Anthropology in the College of Education's Division of Educational Policy and Management at the University of Oregon. He has taught at several American colleges and universities. Wolcott is a Past President of the Council on Anthropology and Education. He is the author of four major monographs, three of which deal directly with educational anthropology: *A Kwakiutl Village and School, The Man in the Principal's Office,* and *Teachers Versus Technocrats.* Wolcott is currently the editor of *Anthropology and Education Quarterly.*